WORLD HISTORY

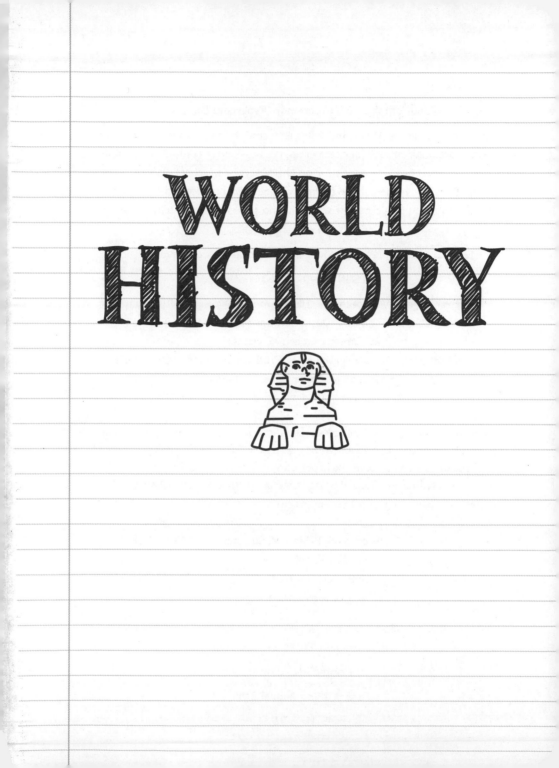

Library of Congress Cataloging-in-Publication Data is available.

ISBN 978-0-7611-6094-6

Writer Ximena Vengoechea   Illustrators Blake Henry, Tim Hall
Series Designer Tim Hall   Designers Gordon Whiteside, Tim Hall
Art Director Colleen AF Venable
Editors Nathalie Le Du, Daniel Nayeri   Production Editor Jessica Rozler
Production Manager Julie Primavera
Concept by Raquel Jaramillo

Workman Publishing Co., Inc.
225 Varick Street
New York, NY 10014-4381
workman.com

WORKMAN, BRAIN QUEST, and BIG FAT NOTE-BOOK are registered trademarks of Workman Publishing Co., Inc.

Printed in Malaysia

First printing August 2016

15 14 13 12

THE COMPLETE MIDDLE SCHOOL STUDY GUIDE

EVERYTHING YOU NEED TO ACE

WORLD HISTORY

IN ONE BIG FAT NOTEBOOK

Borrowed from the smartest kid in class
Double-checked by Michael Lindblad

WORKMAN PUBLISHING
NEW YORK

EVERYTHING YOU NEED TO KNOW TO ACE

WORLD HISTORY

HI!

These are the notes from my world history class. Oh, who am I? Well, some people said I was the smartest kid in class.

I wrote everything you need to ace **WORLD HISTORY**, from the FIRST HUMANLIKE CREATURES to the INTERNET AGE, → and only the really important stuff in between—you know, the stuff that's usually on the test!

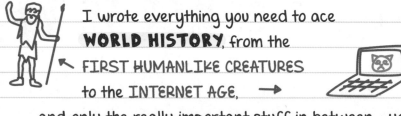

I tried to keep everything organized, so I almost always:

- Highlight vocabulary words in **YELLOW**.
- Color in definitions in green highlighter.
- Use BLUE PEN for important people, places, dates, and terms.
- Doodle a pretty sweet Trojan Horse and whatnot to visually show the big ideas.

AGREED!

If you're not loving your textbook and you're not so great at taking notes in class, this notebook will help. It hits all the major points. (But if your teacher spends a whole class talking about something that's not covered, go ahead and write that down for yourself.)

zzz...WHAT?

Now that I've aced world history, this notebook is **YOURS**. I'm done with it, so this notebook's purpose in life is to help **YOU** learn and remember just what you need to ace **YOUR** world history class.

CONTENTS

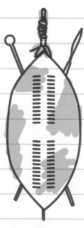

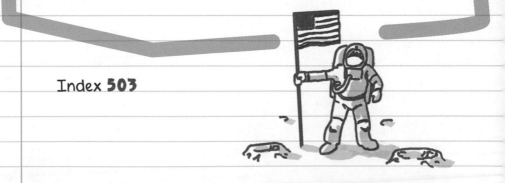

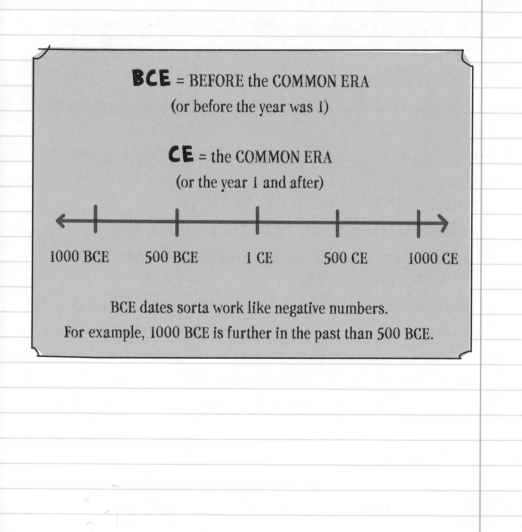

BCE = BEFORE the COMMON ERA
(or before the year was 1)

CE = the COMMON ERA
(or the year 1 and after)

1000 BCE   500 BCE   1 CE   500 CE   1000 CE

BCE dates sorta work like negative numbers.
For example, 1000 BCE is further in the past than 500 BCE.

Unit 1

The First Humans Prehistory– 3500 BCE

What was life like 10,000 or a 100,000 years ago? How have people and cities changed over time? These are some of the questions history tries to answer.

HISTORIANS are the scholars who study our past, using written records and historic art to find the answers. They read letters, look at written laws, and study religious documents and community records.

What if there are **NO** written records of a culture? How can we study **PREHISTORY**, the time before writing was invented?

PREHISTORY
history before
written records

1

The study of prehistory relies on **ARCHEOLOGY** and two groups of people:

> **ARCHEOLOGY**
> the study of human history and prehistory through things people made, used, and left behind

Archaeologists are scientists who study objects made by humans, called ARTIFACTS, to better understand human activity. Artifacts can be tools, instruments, or anything made by humans in past civilizations.

OFTEN FOUND BY DIGGING AROUND IN ANCIENT SITES

EUREKA!

Anthropologists are scientists who also study artifacts but are more interested in the cultural aspects of human society:

- what people in a particular culture wore
- what they ate
- how they learned and created the customs they followed
- how they developed languages

All the things happening now—the presidents of today, the global issues, climate change, cultural change, the sort of lives **WE** lead—will be

THAT SHOE YOU LOST UNDER YOUR BED—IF FOUND THOUSANDS OF YEARS FROM NOW BURIED IN WHAT USED TO BE YOUR BEDROOM, THAT WOULD BE AN ARTIFACT, TOO.

considered part of history someday. Maybe someone will study our "artifacts" and culture. But before that happens, let's go back to the beginning—to the very first humans.

☆ Chapter 1 ☆

THE FIRST HUMANS AND THE PALEOLITHIC ERA

STARTING ROUGHLY 6 TO 7 MILLION YEARS AGO

The first humans looked nothing like us. In fact, scientists think we most likely descended from early forms of apes and the earliest humanlike creatures looked like a cross between them and us.

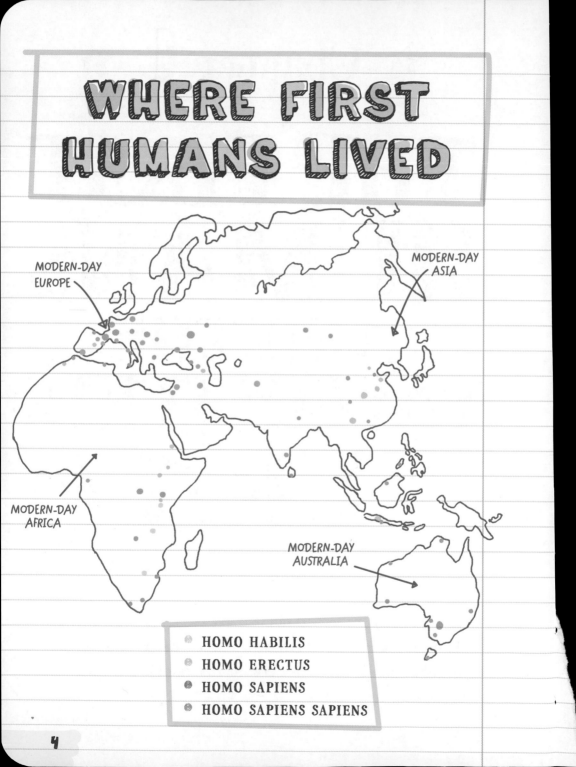

WHERE FIRST HUMANS LIVED

MODERN-DAY EUROPE

MODERN-DAY ASIA

MODERN-DAY AFRICA

MODERN-DAY AUSTRALIA

- HOMO HABILIS
- HOMO ERECTUS
- HOMO SAPIENS
- HOMO SAPIENS SAPIENS

These first humanlike creatures are called HOMINIDS. Hominids had some human attributes, such as the ability to walk upright and OPPOSABLE thumbs (able to move toward and touch the other fingers of the same hand). The earliest hominids lived in Africa four million years ago, evolving over time.

There are many different types of hominids, but here are a few famous types:

THIS SYMBOL MEANS "ABOUT."

Australopithecus (~4 million years ago): AUSTRALOPITHECUS means "southern ape," which tells us that these humanlike apes were probably from eastern or southern Africa. LUCY is a famous *Australopithecus* hominid—she was discovered in 1974 and changed the way scientists looked at the evolution of humankind. It is believed that Lucy is a common ancestor for different types of hominids. She had a very small brain but walked on two legs, nearly two million years before other hominids would walk upright. Walking allowed Lucy to keep her hands free, but she used sticks and stones to dig or break open food instead of making tools. Archeologists once believed that the ability to walk upright led hominids to make tools, but Lucy showed this wasn't true.

LOOK, MA, NO HANDS!

SHOW-OFF!

Homo habilis (~2 million years ago):

HOMO HABILIS means "able man." This short hominid lived in East Africa and had a larger brain than the species *Australopithecus* and was the first *Homo* species to use stone tools.

Homo erectus (~1.5 million years ago):

HOMO ERECTUS, or "upright man," was a more advanced hominid. Even though Lucy and older hominids walked upright, *Homo erectus* had longer arms and legs and looked more like a human. About 500,000 years ago, *Homo erectus* learned to make fire, probably from ← LIKE A BOY SCOUT! rubbing two sticks together or by striking stones together to create a spark. This was a huge help for hunting, protection from animals, cooking, and keeping warm. Fire also meant that these hominids could move to areas with colder climates, which is why *Homo erectus* was probably the first hominid type to leave warm Africa.

Homo sapiens (~400,000 years ago):

HOMO SAPIENS, or "wise man," was a new species of human that quickly became the main species. They made tools from stones, animal bones, and horns. With these tools, they developed new farming and hunting techniques.

Homo sapiens had large brains and small jaws. Their limbs were even longer and straighter than those of *Homo erectus*, and closer to what we look like today.

There are two kinds of *Homo sapiens*: NEANDERTHALS and HOMO SAPIENS SAPIENS. Neanderthals lived in and around present-day Europe and parts of Turkey. They maybe made clothes from animal skins, to keep warm, and were the earliest people to bury their dead. They had large brains but heavier builds and were more slow moving than *Homo sapiens sapiens*, who eventually replaced the Neanderthals.

Homo sapiens sapiens (~200,000 years ago):

Homo sapiens sapiens means "wise, wise human" and is the group that includes today's humans. They first appeared in Africa and then spread out around the world about 100,000 years ago. *Homo sapiens sapiens* had a slow journey out of Africa—archeologists say they may have moved only two or three miles in a whole generation!

THE
PALEOLITHIC
LIFE

The first humans lived in the PALEOLITHIC ERA, or the Old Stone Age (~2,500,000 BCE to around 10,000 BCE). Humans made simple tools from hard stones such as flint. They made:

hand axes and stone spearheads attached to wooden poles, which made hunting large animals easier

the bow and arrow

harpoons and fishhooks of bone, to catch fish and other sea animals

baskets to gather and carry
food, and rope from vines
twisted together

small statues from
stone and ivory and

bone flutes

NOMAD
person who has no
permanent home and
travels to find food

The Paleolithic people were hunters
and gatherers. They probably divided
labor to feed themselves, with men
hunting and women gathering berries, nuts, and plants.
They were **NOMADS**, moving from place to place to survive
in small groups. They followed grazing animals, and they
changed location based on the growing season—when
plants stopped growing, they would move again. Paleolithic
people had no permanent homes and built new shelters
wherever they went.

*THIS WOULD BE LIKE MOVING AROUND FROM
SCHOOL TO SCHOOL WITH YOUR ENTIRE HISTORY CLASS.*

The GREAT MIGRATION

The GREAT MIGRATION was a time of vast movement and long-distance travel for humans, who were beginning to explore other continents. Most humans followed the animals they hunted across the continents, often moving toward wet climates with lakes and fertile lands. The **ICE AGE** pushed humans toward warmer regions and connected

HUMAN
MIGRATION
ROUTES

the continents through land bridges that were uncovered as sea levels lowered. Humans walked from Africa until they reached every continent except Antarctica. It took roughly one million years!

The **ICE AGE** was the most recent glacial period, when much of the earth was covered by ice and oceans were frozen over. It lasted about 100,000 years and ended around 10,000 BCE.

MAJOR EVENTS IN

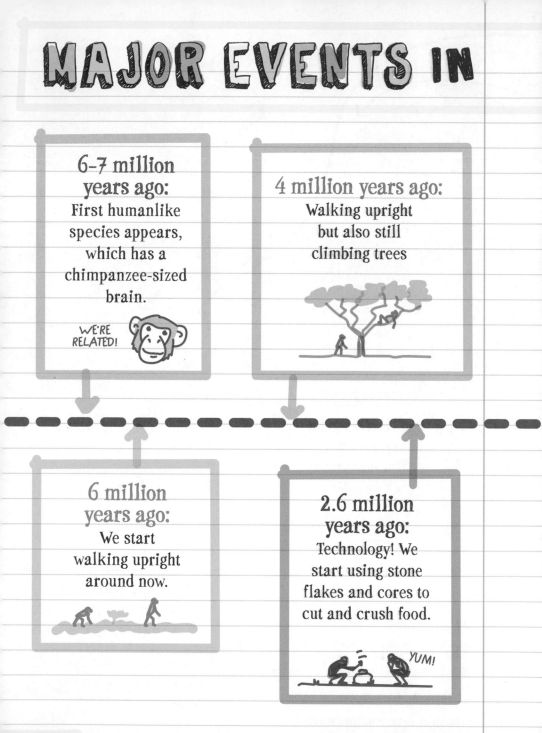

6-7 million years ago: First humanlike species appears, which has a chimpanzee-sized brain.

WE'RE RELATED!

4 million years ago: Walking upright but also still climbing trees

6 million years ago: We start walking upright around now.

2.6 million years ago: Technology! We start using stone flakes and cores to cut and crush food.

YUM!

HUMAN EVOLUTION

500,000 years ago:
We discover fire, which changes our diet, gives us a warm hangout, and helps us to stay safe from predators.

FIRE GOOD.

SOMEONE SHOULD INVENT MARSHMALLOWS...

80,000 years ago:
We leave Africa and begin the Great Migration.

200,000–800,000 years ago:
Our brains rapidly grow bigger, so we communicate better and more of us survive in the harsh environment.

DUH...

INDUBITABLY.

ART was one form of communication for the nomadic Paleolithic people, probably used for telling stories and sharing myths. Sometimes, hunting strategies were drawn on the walls of a cave. Stone lamps filled with animal fat would light the caves while the Paleolithic people painted. Animal fat was also used to make paint: Mixed with various mineral ores, artists used fat to create reds, yellows, and blacks for their work. Artists would use their fingers to draw on the walls of the caves or they would use sticks, leaves, and hollow reeds to blow paint through. Sometimes they left handprints, maybe as a signature. Most cave paintings show animals during a hunt, and some anthropologists think the paintings were created as rituals to ensure a good hunt.

PETROGLYPH
a carving or inscription
on a rock

CHECK YOUR KNOWLEDGE

1. What was the Great Migration and how long did it take?

2. What are some reasons why early humans made cave paintings?

3. How do scientists learn about things that happened in prehistory?

4. When was the Paleolithic era?

5. What effect did the Ice Age have on the planet?

6. What sorts of objects did Paleolithic people make?

ANSWERS

CHECK YOUR ANSWERS

1. The Great Migration was a time when humans traveled from Africa and began to explore every continent except Antarctica. They hunted across the continents and found places with fresh water and fertile lands. The Great Migration took roughly one million years.

2. Early humans used cave paintings to communicate and probably to tell stories and share myths. They also drew hunting strategies and probably used the paintings as part of rituals they hoped would guarantee a good hunt.

3. Scientists learn about prehistory through artifacts, which are objects such as tools, instruments, buildings, pottery, or anything else made by humans. They use these objects to find clues about prehistoric life.

4. The Paleolithic era, or the Old Stone Age, spanned about 2,500,000 BCE to around 10,000 BCE.

5. The cold weather of the Ice Age pushed humans toward warmer regions. Also, sea levels were lower, so land bridges connected continents, and humans used these to travel to distant places.

6. Paleolithic people made simple tools, such as hand axes, stone spearheads, bows, arrows, harpoons, bone fishhooks, baskets, rope, statues, and flutes.

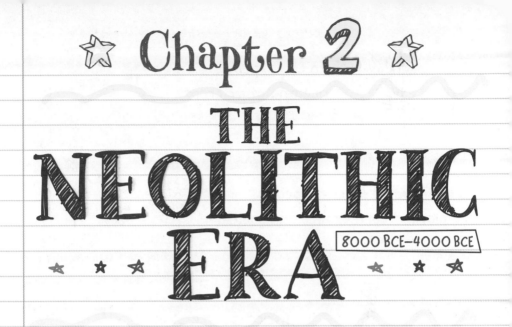

☆ Chapter 2 ☆

THE NEOLITHIC ERA

8000 BCE–4000 BCE

During the Great Migration, humans looked for new, warmer regions with fertile soil to grow their own food and settle down. Early humans were nomads, moving from place to place, but the development of SYSTEMATIC AGRICULTURE in the NEOLITHIC ERA marked a change to a more **SEDENTARY** lifestyle for most humans. The NEOLITHIC REVOLUTION was a fundamental change in the way many humans lived. Humans could now keep animals and grow food on a regular basis, with recurring and more reliable harvests.

> **SEDENTARY**
> staying in one place

UH-OH.

AGRICULTURAL CHANGES

About 9,000 years ago, farmers started planting STAPLE crops—crops people would rely on most for food.

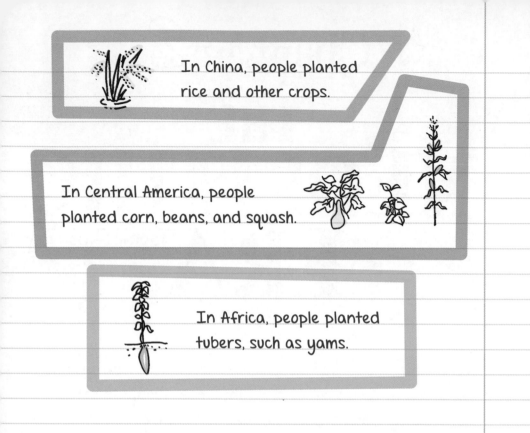

In China, people planted rice and other crops.

In Central America, people planted corn, beans, and squash.

In Africa, people planted tubers, such as yams.

Many crops were important in ancient religions and creation stories. Early farmers discovered that grinding grains makes flour, which can be used to make bread. People figured out where soil was fertile—where plants would grow better. Areas with long springs and summers were popular farming sites, since their climate helped crops thrive. Lakes and rivers were good places to settle too, because they had water and provided an extra source of nutrition through fish and other seafood.

When planting crops, farmers chose seeds from the biggest, best-looking, best-tasting plants. Then they would repeat

that the next time. Slowly but
surely, each harvest would bring
up a better, stronger, tastier round
of crops. This process is called the
DOMESTICATION OF PLANTS.

GOOD PLANT!

DOMESTICATE
to tame or adapt for
your own use

This was a huge leap forward—some
might even say, revolutionary.

The **AGRICULTURAL REVOLUTION** (sometimes called
the **NEOLITHIC REVOLUTION**) refers to the period when
humans transitioned from hunting and gathering to agriculture.
This shift led to sedentary communities, the establishment
of social classes, and the rise of civilizations.

The DEVELOPMENT of SEDENTARY COMMUNITIES

ANIMAL DOMESTICATION began when
humans tamed wild animals like sheep,
goats, and pigs for meat, milk, and wool.
Most likely, the dog was one of the first

EVEN DOGS WERE
ONCE WILD. THEY HAD
TO FIND REAL BONES
BY THEMSELVES TO
CHEW ON.

animals to be domesticated, helping humans hunt larger
animals long before humans settled down. In some parts of
the world, bigger animals were domesticated. In India, for
example, wild elephants were tamed.

Farming techniques like the IRRIGATION SYSTEM were also
crucial for settling early communities. Irrigation systems
were a series of canals built to bring water to the land.

Because sedentary communities grew their own food, they often ended up with a SURPLUS, or more than was needed. A food surplus could feed many more people, so communities could expand and didn't have to follow herds around.

LIKE WHEN YOU PUT LEFTOVERS IN A DOGGY BAG

The EARLY VILLAGES

As more people lived around farms and food surpluses increased, people started to have free time to work on projects that didn't involve just finding or growing food. This led to more DIVISION OF LABOR: people specializing in different roles within a society.

People started to become ARTISANS, workers skilled in a particular craft. They made baskets, tools, pottery, or fabric. Metal tools made from copper and then from BRONZE became more sophisticated. Iron was later used to make strong, durable tools. The WHEEL was also invented around this time. Like fire, the wheel changed everything.

A MIXTURE OF COPPER AND TIN

WOW! BUT WHAT'S THE POINT?

Think of all the things we use **WHEELS** for—cars, bikes, strollers, shopping carts, trains, and buses too! Life would be a lot harder without the wheel!

With so many new goods, people started to buy and sell what they had made. Merchant ships began traveling across seas and rivers to trade goods. Trading with others meant that new technology and farming techniques could be exchanged among cultures. Goods could be **BARTERED**, which means that they were exchanged without money.

> **BARTER**
> to exchange one good for another

LIKE TRADING LUNCHES IN THE CAFETERIA

EARLY GOVERNMENT

Governments eventually formed to regulate trade and other aspects of human activity in these new villages. Villages grew into towns and cities, which sometimes had walls for protection. Villages were probably led by the chiefs of the CLANS or TRIBES (groups of families who lived together). MONARCHS (kings and queens) likely led large groups of cities or groups of tribes. Their job was to keep the kingdom in order through lawmaking.

> **DIVINE RIGHT**
> belief that the right to rule comes directly from a god, not from the consent of the people

Many monarchs claimed to have power based on **DIVINE RIGHT** (the right to rule granted by their **DEITY** or deities).

> **DEITY**
> god, goddess, or divine being

> Religious buildings, such as the ziggurats of Babylon and the pyramids of Egypt, were built. City walls were perhaps less artistic, but more practical, and built for defense purposes.

Societies began dividing according to SOCIAL CLASS (groupings of people ranked by social status). Kings and queens were at the top, with priests and religious authorities beneath them. Next in line were government and military officials. Then came artisans, merchants, and small traders. Farmers (who started it all) were ironically lower still. And finally, some societies had SLAVES, people owned as though they were property, at the bottom of the social order.

KINGS/QUEENS

PRIESTS

GOVERNMENT/MILITARY

MERCHANTS/TRADERS

FARMERS

SLAVES

The FIRST CIVILIZATIONS

As the first **CIVILIZATIONS** developed, the leisure time people gained after settling down and getting a food surplus freed them up for just . . . thinking. People began working out big ideas in mathematics, astronomy, writing, and lawmaking.

CIVILIZATION
society organized around a centralized government, a means of food production, a system of writing, art and architecture, and job specialization

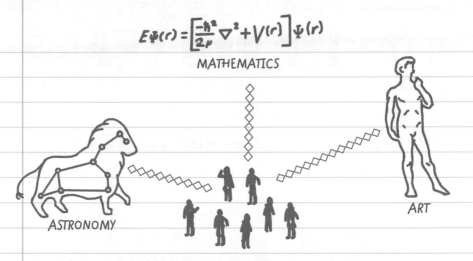

$$E\psi(r) = \left[\frac{-\hbar^2}{2\mu}\nabla^2 + V(r)\right]\psi(r)$$

MATHEMATICS

ASTRONOMY

ART

Writing was particularly important for keeping records of food harvested and goods to be traded. Rulers, priests, merchants, and artisans used writing to keep track of laws, prayers, or their family tree. Writing was used to record the poems, stories, and information that people had passed down through **ORAL TRADITION**, or to create new stories. Painters and sculptors also told stories by illustrating tales about religion or nature and by decorating temples and city buildings.

ORAL TRADITION
passing down information from generation to generation through spoken word and memorization instead of by writing it down

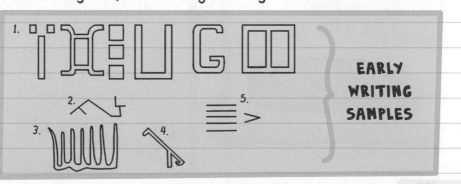

EARLY WRITING SAMPLES

THE LAST 100,000 YEARS

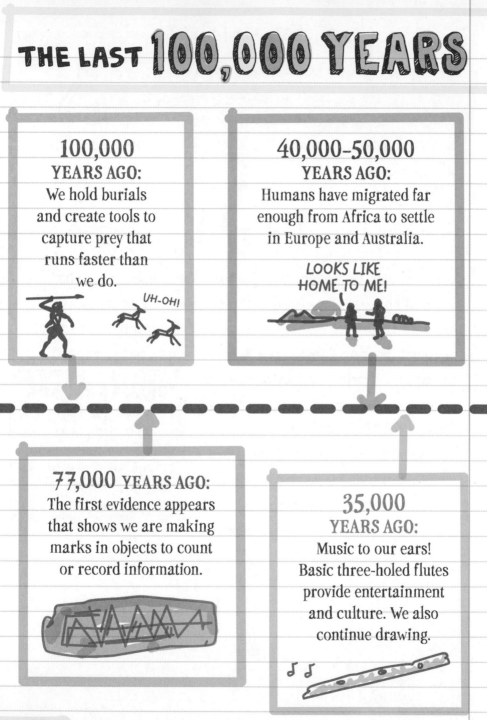

100,000 YEARS AGO:
We hold burials and create tools to capture prey that runs faster than we do.

UH-OH!

40,000–50,000 YEARS AGO:
Humans have migrated far enough from Africa to settle in Europe and Australia.

LOOKS LIKE HOME TO ME!

77,000 YEARS AGO:
The first evidence appears that shows we are making marks in objects to count or record information.

35,000 YEARS AGO:
Music to our ears! Basic three-holed flutes provide entertainment and culture. We also continue drawing.

IN HUMAN EVOLUTION

30,000–23,000 YEARS AGO:
We begin using needles made from bone to sew clothes that fit us better.

8,000 YEARS AGO:
The first written documents are created using symbols. During the next few thousand years, symbols will be replaced with words.

IT SAYS, "TURN LEFT AT THE BIG ROCK"!

NO, IT SAYS, "LOOK OUT FOR BEARS"!

9,000 YEARS AGO:
We start domesticating plants and animals, which leads to sedentary communities.

20 YEARS AGO:
Human population doubles in just 40 years, from 3 billion to 6 billion people.

OOF!

The first civilizations formed mostly in and around Mesopotamia, Egypt, the Indus Valley, China, and Central America, beginning in about 4500 BCE.

RECIPE FOR CIVILIZATION

INGREDIENTS:

- workers
- writing
- art
- government

Put them all together, and let cook for a few thousand years.

CHECK YOUR KNOWLEDGE

1. Why did people abandon their nomadic lifestyle during the Neolithic era?

2. What new farming techniques did the Neolithic people use?

3. What do we mean when we say "division of labor"?

4. Give an example of bartering.

5. What was the role of monarchs in these new societies?

6. How did having leisure time advance civilizations?

7. What is a surplus, and why was it so important for the development of civilizations?

8. Where were the first civilizations mostly found?

CHECK YOUR ANSWERS

1. People stopped being nomadic because they developed systematic agriculture. During the Neolithic era, people began farming and could settle down in one place rather than chase animals for food.

2. People began picking and choosing the seeds from the biggest, best plants and planting only those in order to grow even bigger crops (this is called the domestication of plants). Farmers also used an irrigation system to control the flow of water to different areas of land by using canals.

3. Division of labor means that tasks in a society are performed by separate groups.

4. An example of bartering is trading a woven basket for an iron pot.

5. Monarchs were the new leaders of towns and cities. They used laws to keep order, and many claimed to have power based on "divine right."

6. Leisure time advanced civilizations because people had time to explore ideas and be creative.

#4 has more than one correct answer.

7. A surplus is an excess of food, and it is important because that is what created leisure time. It also meant that populations could expand and that people did not have to follow a herd for food anymore.
8. The first civilizations were mostly found around Mesopotamia, Egypt, the Indus Valley, China, and Central America.

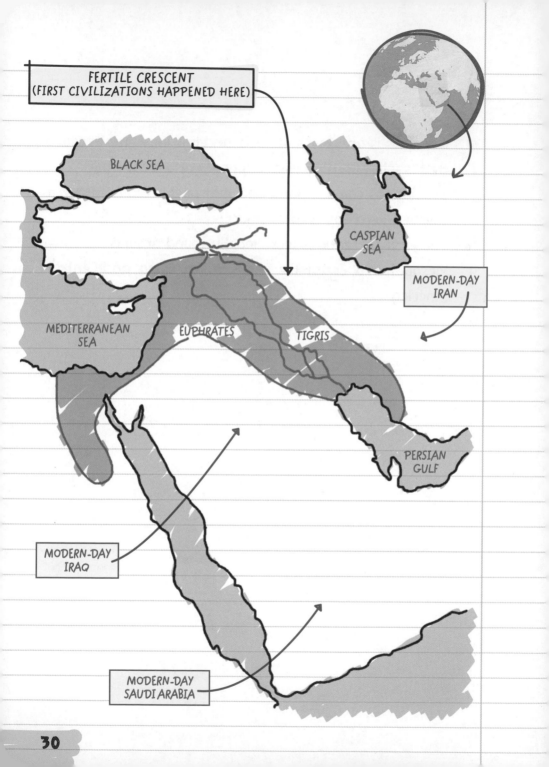

FERTILE CRESCENT
(FIRST CIVILIZATIONS HAPPENED HERE)

BLACK SEA

CASPIAN SEA

MODERN-DAY IRAN

MEDITERRANEAN SEA

EUPHRATES

TIGRIS

PERSIAN GULF

MODERN-DAY IRAQ

MODERN-DAY SAUDI ARABIA

Unit 2

First Civilizations
3500 BCE – 300 CE

The world's first complex civilizations were the first to create systems of writing, economic trade, and governments.

The first civilizations started in a crescent-shaped area extending from the Mediterranean Sea to the Persian Gulf in the FERTILE CRESCENT (what is now Iraq). It had rich soil and produced abundant crops. Within the Fertile Crescent, two rivers, the TIGRIS and the EUPHRATES, hugged a valley that became known as MESOPOTAMIA. Mesopotamia could support large populations because its location was ideal for both trade and agriculture. ←PROBABLY WHY THE FIRST HIGHLY ORGANIZED SOCIETIES STARTED HERE

☆ Chapter 3 ☆

MESOPOTAMIA

4000 BCE–612 BCE

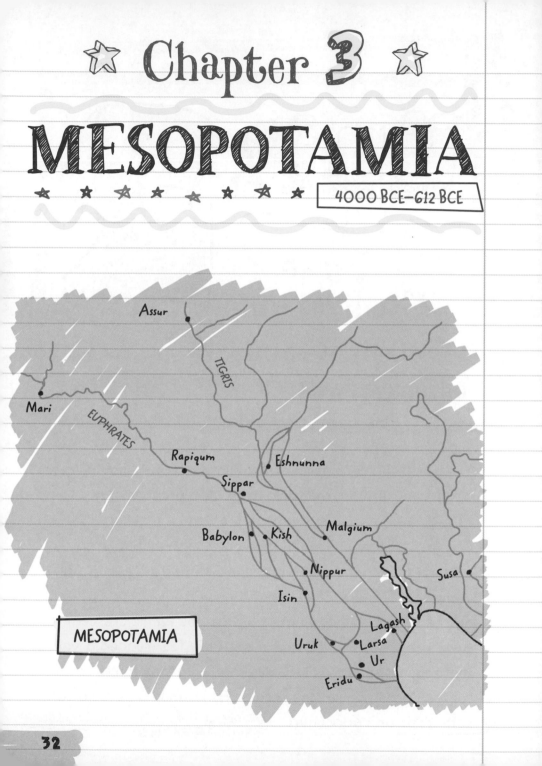

MESOPOTAMIA

TIGRIS

EUPHRATES

Assur

Mari

Rapiqum

Sippar

Eshnunna

Babylon • Kish

Malgium

Nippur

Isin

Susa

Uruk

Lagash

Larsa

Ur

Eridu

SUMERIA

SUMERIA was the first civilization in Mesopotamia and developed around 4000 BCE. The SUMERIANS relied on annual floods to deposit rich soil onto the riverbanks every spring. The Sumerians used irrigation and drainage ditches to control the flow of water. But there were still surprise floods that washed entire areas out. This convinced the Sumerians that other forces were at work; people turned to religion to explain destructive floods.

Religion and the Ruling Class

The Sumerians were a **POLYTHEISTIC** people. They

> **POLYTHEISM**
> the belief in many gods; from **POLY** (more than one) and **THEISM** (belief in a god or gods)

hoped that if they obeyed and served the gods, they'd get a good harvest. They built and dedicated **ZIGGURATS** to the chief god or goddess of a city.

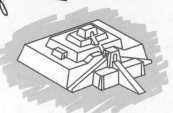

ZIGGURATS were temples shaped like pyramids. The Sumerians' ziggurats were massive towers made of clay bricks, with steps leading to the top, but they didn't last through time like the stone pyramids of Egypt.

So, if most of the Sumerian ziggurats were destroyed, how do we know of their existence today? Well, technically not ALL of the ziggurats were destroyed. As a result of slow erosion and, later, construction over their sites, many ziggurats were buried. Over time, archaeologists were able to dig up the ruins and find clues of the ziggurats' former existence.

Sumeria was a **THEOCRACY** in which priests held an authoritative role, because Sumerians believed gods ultimately ruled the land. Kings ruled by divine right and lived in large palaces.

The Mesopotamians named nearly 3,000 gods and goddesses!

Writing and Education

Around 3000 BCE, the Sumerians created CUNEIFORM, a form of writing based on making wedge-shaped impressions with reeds on soft clay tablets.

FISH

OX

BIRD

OBJECT → PICTURE → CUNEIFORM → WORD!

Once the impressions were made, the tablets were put in the sun to dry, and there could be no more changes!

NO "EDIT UNDO" POSSIBLE

Cuneiform was used to keep records and write stories and poems. It took a long time to make a tablet, so it was important to have professional writers, called SCRIBES. Scribes studied at schools and then went to work as copyists, teachers, lawmakers, and leaders. They were an important part of Sumerian society, and thanks to them, history was recorded in words.

Writing wasn't used just for record keeping. The Sumerians created some of the earliest surviving works of literature, like **GILGAMESH**, an **EPIC** about the adventures of a legendary king and his best friend, Enkidu.

EPIC
a long poem, usually centered on a hero

> The Sumerians started the very first schools, which focused on the brand-new invention of writing with cuneiform.

THANKS A LOT, SUMERIANS.

City-States

The Sumerian kingdom was made up of CITY-STATES, which were cities that also acted as politically independent states. Each had its own government, army, and king. Trade between city-states was regulated through religious temples, which also functioned as storage units for surplus goods. Goods like wool and wheat were bartered for timber and imported copper. Priests often collected rent from farmers and acted as tax collectors in each city-state.

BUT the city-states also fought each other for land and water, eventually leading to the downfall of Mesopotamia's first civilization.

SUN'S RAYS

SUNRISE →

←SUNSET

AROUND 5 PM

THE SUMERIANS invented the system of units that we use today to tell time:

60 seconds = 1 minute
60 minutes = 1 hour

AKKADIA

AKKADIA was led for over 50 years (around 2334-2279 BCE) by KING SARGON I, who is considered the first great king in history. King Sargon I united the Sumerian city-states. Around 1900 BCE the Sumerian city-states fell to a northern rival, BABYLONIA.

The Akkadians spoke a **SEMITIC LANGUAGE**, one of a group of languages that rose and spread throughout early North Africa and Southwest Asia. Akkadian dialects were the chief language of Mesopotamia during Akkadia's control of Sumeria, but there were others, including Sumerian, Eblaite, and Babylonian, which all came from Mesopotamia. Arabic is a Semitic language spoken by millions of people today.

BABYLON

The Babylonians lived in the western half of the Fertile Crescent. The most well-known Babylonian leader was HAMMURABI, who conquered northern Sumerian cities such as Sumer and Akkad to create the BABYLONIAN **EMPIRE** around 1800 BCE. The Babylonians built roads to encourage trade and make travel easier. Goods like cloth and spices could come in from as far as India and Egypt. Merchants and traders managed their own businesses.

EMPIRE
a large area of many territories and peoples, all controlled by one government

Hammurabi is most famous for a list of 282 laws called HAMMURABI'S CODE. This was the first time laws were written out, and therefore the first time people could know how they would be punished if they committed a crime. The laws were based on the idea of "an eye for an eye," meaning that the punishment should be equally as bad as the crime. However, the punishment varied according to the class of the victim and the lawbreaker. The code covered all aspects of daily life—punishments for everything from judges who incorrectly ruled on a case to builders who built houses that collapsed.

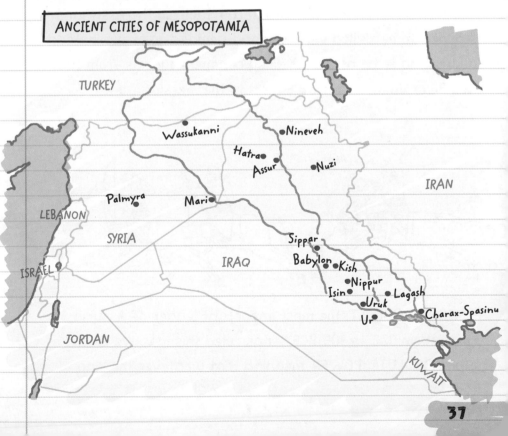

ANCIENT CITIES OF MESOPOTAMIA

TURKEY

Wassukanni

Nineveh

Hatra
Assur

Nuzi

IRAN

Palmyra

Mari

LEBANON

SYRIA

IRAQ

Sippar

Babylon
Kish

ISRAEL

Isin

Nippur

Uruk

Lagash

Ur

Charax-Spasinu

JORDAN

KUWAIT

Men held the most power in the **PATRIARCHAL** society of Mesopotamia, and they could also punish women and children. Hammurabi's empire was conquered and destroyed in the early 1500s BCE.

> **PATRIARCHY**
> a form of social organization in which the father is the supreme authority

ASSYRIA

The kingdom of ASSYRIA arose around 1400 BCE and was one of the first new empires in Mesopotamia. The Assyrian Empire occupied the northern part of Mesopotamia, in what is now northern Iraq. The land where Assyria was located was easy for outsiders to get into and attack, so the Assyrians learned to be skilled warriors and decided to strike instead of waiting to be attacked. They conquered lands from the Nile River (in modern-day Egypt) to the Persian Gulf.

say "Ahh..."

Pew!

KING SARGON II, the most important leader of Assyria, ruled from 722 to 705 BCE. Kings ruled this massive empire with ABSOLUTE POWER, meaning that whatever the king decided became the law. The Assyrians developed a system of communication, with riders on horses delivering messages across the empire within a week. This kept the king and his governors in contact. They also developed trade networks as far as the Mediterranean.

NINEVEH, Assyria's capital city, became a center of learning; it housed one of the world's first libraries, storing a collection of dried clay tablets.

The Assyrians were defeated by the Medes, the Persians, and the Scythians in 612 BCE.

CAPPADOCIA

ASSYRIAN EMPIRE

CASPIAN SEA

Nineveh

MESOPOTAMIA

GREAT SEA

Jerusalem

Persepolis

EGYPT

PERSIAN GULF

BABYLON and the CHALDEANS

Around 612 BCE, Babylon rose again under the CHALDEANS, who were masters of mathematics and astronomy. The Babylonians were the first to identify five of the other planets: Mercury, Venus, Mars, Jupiter, and Saturn. They learned about the planets and stars by actually assigning workers to chart them every night.

SUN

MERCURY

VENUS

EARTH

MARS

JUPITER

SATURN

Remember the order of the first civilizations of Mesopotamia with this mnemonic device:

Starving (Sumerians)

Apes (Assyrians)

Attacked (Akkadians)

Bananas (Babylonians)

CHECK YOUR KNOWLEDGE

1. What is the name of the first civilization in Mesopotamia?

2. How did geography help civilizations develop in the area?

3. What is cuneiform, and why was it important to Sumerian society?

4. What is a city-state?

5. Who was King Sargon I of Akkadia, and why was he so important?

6. What were some of the accomplishments of the Babylonians?

7. Who was Hammurabi, and what was his contribution to the Babylonian Empire?

ANSWERS

CHECK YOUR ANSWERS

1. The first civilization in Mesopotamia was Sumeria.

2. The first civilizations started in the Fertile Crescent, where the rich soil produced abundant crops for people to grow food and thrive.

3. Cuneiform is a form of writing created by the Sumerians using reeds on clay tablets. It was important because Sumerians used it to keep records and write down stories and poems.

4. A city-state is a city that is politically independent, with its own government, army, and king.

5. King Sargon I was the leader of Akkadia for over 50 years and united the Sumerian city-states.

6. The Babylonians built roads to encourage travel and trade goods from India and Egypt. Merchants and traders ran their own businesses.

7. Hammurabi was the leader of Babylon who conquered northern Sumerian cities to create the Babylonian Empire. He is most famous for his list of 282 laws, called Hammurabi's Code. This was the first time laws were written down.

Chapter 4

ANCIENT
★ ★ ★ ★ ★ ★ ★ ★ ★ ★ ★ ★
AFRICA

3100 BCE–32 BCE

EGYPT

Egypt was one of the first river-valley civilizations, nestled on the banks of the Nile River. The longest river in the world, the Nile flows north through Africa for over 4,000 miles (6,437 kilometers). It splits into multiple channels in a **DELTA** just before emptying into the Mediterranean Sea. The Nile Delta is called **LOWER EGYPT**. The land south of it is called **UPPER EGYPT**.

> ABOUT THE SAME DISTANCE AS FROM NEW YORK TO ALASKA

> **DELTA**
> plain at the mouth of a river

The Nile's annual flooding deposited rich, dark soil on the riverbanks. This land was called KEMET, or "black land," and the dry desert land was called "red land."

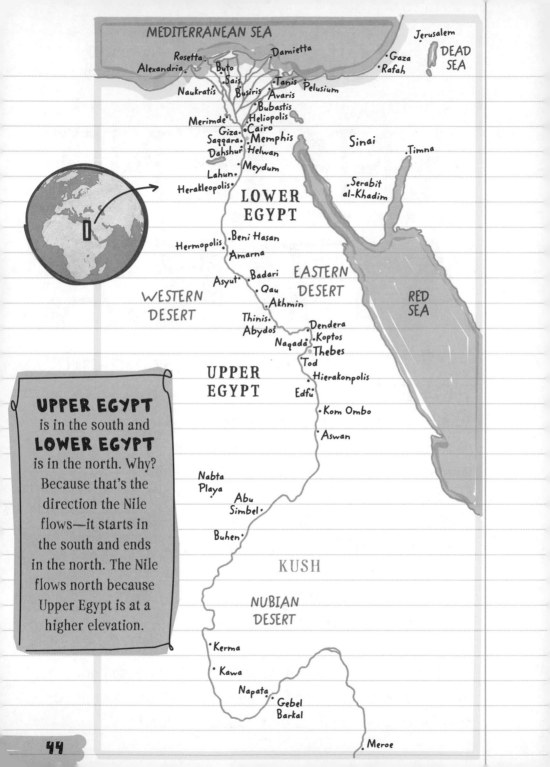

MEDITERRANEAN SEA

Jerusalem

DEAD SEA

Rosetta
Alexandria
Damietta
Gaza
Rafah
Buto
Sais
Naukratis
Busiris
Tanis
Pelusium
Avaris
Bubastis
Merimde
Heliopolis
Giza
Cairo
Saqqara
Memphis
Dahshur
Helwan
Meydum
Lahun
Herakleopolis

Sinai

Timna

LOWER EGYPT

Serabit al-Khadim

Hermopolis
Beni Hasan
Amarna

WESTERN DESERT

Asyut
Badari
Qau
Akhmin

EASTERN DESERT

RED SEA

Thinis
Abydos
Naqada
Dendera
Koptos
Thebes
Tod
Hierakonpolis
Edfu

UPPER EGYPT

Kom Ombo

Aswan

Nabta Playa
Abu Simbel

Buhen

KUSH

NUBIAN DESERT

Kerma

Kawa

Napata
Gebel Barkal

Meroe

UPPER EGYPT is in the south and **LOWER EGYPT** is in the north. Why? Because that's the direction the Nile flows—it starts in the south and ends in the north. The Nile flows north because Upper Egypt is at a higher elevation.

The Kemet was perfect for farming, leading to a surplus of food and a well-fed people. The regular flooding led to accurate recording of the

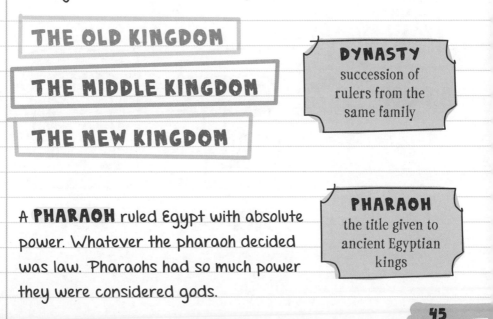

The Egyptians (and the cyclically flooding river) are responsible for our 365-days-a-year calendar.

calendar—dates, times, and numbers. The Nile was also perfect for transportation and communication. HAPI, the Egyptian god of the Nile, was praised highly by the people, along with AMON-RE (the king of the gods), ISIS (the goddess of healing, motherhood, and many other things), and Isis's husband, OSIRIS (the god of the afterworld). The Egyptians had hundreds of gods, including many female gods.

Egyptian Rule

Egypt was ruled by 31 different **DYNASTIES** over about 3,000 years, divided into three periods:

THE OLD KINGDOM

THE MIDDLE KINGDOM

THE NEW KINGDOM

DYNASTY
succession of rulers from the same family

A **PHARAOH** ruled Egypt with absolute power. Whatever the pharaoh decided was law. Pharaohs had so much power they were considered gods.

PHARAOH
the title given to ancient Egyptian kings

45

EGYPTIAN GOD FAMILY TREE

(ONE OF THEM)

ATUM

TEFNUT

GED

SHU

NUT

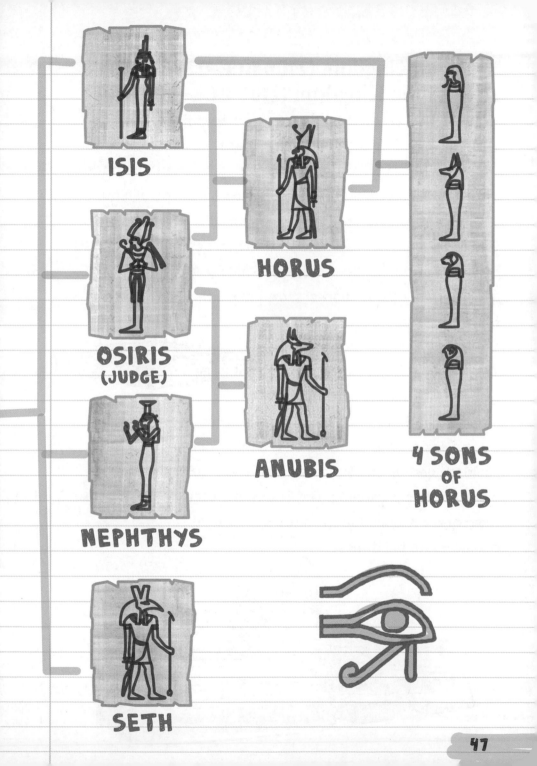

ISIS

HORUS

OSIRIS
(JUDGE)

ANUBIS

4 SONS
OF
HORUS

NEPHTHYS

SETH

47

The Old Kingdom (2700 BCE–2200 BCE) and Middle Kingdom (2100 BCE–1800 BCE)

KING MENES created the first united Egyptian dynasty when he joined Upper and Lower Egypt. He built his capital city of MEMPHIS near modern-day Cairo. The Old Kingdom also saw the construction of the great pyramids of Egypt, which were built for the burial of pharaohs and their families. Historians estimate that the largest of the over 30 Egyptian pyramids, the GREAT PYRAMID AT GIZA, took 20 years, up to 100,000 workers, and more than 2 million stones to build.

JUST 100 MORE STORIES TO GO!

The GREAT SPHINX, a giant statue that is half man and half lion, was built to protect the GREAT PYRAMID. During the annual flooding of the Nile, farmers couldn't work in the fields, so they were put to work building pyramids. The Egyptians used their great knowledge of math, specifically geometry, to build these massive pyramids.

THERE IS SOME EVIDENCE THAT THESE FARMERS AND WORKERS WERE SLAVES.

The massive pyramids in Egypt obviously took a lot of time and hard work to build. Most historians believe that workers pushed stones across the sand on sleds or rolled them on logs to accomplish the construction. Ramps made from packed earth and sand were constructed at the base of the pyramid to allow workers to keep moving up as the pyramids grew taller and taller.

THE GREAT PYRAMID AT GIZA

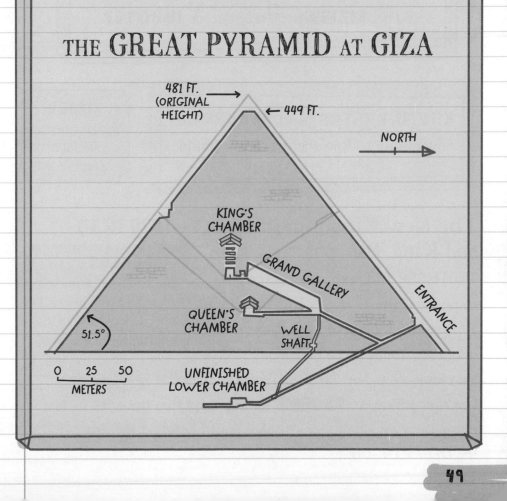

481 FT. (ORIGINAL HEIGHT)

← 449 FT.

NORTH

KING'S CHAMBER

GRAND GALLERY

QUEEN'S CHAMBER

WELL SHAFT

ENTRANCE

51.5°

0   25   50
METERS

UNFINISHED LOWER CHAMBER

The Middle Kingdom was a stable period of expansion. KUSH, or Nubia, an area south of Egypt, was conquered. Pharaohs provided aid for public projects, such as draining swampland and digging canals.

Some famous pharaohs of the Old Kingdom were:

DJOSER: had the first pyramid built for him by his **VIZIER**/architect/doctor **IMHOTEP**

KHUFU, KHAFRA, and **MENKAURA:** oversaw building the great pyramids

VIZIER
a high-ranking official or counselor

The New Kingdom (1500 BCE–1070 BCE) and King Tut

THUTMOSE III was next in the royal bloodline to become pharaoh in about 1473 BCE, but because he was only about three years old, his stepmother HATSHEPSUT ruled

REGENT
an adult who rules in the place of a ruler who is a child and inherited a kingdom too young, a ruler who is absent, or a ruler who is disabled

for him, acting as **REGENT** for the first two decades of his reign. Once he finally took power, Egypt entered the era of the NEW KINGDOM.

Hatshepsut was a mostly peaceful leader who encouraged trade with cities in other parts of Africa, such as Punt on the east coast. This exchange introduced ivory and incense to Egypt. When it was Thutmose III's turn to rule, he led an army of 20,000 to extend Egypt's control into Syria and Palestine.

I WAS ONLY 19!

One of the most famous Egyptian pharaohs to people today, KING TUTANKHAMEN, or KING TUT, was crowned at nine years old and ruled from approximately 1333 to 1323 BCE. King Tut only lived until he was nineteen. He was buried in a tomb containing over 5,000 expensive objects, which were meant to accompany him into the afterlife. King Tut's body was MUMMIFIED, which means that it was preserved; Egyptians believed the soul could continue its life after death, but that it needed the body as a sort of home base. They buried mummies deep below the desert where the cool temperature would help preserve them. The Egyptians gained extensive knowledge of human anatomy and surgery from the process of mummification.

The New Kingdom collapsed in 1070 BCE. Alexander the Great of Macedonia eventually conquered Egypt in about 332 BCE. In 51 BCE, QUEEN CLEOPATRA VII would be the last Macedonian ruler. She waged war with factions of the Roman Empire. After her, Egypt would not be independent again for nearly 2,000 years.

Some other famous pharaohs of the New Kingdom:

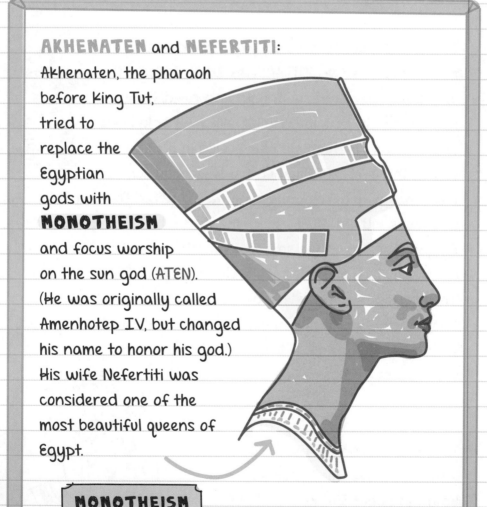

AKHENATEN and **NEFERTITI**:
Akhenaten, the pharaoh before King Tut, tried to replace the Egyptian gods with **MONOTHEISM** and focus worship on the sun god (ATEN). (He was originally called Amenhotep IV, but changed his name to honor his god.) His wife Nefertiti was considered one of the most beautiful queens of Egypt.

MONOTHEISM
belief in one god

RAMSES THE GREAT: reigned for 66 years (1279–1213 BCE), was known as a great warrior, and signed the world's first peace treaty (with his enemies the Hittites). He also had many monuments built that can still be seen today.

The Egyptians created beautiful illustrations, but often they looked a lot alike. Artists and sculptors were expected to follow a formula, not come up with original ideas. For instance, Egyptians are often pictured in a half-profile pose (partly facing forward, partly facing to the side). So while the art was lovely and consistent, and although artists sometimes drew fun sketches, they did not use a new style for thousands of years.

WHERE'S MY COOL HEAD?

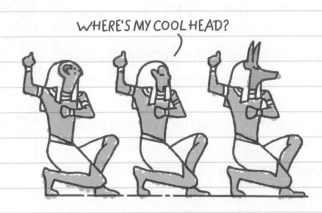

HIEROGLYPHICS

The Egyptians invented **HIEROGLYPHICS**, picture-like symbols used for writing. Hieroglyphics were complicated—to write a word you might have to spell it out **AND** add an extra picture to show what it meant. Only members of the upper and middle classes of society were trained as scribes. A simplified version of hieroglyphics, **HIERATIC SCRIPT**, was used for everyday business.

READ LIKE AN EGYPTIAN!

PAPYRUS

Although they first wrote on clay tablets, the Egyptians later invented **PAPYRUS**, a type of paper made from the papyrus plant. Papyrus most likely no longer grows in Egypt, but historians are pretty sure that it would have been a common plant along the Nile River in ancient times. Papyrus plants like to grow near marshy riverbanks because they need a lot of water. The Nile River Valley would have been ideal.

Egyptians wrote in hieroglyphics on papyrus in order to communicate across their empire and keep records of their history and achievements. The oldest papyrus scroll has been linked to the reign of Pharaoh Khufu, who ruled between 2575 and 2465 BCE.

PAPER LIKE WE USE TODAY WAS INVENTED BY THE CHINESE AND INTRODUCED TO THE MIDDLE EAST DURING THE 800s CE.

Papyrus was also popular in ancient Greece, Rome, and various Arabic regions.

Historians study papyrus documents that have survived many thousands of years. The sheets were formed by laying strips of papyrus stalks first diagonally and then horizontally. The damp layers were then pressed together and left to dry. Papyrus was normally made into rolls and stuck together with a paste. Egyptians wrote hieroglyphics mostly in black or red ink, but a skilled painter would also use white, blue, green, yellow, and orange ink.

ANCIENT EGYPT

3300–3200 BCE:
Egyptians develop hieroglyphics to communicate through writing.

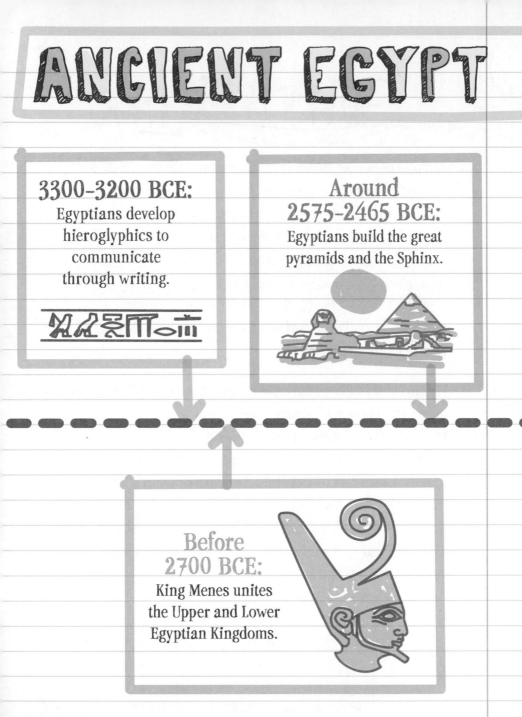

Around 2575–2465 BCE:
Egyptians build the great pyramids and the Sphinx.

Before 2700 BCE:
King Menes unites the Upper and Lower Egyptian Kingdoms.

TIMELINE

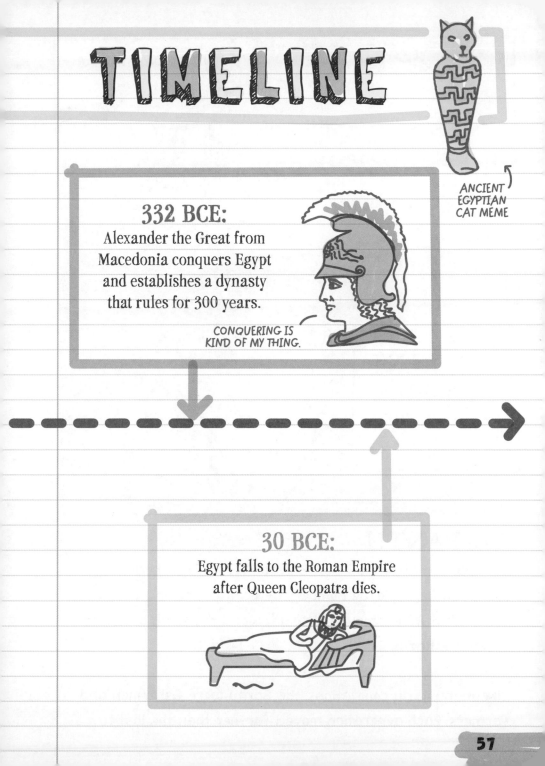

ANCIENT
EGYPTIAN
CAT MEME

332 BCE:
Alexander the Great from Macedonia conquers Egypt and establishes a dynasty that rules for 300 years.

CONQUERING IS
KIND OF MY THING.

30 BCE:
Egypt falls to the Roman Empire after Queen Cleopatra dies.

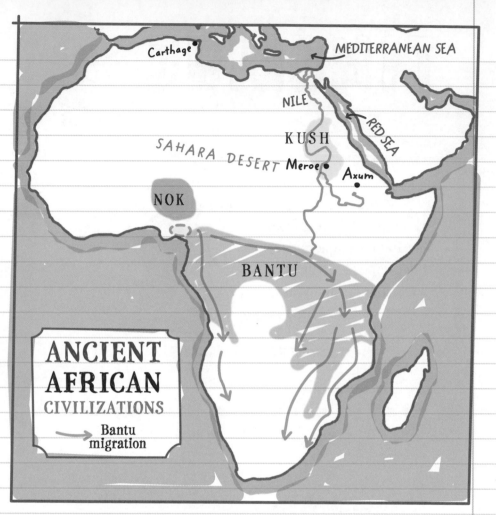

ANCIENT AFRICAN CIVILIZATIONS

→ Bantu migration

Map labels: Carthage, MEDITERRANEAN SEA, NILE, KUSH, RED SEA, SAHARA DESERT, Meroe, Axum, NOK, BANTU

The BANTU

In approximately 1500 BCE, BANTU MIGRATION began.
For 2,000 years, large numbers of Bantu-speaking people
from West Africa moved slowly toward the south and east
of the continent.

Like many early civilizations, the Bantu were fishermen and
farmers. Each generation moved farther than the last to

find more fertile land and better grazing for their animals. The villages were composed of clans that at times would move into already inhabited areas to share cultures and crops (yams, for example). The Bantu brought metalworking techniques with them, and iron tools and weapons. If their new neighbors weren't welcoming, the Bantu would put these weapons to use.

The KINGDOM of KUSH

The KINGDOM OF KUSH was at its most powerful between around 2000 BCE to 1500 BCE. Also called Nubia, it was an African civilization located on the Nile River south of Egypt. At first it was under Egyptian rule. Its major city was Meroe, which was the main residence of the rulers. The Kushites were farmers turned traders. They made iron weapons and tools, and they traded ivory, gold, ebony, and slaves to India, Arabia, and the Roman Empire.

The **ISLAND OF MEROE** ↰ NOT REALLY AN ISLAND was the capital and heart of the Kingdom of Kush. Home to Kush's leaders, and an important center of Egyptian and African civilization until the 4th century CE, the city includes a cemetery, pyramids, temples, palaces, domestic buildings, and evidence of Egyptian water management.

AFRICAN

Rock painting is Africa's oldest and longest-lasting
art form. The paintings show graceful human figures,
colorful animals, and **THERIANTHROPES**,
or figures with both human and animal
characteristics. At first glance, the rock
paintings across the continent seem very
similar, but a trained eyed can notice subtle
but distinct regional differences. Historians
have categorized three different
geographical styles: southern,
central, and northern.

Of these three regions, the rock paintings of Central
Africa are the most unusual. In the north and south,
images of animals and human beings are common,
but the rock paintings of Central Africa are usually
finger-painted, and mostly show geometric images.

ROCK ART

Paintings from the Kasama hills in Zambia show figures made of circles and lines in winding patterns that are as mysterious as they are beautiful. Across the millennia, generations, and cultures, African rock paintings capture a unique sense of movement and nature.

The NOK people lived to the south and west of the Sahara Desert in approximately 500 BCE. Each town had its own king, who ruled over communities of large families. The Nok worked as farmers, merchants, metalworkers, and craft workers specializing in clay figures. →

CARTHAGE was a city founded by the Phoenicians around about 800 BCE on the coast of North Africa. It became a large trading empire with colonies near and far, like in Spain and Sicily. Carthage was hugely powerful for about 600 years, until it fought Rome in three deadly wars. Three strikes and they were out.

In East Africa, a major trading center developed in the coastal city of AXUM in about 100 CE. Axum's trading center lasted for hundreds of years, controlling routes between the Mediterranean Sea and Asia.

There are very few written records for many ancient African cultures, which relied on ORAL TRADITIONS to transmit information from generation to generation. Historians also rely heavily on **ORAL HISTORIES** to gather the pieces of ancient Africa.

ORAL HISTORY
an account of the past handed down through spoken word, usually by the people who are considered to be the tradition keepers of a culture or society—elders, priests, etc.

CHECK YOUR KNOWLEDGE

1. How did the Nile River help the Egyptian people?

2. Describe the form of government in ancient Egypt.

3. What major feat was accomplished during the Old Kingdom?

4. What was important about the Middle Kingdom?

5. The Egyptians started out writing on clay, but eventually switched to a different material. What was it?

6. Were any women powerful in Egyptian society? Give an example.

7. Oral histories are stories of the past that people pass down by word of mouth. Why are oral histories more important in understanding ancient Africa than in understanding some other civilizations?

8. What civilization founded Carthage?

9. Where was the city of Carthage located, and how long did Carthage stay in power?

ANSWERS

CHECK YOUR ANSWERS

1. The Nile flooded every year and deposited rich soil on its banks, which helped with farming and led to a surplus of food. The annual flooding also helped the Egyptians create a calendar, travel, and communicate.

2. Egypt was ruled by a pharaoh with absolute power, which meant that whatever the pharaoh decided was law.

3. Both the great pyramids of Giza and the Great Sphinx were constructed during the Old Kingdom.

4. The Middle Kingdom was a stable period of expansion, and the pharaohs funded public projects like draining swampland and digging canals.

5. Egyptians switched to papyrus, which is a type of paper that is made from grass.

6. Yes, some were. Hatshepsut and Cleopatra ruled Egypt, and many Egyptian gods were female.

7. Oral histories are important in understanding ancient African history because there are very few written records for many ancient African cultures. Some other ancient civilizations had written records, so historians could use those records instead.

8. Carthage was founded by the Phoenicians.

9. Carthage was located on the coast of North Africa. Carthage stayed in power for about 600 years, until it fought Rome in three wars.

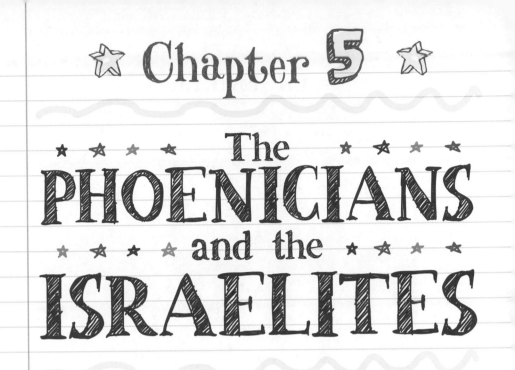

☆ Chapter **5** ☆

The PHOENICIANS and the ISRAELITES

PHOENICIA

The PHOENICIANS were a polytheistic, seafaring people who settled on the eastern coast of the Mediterranean Sea and lived there from 1550 to 300 BCE. They were best known for two things: their trade and their alphabet.

The Phoenicians told stories of sea monsters to scare off other people from trying to compete with them for trade.

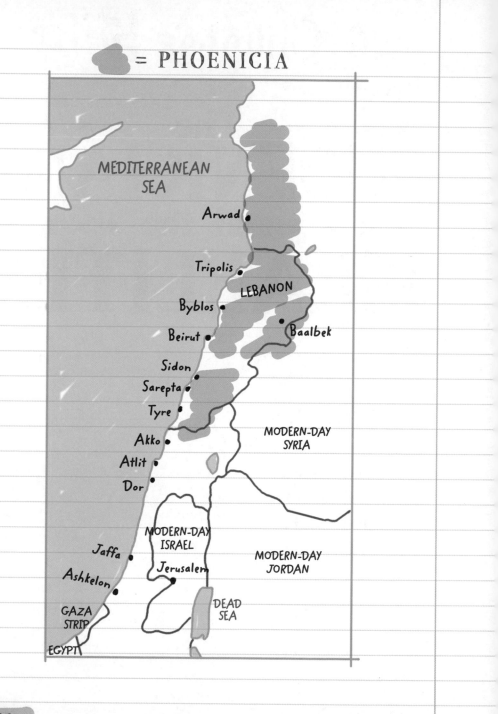

= PHOENICIA

MEDITERRANEAN
SEA

Arwad

Tripolis

LEBANON

Byblos

Beirut   Baalbek

Sidon

Sarepta

Tyre

Akko   MODERN-DAY
                  SYRIA
Atlit

Dor

            MODERN-DAY
            ISRAEL   MODERN-DAY
Jaffa   JORDAN

      Jerusalem

Ashkelon

GAZA   DEAD
STRIP   SEA

EGYPT

The Phoenicians traveled and traded as far as the Atlantic Ocean and built a colony in CARTHAGE in North Africa.

They built large ships, sailing from the central coastal town of Tyre and trading lumber from cedar forests and purple dye made from snails in exchange for figs, olives, and spices. The purple dye was used by the Phoenicians to dye cloth. Purple was a pretty fancy color at the time—it eventually came to signify royalty.

The Phoenicians' system of writing consisted of an alphabet of 22 characters to represent the sounds of their language. It was easier to spell out words with sounds than to use pictures for objects. This new alphabet wasn't just for scribes. It was created to help Phoenicians trade goods with peoples who spoke different languages. It spread as the Phoenicians traded with new lands. This alphabet would eventually be passed on to the Greeks, and then to the Romans, who created the alphabet we use today.

ISRAEL

The ISRAELITES lived south of Phoenicia in the land of Israel from around 1250 to 700 BCE. The TORAH, the sacred text of the Israelites, is used by historians looking for clues about ancient history. The Israelites' leader was ABRAHAM, who taught the Israelites monotheism. According to the Torah, Abraham received a divine command to leave Mesopotamia, so he led his people to Canaan (the modern-day regions of Israel, Lebanon, and the Palestinian territories) in perhaps 2000 BCE. Because of drought and famine, the Israelites moved to Egypt, where they were eventually enslaved, and were freed only when MOSES led them out of Egypt in the **GREAT EXODUS**, possibly between 1450 and 1200 BCE. Eventually, the Israelites returned to Canaan.

> **EXODUS**
> any kind of mass departure

JERUSALEM

After defeating the Philistines in Canaan, King David developed Israel into a united kingdom and made JERUSALEM its capital in 1000 BCE. David's son, King Solomon, built the Temple of Jerusalem. When Solomon died around 931 BCE, the kingdom split into two parts: the kingdom of Israel in the north, and the kingdom of Judah in the south.

> AS IN DAVID AND GOLIATH

The Assyrians took advantage of the unrest to gain control. Then, in turn, the Chaldeans conquered them, destroyed Jerusalem, and **EXILED** the people to Babylonia. Next in line to

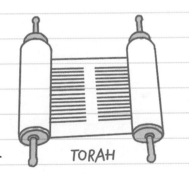

EXILE
to force people out of their country or homeland

conquer the region were the PERSIANS, who allowed the Israelites to return and rebuild Jerusalem and its temple. The Israelites eventually became known as the Jewish people, and their religion is called Judaism.

JUDAISM

The ancient Israelites' religion was JUDAISM. It is characterized by a **COVENANT** between the Israelites and their monotheistic God. The contract, according to their sacred text (the Torah), promised Abraham that his people would become kings and build nations if they followed God's laws. Later, Moses promised to lead the Israelites back to Canaan, or "the promised land."

COVENANT
a contract or agreement

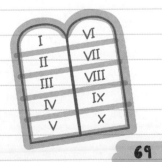

TORAH

The TEN COMMANDMENTS are Judaism's divine laws on proper behavior toward God and each other

I	VI
II	VII
III	VIII
IV	IX
V	X

and are believed to have been given to the Israelites through Moses. In ancient times, Judaism had PROPHETS, religious teachers who spoke for God. The prophets advised people on how God wanted them to live.

CHECK YOUR KNOWLEDGE

1. Which people practiced monotheism—the Phoenicians or the Israelites?

2. What are the Phoenicians famous for?

3. Why was the Phoenician alphabet so useful?

4. What is the sacred text of the Israelites, and what does it say about Abraham and Moses?

5. What did the Persians do when they conquered the Chaldeans?

6. What are the major features of Judaism?

7. What did the Israelites believe about prophets?

ANSWERS ▶

CHECK YOUR ANSWERS

1. The Israelites practiced monotheism.
2. The Phoenicians were famous for their extensive trade and for their alphabet.
3. The Phoenician alphabet could be learned by anyone, so it helped Phoenicians trade goods with peoples who spoke different languages.
4. The sacred text of the Israelites is the Torah. According to the Torah, Abraham taught the Israelites monotheism and was commanded by God to leave Mesopotamia and lead them to Canaan. The Torah says that when the Israelites were enslaved in Egypt, Moses led them out of Egypt in the Great Exodus and gave them the Ten Commandments, which were divine laws.
5. When the Persians conquered the Chaldeans, they allowed the Israelites to return to Israel and rebuild Jerusalem and its temple.
6. Judaism is characterized by monotheism, a contract between the Israelites and God, the Ten Commandments, and prophets.
7. The Israelites believed that prophets were religious teachers who could speak for God and tell people about how God wanted them to live.

Chapter 6

ANCIENT INDIA

2600 BCE–500 CE

India is separated from other countries in Asia by the HIMALAYAS, the highest mountain range in the world. Small gaps in this wall of mountains allowed people to pass through and settle in places like the INDUS RIVER VALLEY.

The INDUS RIVER VALLEY

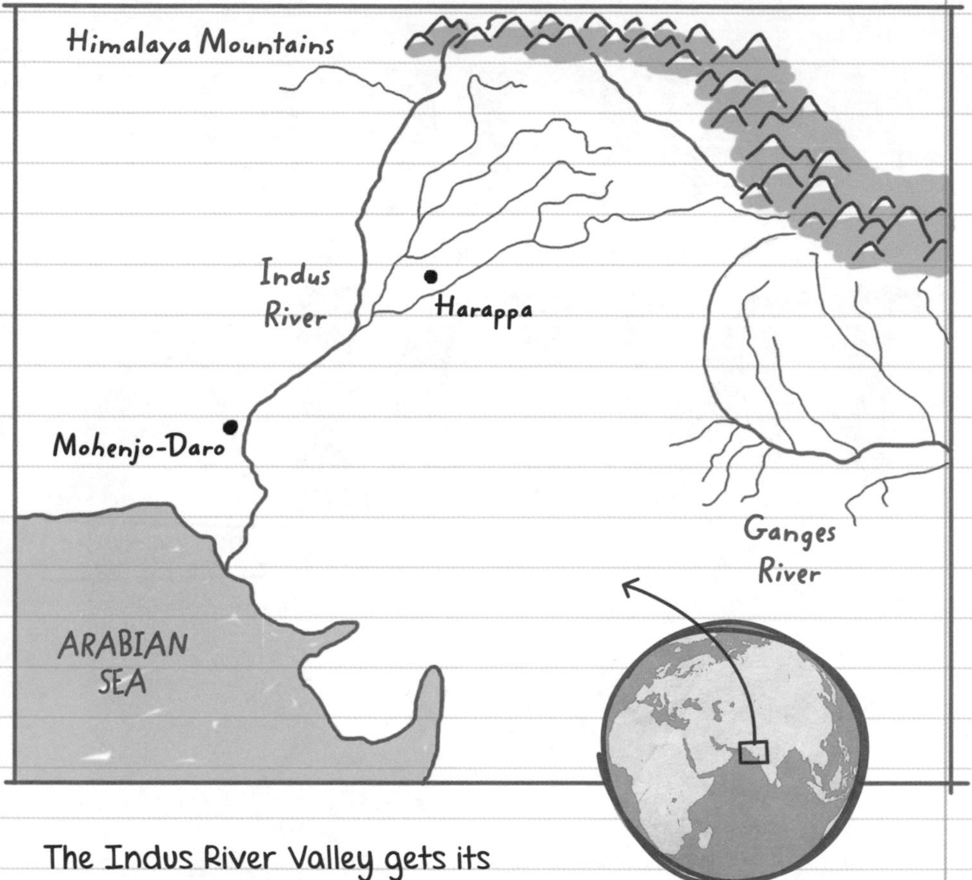

Himalaya Mountains

Indus
River

Harappa

Mohenjo-Daro

ARABIAN
SEA

Ganges
River

The Indus River Valley gets its
name—and its rich soil—from the
INDUS RIVER, which crosses the Himalayas and flows as
far as the Arabian Sea. Another river, the GANGES, also cuts
through the Himalayas; it empties into the Bay of Bengal.
The two rivers created fertile land for farming, and their
banks became the sites of major cities. In the Indus River
Valley, the cities of HARAPPA and MOHENJO-DARO emerged

around 2600 BCE and grew to nearly 40,000 people. The cities were carefully laid out in a grid.

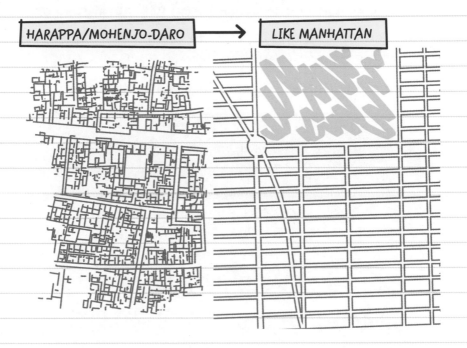

HARAPPA/MOHENJO-DARO → LIKE MANHATTAN

A **CITADEL** on each city's highest point protected its most important buildings, like the grain storage houses. These cities had advanced drainage systems. There were

CITADEL
a fortress that overlooks the city

public wells, and many buildings had a bathroom (this was a really great new invention). Trade was prosperous; copper and lumber were the main exports. They traded with Sumer, and similarities in art suggest the two cultures mimicked each other's best work.

Around 2000 BCE the Indus valley farmers began to abandon their land—maybe because of natural disasters and invasions by nomads. Around 1500 BCE, ARYANS moved in from Central Asia and mixed with the original inhabitants of the Indus Valley, creating a new culture that eventually spread into the GANGES VALLEY, located to the east.

> Around 1550 BCE, a system of writing called **SANSKRIT** was developed in India. The oldest text in the language is the RIG VEDA, an ancient religious document from the northern midlands of India. While Sanskrit is no longer spoken by many people, Dravidian, an ancient relation of Sanskrit, is still spoken in southern India.

तकराञामाञरीाांडइस्डञलिाञगण गोब्लिड्माबननिवाञलयलिसुडेारा

SOCIAL STRUCTURE

This new culture was organized by a **CASTE SYSTEM** called VARNAS:

CASTE SYSTEM
a social structure in which classes are determined by birthright

BRAHMANS: the highest caste; they performed religious services

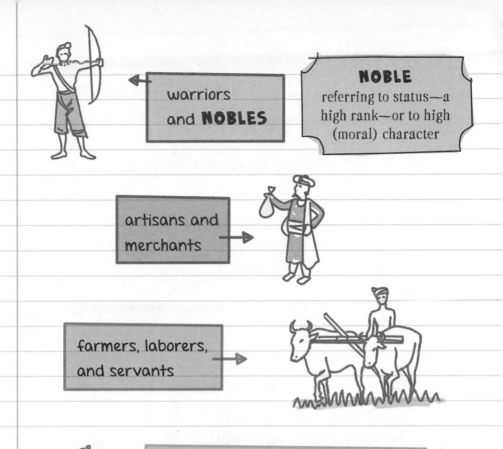

warriors and NOBLES

NOBLE referring to status—a high rank—or to high (moral) character

artisans and merchants

farmers, laborers, and servants

UNTOUCHABLES: at the bottom; people considered them so impure their only work could be burying bodies or collecting trash

Under the caste system, there was no upward mobility for individuals; a person born to servant parents was stuck being a servant. A farmer couldn't become a warrior, and a warrior couldn't become a Brahman. No one asked what you wanted to be when you grew up; it was already determined by your lineage.

HINDUISM

Two major religions originated in India: HINDUISM and
BUDDHISM. Hinduism originated about 1500 BCE from the
blending of Aryan beliefs with the cultures of the original
settlers of India. According to Hindu beliefs, there is
one prevailing spiritual power that lives in everything.
Hindus also believe in many gods and goddesses, including
BRAHMA (the Creator), VISHNU (the Preserver), and SHIVA
(the Destroyer).

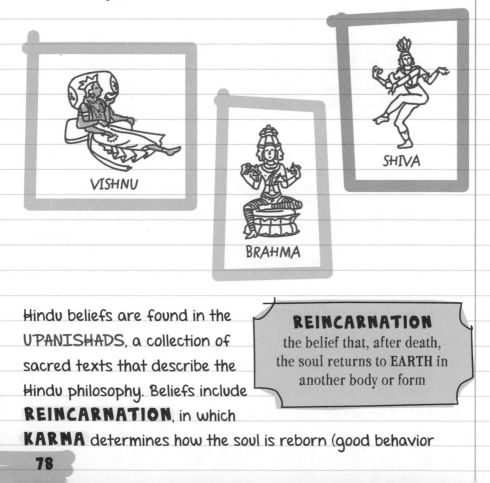

VISHNU

BRAHMA

SHIVA

Hindu beliefs are found in the
UPANISHADS, a collection of
sacred texts that describe the
Hindu philosophy. Beliefs include
REINCARNATION, in which
KARMA determines how the soul is reborn (good behavior

REINCARNATION
the belief that, after death,
the soul returns to EARTH in
another body or form

may lead to rebirth into a higher caste; bad behavior is punished). If you led a perfect life, you would be freed from the cycle of death and rebirth and become one with the BRAHMAN, the spiritual center of

the universe. Believers must obey their DHARMA, a divine law of religious and moral duties unique to each individual. Other ways of uniting with Brahman were through yoga, which is widely popular today as a workout, but according to Hindu beliefs, it is a form of exercise that frees the soul.

DON'T CONFUSE THESE:

BRAHMAN: top of the caste system
BRAHMA: a top deity
BRAHMAN: spiritual top of the universe

BUDDHISM

Buddhism appeared as a rival religion in the sixth century BCE. SIDDHARTHA GAUTAMA, a young Hindu prince living in the lap of luxury, left his palace and saw the devastation of the real world. In the foothills of the Himalayas he found sickness and poverty, sorrow, greed, love, and death. Siddhartha decided to abandon his riches to seek the meaning of life and the cure for human suffering.

He's the founder of Buddhism and became known as the BUDDHA, or "Enlightened One."

Siddhartha took up the Hindu practice of **MEDITATION**, focusing his mind to reach a higher level of awareness. Buddhists believe that he achieved

> **MEDITATION**
> thinking deeply or focusing one's mind in silence or with chanting

enlightenment and came to understand the meaning of life. Siddhartha spent the rest of his life spreading his FOUR NOBLE TRUTHS, which teach that feelings of suffering in our lives will end when we stop trying to satisfy selfish goals, overcome the desire for material objects, and begin to see others as extensions of ourselves. Siddhartha broke this idea down for his followers in his EIGHTFOLD PATH.

The Eightfold Path teaches that we must overcome selfish desires for power and wealth and learn to be wise so that we may reach NIRVANA: everlasting peace where the self ends and reunites with the Great World Soul. After Siddhartha's death, which was somewhere between 410 and 370 BCE, his followers continued to spread his message, building monasteries to promote his teachings.

> NIRVANA CAN BE REACHED BY YOU, THE PRESIDENT, OR PEOPLE OF ANY SOCIAL CLASS.

The principles of the Eightfold Path are:

RIGHT UNDERSTANDING –
Understanding the Buddha's teachings

RIGHT INTENTION – Improving yourself
mentally and ethically

RIGHT SPEECH – Saying no hurtful or
negative things; telling no lies

RIGHT ACTION – No killing, stealing,
or harming others

RIGHT LIVELIHOOD – Living and
working in a peaceful way

RIGHT EFFORT – Thinking positively

RIGHT MINDFULNESS – Being aware of your
own—and others'—bodies, feelings, and thoughts

RIGHT CONCENTRATION – Thinking
clearly and being "in the moment"

**Remember the main principles of the Eightfold Path
of Buddhism with this mnemonic device:**

Unicorns (Understanding)

In (Intention)

Saris (Speech)

Always (Action)

Love (Livelihood)

Eating (Effort)

My (Mindfulness)

Curry (Concentration)

CURRY?
FOR ME?!
I LOVE
CURRY!

ANCIENT INDIA

2600 BCE:

A civilization develops around the Indus River Valley that uses crops grown on the fertile land around the river for trade. At its peak, the Indus River Valley is the largest ancient empire.

2000 BCE:

The Indus River Valley Empire falls, most likely because of extreme flooding, invaders, or because the Indus River changed its course.

1500 BCE:

The Aryan people from an Indo-Europe region invade from the north. They settle as far as the Ganges Valley.

TIMELINE

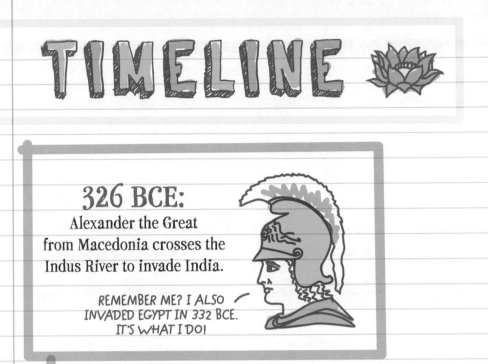

326 BCE:
Alexander the Great from Macedonia crosses the Indus River to invade India.

REMEMBER ME? I ALSO INVADED EGYPT IN 332 BCE. IT'S WHAT I DO!

50 CE:
The Romans trade with India for pearls, ivory, silk, spices, cloths, and precious stones.

320 CE - 550 CE:
India enters a golden age under the Gupta Empire. Hinduism becomes the major religion, and the population makes great leaps in literature, art, architecture, and science.

The MAURYA EMPIRE and the GUPTA DYNASTY

Around 322 BCE, CHANDRAGUPTA MAURYA founded the MAURYA EMPIRE, overthrowing kingdoms along the Ganges River and extending his power over most of northern and central India. His armies were powerful, and he had a herd of 9,000 war elephants. Chandragupta governed by ABSOLUTE RULE,

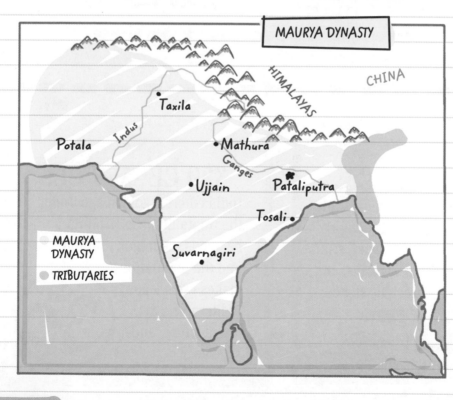

MAURYA DYNASTY

HIMALAYAS

CHINA

Taxila

Indus

Potala

Mathura

Ganges

Ujjain

Pataliputra

Tosali

MAURYA DYNASTY

TRIBUTARIES

Suvarnagiri

complete power over his people. He
constantly feared for his life. He
made servants taste his food to test
for poison, and he never slept in the
same bed two nights in a row.

Chandragupta's grandson AŚOKA
was another powerful leader. He converted to Buddhism
after waging a violent war in Kalinga and seeing the
devastation it had caused. He spread Buddhism throughout
the empire, built hospitals, and practiced religious tolerance.

After Aśoka's death, the Maurya Empire weakened and was
plagued by foreign invasions until 320 CE, when the GUPTA
dynasty took over. The people enjoyed a golden age of
Indian culture:

Techniques for printing on cloth were devised.

Schools of philosophy developed.

KALIDASA, one of the great Indian poets, wrote
the popular Sanskrit poem *The Cloud Messenger.*

Hindu and Buddhist temples and shrines were built.

The DECIMAL SYSTEM and the
concept of ZERO were invented.

This golden age of culture and trade lasted until the HUNS
invaded in the late fifth century CE and fractured India.
Northern India would remain splintered for hundreds of years.

CHECK YOUR KNOWLEDGE

1. Why were India's earliest civilizations formed alongside rivers? How were they laid out?

2. What mountain range separates India from other countries?

3. What is a caste system? Who was at the top of the caste system and who was at the bottom?

4. What are the two major religions that originated in India?

5. Briefly describe how each religion was formed. What are the major texts and principles each religion is founded upon?

6. Why do you think Buddhism became such a popular religion in so many countries outside of India?

7. How long did the golden age of Indian culture last, and what was invented during this time?

ANSWERS

CHECK YOUR ANSWERS

1. India's early civilizations were formed alongside rivers in order to take advantage of the fertile soil for farming. Harappa and Mohenjo-Daro were laid out in grids.

2. The Himalayas, the highest mountain range in the world

3. A caste system is a social system that separates people into different classes according to the families they were born into. A person born to servant parents must be a servant, and people can't change the class that they were born into. The Brahmans were at the top of the caste system, and the untouchables were at the bottom.

4. Hinduism and Buddhism originated in India.

5. Hinduism was formed by blending Aryan beliefs with the cultures of India's original settlers. Hindus believe in one spiritual power that lives in everything and also believe in many gods and goddesses, reincarnation, and karma. Their sacred text is the Upanishads. Buddhism was founded by Siddhartha Gautama. Buddhism's Eightfold Path says that people must overcome selfish desires and learn to be wise so that they can reach nirvana.

6. There are lots of possible reasons, but some might be because of Buddhism's focus on personal enlightenment, giving up selfishness to end suffering, finding inner peace, and practicing yoga and other exercises to free the mind and soul.

7. The golden age lasted about 200 years. It started when the Gupta dynasty took over and lasted until the Huns invaded. During this time, Indians invented a technique for printing on cloth, the decimal system, and the concept of zero.

Chapter 7
ANCIENT CHINA

1750 BCE–220 CE

As in other great early civilizations, the people of ancient China farmed, and they settled near major rivers in what would later become important cities. More than 5,000 years ago, farming in China was primarily done in the valley of the Huang He, or Yellow River. Rice farming was especially important to the area. The land was fertile, though great MONSOONS, or seasonal winds causing heavy rain and floods, destroyed the surrounding areas.

The SHANG DYNASTY

THE SHANG DYNASTY built China's first cities in about 1760 BCE. Dynasties passed down ruling power from one generation to the next. During the Shang dynasty, bronze work and expert toolmaking flourished. Also during this time, the people invented the first Chinese writing system. Farming was important but was under **ARISTOCRATIC** control: Farmers supplied food to their local nobleman in exchange for protection. These aristocrats relied on land for wealth and passed this power on from generation to generation.

> **ARISTOCRACY**
> a group of people holding the highest rank, usually by birthright; the elite

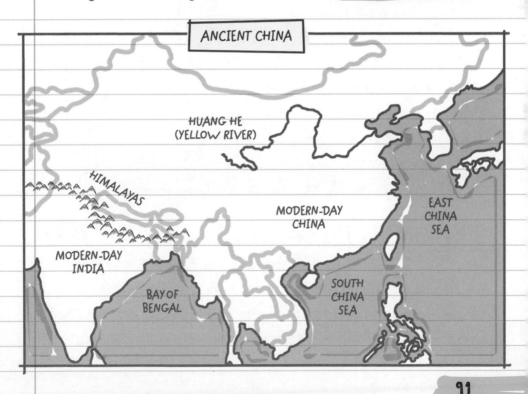

ANCIENT CHINA

HUANG HE
(YELLOW RIVER)

HIMALAYAS

MODERN-DAY
CHINA

EAST
CHINA
SEA

MODERN-DAY
INDIA

BAY OF
BENGAL

SOUTH
CHINA
SEA

Around the time of the Shang dynasty, the first Chinese writing system was created with characters to represent words. (Historians don't know exactly how long this system was in place, but the oldest examples from the Shang dynasty era show writing that was very well developed.) The kings of the Shang dynasty believed their ancestors could advise them after death. They carved questions and answers onto pieces of ox bones or turtle ➔ shells in order to ask questions such as, "When is the best time to grow crops?"

The ZHOU DYNASTY

HEY, HOW ABOUT USING SOME PAPYRUS?

THE ZHOU DYNASTY took control around 1050 BCE and ruled for nearly 800 years. The kings built forts and walls to defend their land against each other. Like the Shang, the Zhou kingdom was divided into territories governed by officials.

Those who owned the land that the peasants farmed kept a large share of the harvested crops for themselves. These states fought each other for power in the period called the WARRING STATES (about 475 BCE–221 BCE).

After about 500 years of fighting, the first emperor of China, the QIN ruler Shih Huang-di, gained control. He began construction of the GREAT WALL OF CHINA, one of the largest frontier defenses in the world. It is longer than the distance from New York City to Milan, Italy. The wall was built by millions of poor Chinese workers; this led to uprisings by both the army and the peasants after Shih Huang-di's death.

The HAN DYNASTY

THE HAN DYNASTY followed this rebellion, beginning around 206 BCE. The first Han emperor, LIU BANG, started out as only a minor official whose parents had been peasants. Under his great-grandson WUDI's rule, the Great Wall and the army were strengthened. The Han dynasty began trading with the Western world through the SILK ROAD, a trade route from China all the way to the Mediterranean Sea. The main Chinese export was silk, made by silkworms. Europeans weren't used to such smooth, soft material (great for underwear).

SO SOFT!

THE GREAT WALL OF CHINA

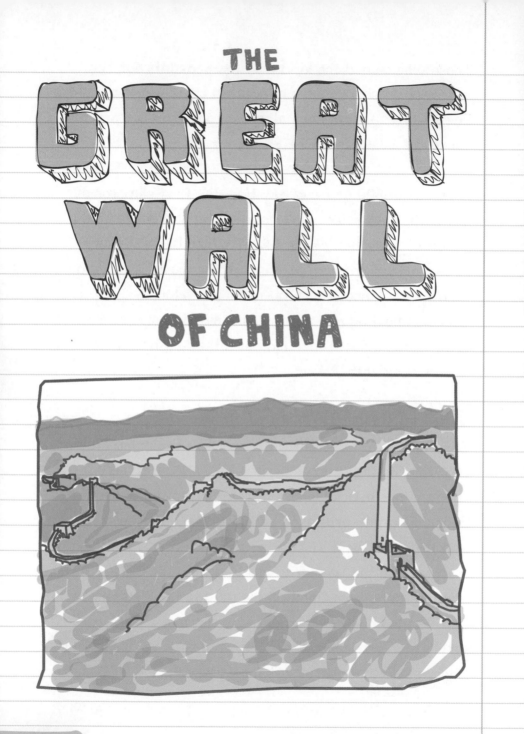

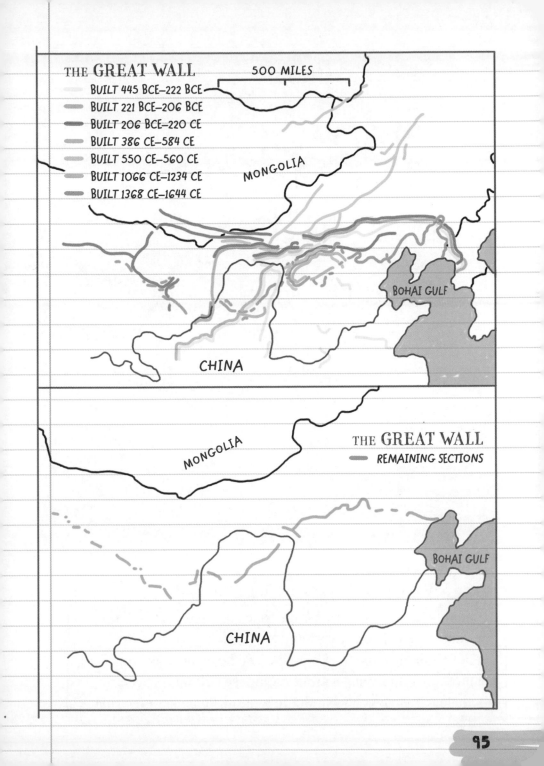

THE GREAT WALL   500 MILES
— BUILT 445 BCE–222 BCE
— BUILT 221 BCE–206 BCE
— BUILT 206 BCE–220 CE
— BUILT 386 CE–584 CE
— BUILT 550 CE–560 CE
— BUILT 1066 CE–1234 CE
— BUILT 1368 CE–1644 CE

MONGOLIA

BOHAI GULF

CHINA

MONGOLIA

THE GREAT WALL
— REMAINING SECTIONS

BOHAI GULF

CHINA

95

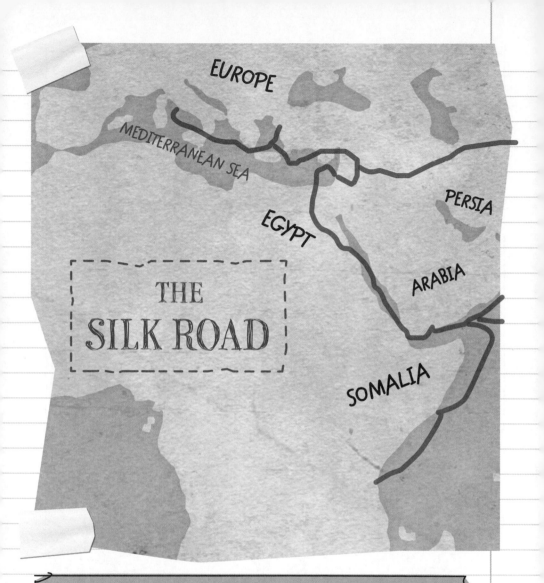

THE
SILK ROAD

The **SILK ROAD** was not actually one road—it was more of a 4,000-mile-long system of trade routes that connected China to Europe, the Middle East, and North Africa. Travel was not safe on the Silk Road, which could be home to bandits, murderers, and Mongol armies. Chinese silk was especially valuable in Rome, though, where wealthy Romans were proud

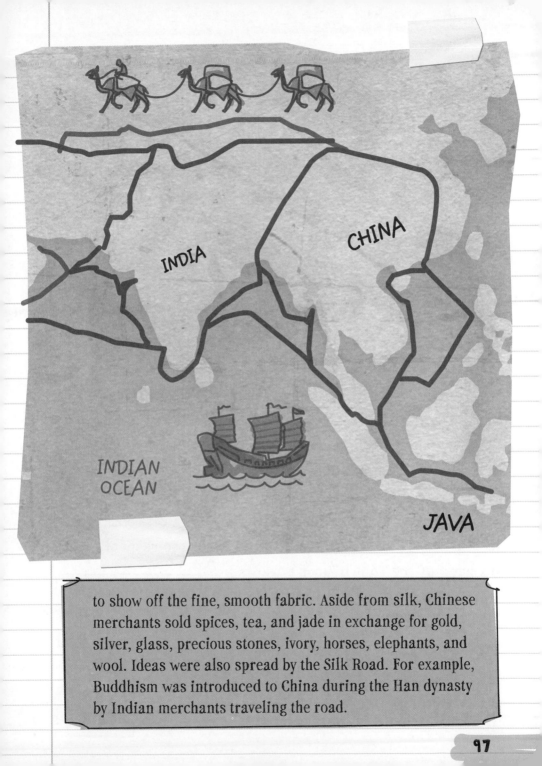

to show off the fine, smooth fabric. Aside from silk, Chinese merchants sold spices, tea, and jade in exchange for gold, silver, glass, precious stones, ivory, horses, elephants, and wool. Ideas were also spread by the Silk Road. For example, Buddhism was introduced to China during the Han dynasty by Indian merchants traveling the road.

The Chinese created the sailboat rudder, manufactured steel, and made paper from wood pulp. They made medicinal advances, like what became known as ACUPUNCTURE (placing needles on various spots in the body to treat ailments—it doesn't hurt!). They invented herbal medicines and also traded in spices, tea, and porcelain.

> Gunpowder is also said to have been discovered in ancient China, but not until the Tang dynasty in the ninth century CE.

THE MANDATE OF HEAVEN: The rulers of
ancient China believed that they were destined to rule by a MANDATE (command) from heaven. The ruler was considered the link between heaven and earth. He was expected to be virtuous and rule to please the gods. Ancient Mandarin and Confucian scholars influenced Chinese kings to honor the mandate by taking care of the people.

Family came first in Chinese society; you were responsible to your family above all. You also had a duty to respect the head of the family (your parents, elders, and ancestors), an idea called **FILIAL PIETY**. EXTENDED FAMILIES lived together: mother, father, children, cousins, uncles, aunts, great-aunts, grandmothers, great-grandmothers, great-great-grandmothers, and so on and so on.

FILIAL
the relationship between children and parents

PIETY
respect

98

There could be as many as five generations living together, and maybe people from age one to one hundred! The early Chinese practiced ancestor worship in **HOMAGE** to their deceased family members.

HOMAGE
an expression of high regard; respect

CONFUCIANISM

Confucius was a famous Chinese teacher and philosopher. Born in 551 BCE to a noble but poor family, he worked to pass on the forgotten teachings of thinkers from an earlier age and to bring peace and stability to the people of China, starting with family and friends.

CONFUCIANISM holds that there are five human relationships:

1. RULER AND RULED

2. FRIEND AND FRIEND

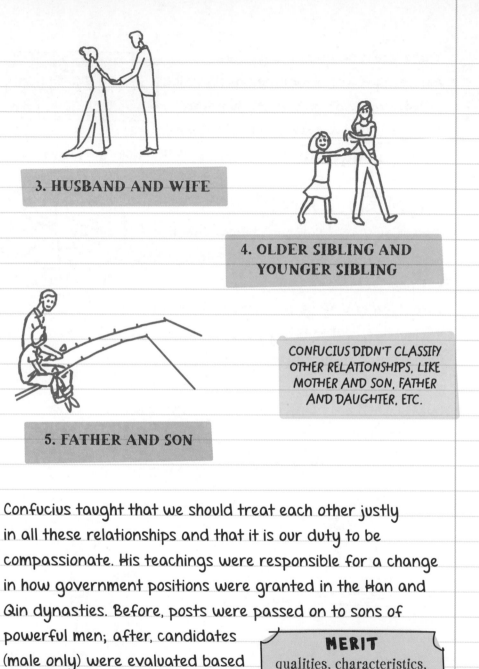

3. HUSBAND AND WIFE

4. OLDER SIBLING AND YOUNGER SIBLING

CONFUCIUS DIDN'T CLASSIFY OTHER RELATIONSHIPS, LIKE MOTHER AND SON, FATHER AND DAUGHTER, ETC.

5. FATHER AND SON

Confucius taught that we should treat each other justly in all these relationships and that it is our duty to be compassionate. His teachings were responsible for a change in how government positions were granted in the Han and Qin dynasties. Before, posts were passed on to sons of powerful men; after, candidates (male only) were evaluated based on **MERIT**.

MERIT
qualities, characteristics, or achievements

TAOISM

TAOISM is another philosophy developed around the time of Confucianism, in the 500s BCE. It is based on the writings of LAOZI (also spelled LAO-TZU). Followers believe happiness comes from leading a balanced life in harmony with nature, through living simple and selfless lives. Both Taoism and Confucianism are considered philosophies, rather than religions, because they examine human behavior rather than search for a divine meaning to the universe.

Over time, Taoism grew into an organized religion. More writing, gods, and schools with different ideas were created. In today's China, Buddhism and Taoism are the two most popular religions in the country.

The **YIN** and the **YANG** is probably the most well-known Taoist symbol in the modern world. Yin, the dark side, represents shade, water, west, and the tiger. Yang, the light side, is associated with light, fire, east, and the dragon. Separately, Yin and Yang represent opposing ideas, but together, their balance brings harmony to the universe.

DIVIDED CHINA

By 220 CE, warlords had taken control from the Han dynasty. Civil war divided China into smaller kingdoms, and it would take 400 years before the next great dynasty emerged.

DIVIDED CHINA

BEI
(NORTHERN WEI)

HIMALAYAS

CHENGDU

EAST
CHINA
SEA

NAN
(SOUTHERN QI)

HANOI

SOUTH
CHINA
SEA

CHECK YOUR KNOWLEDGE

1. What was China's first civilization, and what was invented during that period?

2. Why do you think that China's first civilizations formed alongside rivers? How can you connect this to what you have learned so far about other ancient civilizations, such as Mesopotamia, Egypt, and India?

3. A very important export developed during the Han dynasty. What was it?

4. Why are Confucianism and Taoism considered philosophies rather than religions?

5. Describe ancient Chinese rulers' relationship to power. Was power something they gained over a lifetime or something they were born with?

6. What were some of the ruler's duties in ancient China?

7. Monsoons occur every season in China and parts of India. What are they?

ANSWERS 103

CHECK YOUR ANSWERS

1. China's first civilization was the Shang dynasty, and the first Chinese writing system was invented during that time.

2. As in other early civilizations, the people of ancient China farmed and settled near major rivers because the land was fertile. Easier farming and reliable sources of food make it more possible for people to settle in cities and start doing things with their time other than hunting for food.

3. The Han dynasty began trading silk with the Western world through the Silk Road.

4. Taoism and Confucianism are considered philosophies because they analyze human behavior instead of search for a holy meaning to life.

5. The rulers of ancient China believed in the Mandate of Heaven, which was a command from heaven that destined them to rule. Therefore, they were born with power, and the king was considered the link between heaven and earth.

6. The king was expected to be good and rule to please the gods.

7. Monsoons are seasonal winds causing heavy rains and floods. They can destroy lands surrounding rivers.

Chapter 8

ANCIENT GREECE

3000 BCE–1 CE

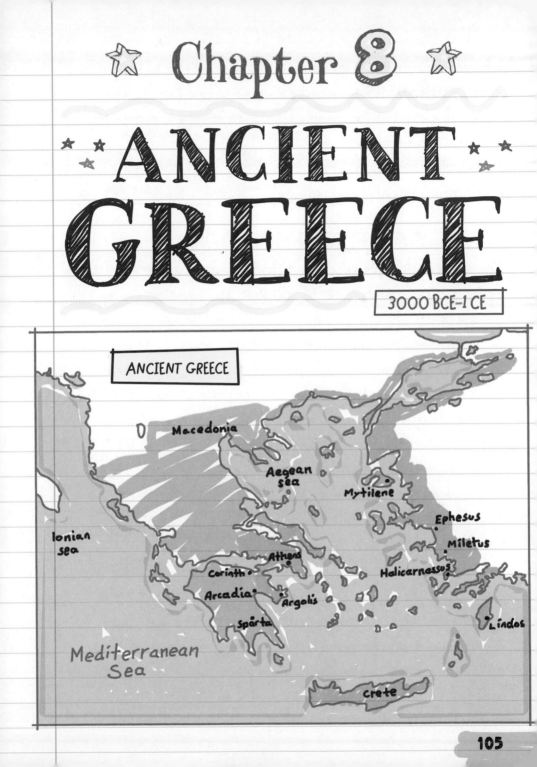

ANCIENT GREECE

Macedonia

Aegean Sea

Mytilene

Ionian Sea

Ephesus

Miletus

Athens

Corinth

Halicarnassus

Arcadia

Argolis

Sparta

Lindos

Mediterranean Sea

Crete

Greece was (and still is) made up of many little islands and slim **PENINSULAS** bunched together in one big cluster.

This made it hard for people from different islands to connect to each other (geographically and culturally).

> **PENINSULA**
> a mass of land that projects out and is surrounded by water on three sides

EARLY GREEK HISTORY

The MINOANS were successful traders who lived on an island called CRETE around 3000 to 1100 BCE. They had an elegant palace in the ancient city of Knossos. The Minoan civilization declined when invaders from mainland Greece, probably the MYCENAEANS, took over around 1400 BCE. The Mycenaeans lived principally on the mainland, in the city of Mycenae. They used writing, as the Minoans had done. The Mycenaean writing system (Linear B) is the earliest form of written Greek. No one has figured out the hundreds of symbols in the Minoan writing system (Linear A) yet.

> To remember which early Greek civilizations fared better than the other, think:
> The **Mighty Mycenaeans** beat the minnow-like **Minoans**.

GEE, THANKS!

Then came the Trojan War, which took place around 1194-1184 BCE. Historians disagree about whether this war was really fought or whether it's a mixed-up memory of a lot of different events, but it marks the decline of Greek civilization and the beginning of the DARK AGES in Greece (1100s-750 BCE). It is believed that large-scale trading ended and poverty spread. Things were desperate. We have no written records of this time.

THE TROJAN HORSE

According to Greek legend, Greek soldiers hid in a giant wooden horse to sneak into the city of Troy and conquer it! You can read all about it in two epic poems that recount the Trojan War, the *Aeneid* and the *Odyssey*.

Sometime around 800 BCE, CITY-STATES began to form and written records reappeared. Usually led by aristocrats and military rulers, the city-state (also called the POLIS) was the center of Greek life. Eventually some citizens came up with the idea to form a type of government called DEMOCRACY, where citizens govern themselves (more on that later).

Around 750 BCE, the Greek poet **Homer** tells the story of the Trojan War in his epic poem the *Iliad*. It describes the city of Troy waging a war against ancient Greece for ten years. The fighting started because the Trojan prince Paris abducted Helen, who was the wife of the Spartan King Menelaus. In the first century BCE, Virgil, a great Roman poet, also wrote an epic poem about the Trojan War— the *Aeneid*. In Virgil's poem, the Greek gods take sides. It ends with a mythical prince named Aeneas escaping as the city of Troy burns down. In the poem, Aeneas goes on to found the Roman state.

HOMER

The GOLDEN AGE

By 700 BCE, Athens was the city-state where everything was happening. At first it was ruled by a king. Later, the Athenian leader SOLON reformed the economy and government in 594 BCE. He made changes like freeing people who had fallen into slavery from debt, and then he canceled debt altogether. Still, only one in five Athenians was considered a citizen.

Soon there was the golden age of Greece, a period during which Athens grew rich from silver and trade and made important cultural achievements. From 479 BCE to 431 BCE, the people of Greece were busy developing their philosophy, religion, art, and architecture.

GREEK RELIGION

The Greeks worshipped a family of gods and goddesses led by ZEUS and HERA, the king and queen of the gods. Gods ruled different areas of life, like war (ARES), love (APHRODITE), and the sea (POSEIDON). The Greeks believed that the most powerful gods formed a family called the Olympians.

NOT REALLY A NORMAL FAMILY, BUT WHAT'S A NORMAL FAMILY, ANYWAY?

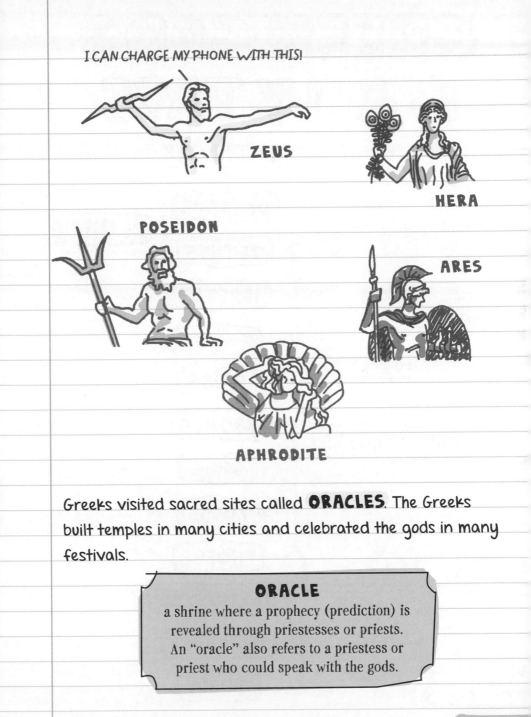

I CAN CHARGE MY PHONE WITH THIS!

ZEUS

HERA

POSEIDON

ARES

APHRODITE

Greeks visited sacred sites called **ORACLES**. The Greeks built temples in many cities and celebrated the gods in many festivals.

ORACLE
a shrine where a prophecy (prediction) is revealed through priestesses or priests. An "oracle" also refers to a priestess or priest who could speak with the gods.

GREEK GODS FAMILY TREE

THE TITANS

GAEA

OURANOS

THE CYCLOPES

OCEANUS

CLYMENE

TETHYS

IAPETUS

THEMIS

KRIOS

KRONOS

RHEA

POLOS

PHOEBE

MNEMOSYNE

HYPERION

THEIA

THE **OLYMPIANS**

DIONYSOS

ATLAS

ATHENA

PROMETHEUS

HERMES

EPIMETHEUS

MENOITIOS

ZEUS

ARES

HERA

HEPHAISTOS

DEMETER

HADES

APHRODITE

↳ NOT AN OLYMPIAN

↑ BORN FROM FOAM!

LETO

POSEIDON

HESTIA

ARTEMIS

APOLLO

111

THE OLYMPIC GAMES

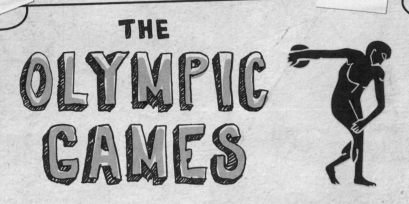

The Olympic Games began around 776 BCE as a festival for the Olympians. Athletic games were a way of honoring the gods. According to some myths, Zeus defeated Kronos in a fight for the throne of the gods. Later, Herakles (also known as Hercules), a demigod, staged the games in honor of Zeus. The first real games were held on the ancient plains of Olympia. They were held for nearly 12 centuries, until Emperor Theodosius banned them in 393 CE because he believed they were a pagan ritual.

The ancient Olympic Games included poetry competitions and:

RUNNING – 200-meter and 400-meter footraces

JUMPING – Halteres (stone or lead weights) were used to increase the distance of athletes' jumps. They held the weights until the end of their jump, then threw the weights backward.

DISCUS THROW – The techniques used in the ancient games are very similar to today's techniques.

WRESTLING – Matches ended only when one contestant admitted defeat.

BOXING – The fighters sometimes wrapped their hands in hard leather, which caused disfigurement to their opponents' faces.

PANKRATION – This was a primitive form of martial arts that mixed boxing and wrestling. The ancient Greeks believed it was founded when Theseus defeated the Minotaur.

HORSE AND CHARIOT RACES – Races were held in the hippodrome, which was a stadium built for horse racing.

GREEK PHILOSOPHY

Early Greek philosophers focused on the development of rational thought. They were trying to come up with a system of thinking to explain the universe.

Several important philosophers taught in Athens:

SOCRATES taught people how to think and figure things out by asking questions (the SOCRATIC METHOD). Sometimes he disagreed with the rulers or doubted the existence of the gods, and eventually he was executed by being made to drink hemlock, a poison.

SOCRATES

PLATO studied under Socrates. He wrote a book called THE REPUBLIC and believed society should be divided into three groups: workers, soldiers, and philosopher-rulers. He taught his students how to live by a code of ethics that would lead them to moral, happy lives.

PLATO

Unlike Socrates, who never wrote anything down, Plato wrote down **EVERYTHING**—about reality and objects, war and government, and justice and society. He founded and taught at an Athenian school, called the **ACADEMY**, to train government leaders.

ARISTOTLE studied under Plato. Like Plato, Aristotle believed people's happiness was connected to their behavior. He also worked to define categories of logic, biology, and physics; he was fascinated

ARISTOTLE

by nature, and he classified plants and animals in a scientific method that's the foundation of the method used today. He wrote about politics too—his ideas were different from Plato's. Aristotle thought there were three good forms of government: monarchy, aristocracy, and (a sort of) democracy. Aristotle founded his own school, the **LYCEUM**. Aristotle tutored the famous conqueror Alexander the Great.

GREEK ART, ARCHITECTURE, and SCULPTURE

The Greek playwrights wrote tragedies and comedies. Their plays usually consisted of dialogue mixed with a chorus singing or chanting. The chorus was a way for the author to include background information and to comment on the plot.

Three major Greek playwrights were **AESCHYLUS**, **SOPHOCLES**, and **EURIPIDES**.

AESCHYLUS wrote a trilogy called THE ORESTEIA—a set of three plays about the family of Agamemnon, who was the king of the city-state Argos during the Trojan War.

SOPHOCLES is best known for his play OEDIPUS REX, a family tragedy where an oracle predicts that Oedipus will kill his father and marry his mother (!!!).

EURIPIDES went for more realistic characters and hot topics like war and human suffering. One of his plays is MEDEA.

All three were a big deal then, and their plays are still read and performed today.

Some famous epic poems came out of Greece at this time. At the very end of the Dark Ages, the work of Homer came to light, including the ODYSSEY and another epic poem, the ILIAD. They're each hundreds of pages long, and they teach about courage and honor and the gods. Orators would memorize the epics and perform them as part of Olympic competitions! The concept of the Greek hero owes a great deal to Homer.

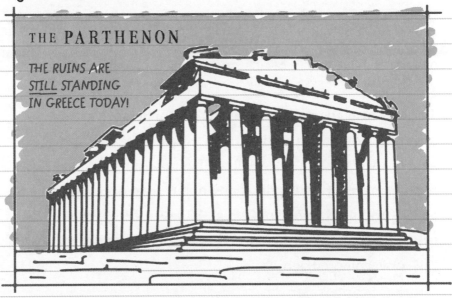

THE PARTHENON

THE RUINS ARE STILL STANDING IN GREECE TODAY!

In architecture, the great temple of Athena, the PARTHENON, was built in Athens between 447 BCE and 432 BCE. It was dedicated to both Athena and the Athenians and was a symbol of the pride of Athens itself. Constructed under the leadership of PERICLES, the Parthenon was severely damaged by an explosion in 1687 CE. But its ruins remain on the hilltop in Athens to this day.

HIPPOCRATES was an ancient Greek doctor who believed that diseases were caused naturally and not caused by a god or affected by superstition. Doctors today still take the **HIPPOCRATIC OATH** to help patients and do no harm.

The AGE of PERICLES

Pericles was one of the most influential leaders in ancient Greece. Around 460 BCE he introduced reforms like having the city pay a salary to its officials. This may seem logical (you work, you get paid), but before this, no poor citizen could afford to hold public office and work for free.

Pericles also encouraged citizens to participate in the governing assembly and vote on major issues, a concept known as a DIRECT DEMOCRACY because citizens could give their opinions on laws, decisions about war, and foreign policy, and elect public officials. However, only a male Athenian with two Athenian parents was considered a free, self-governing citizen.

ATHENS and SPARTA

ATHENS and SPARTA were two major Greek city-states in early Greece, but they couldn't have been more different. Athenians wrote plays and made pottery, sold goods, and chatted about philosophy in the marketplace. They had what has been estimated to be 100,000 slaves. Athens was PROSPEROUS (well-off) at the cost of others.

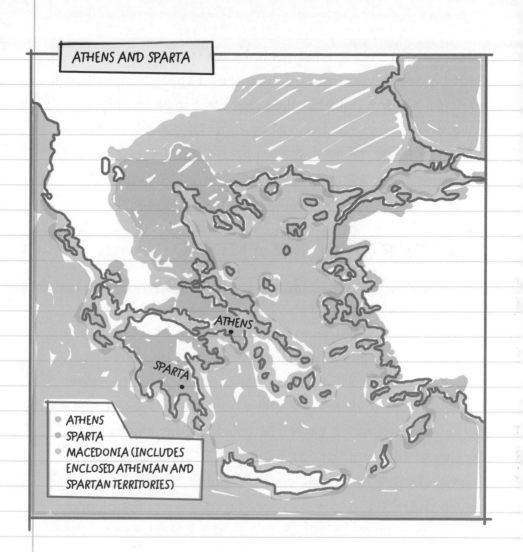

ATHENS AND SPARTA

- ● ATHENS
- ● SPARTA
- ● MACEDONIA (INCLUDES ENCLOSED ATHENIAN AND SPARTAN TERRITORIES)

Sparta, a city-state in southern Greece, was prosperous in a different way: in battle. The Spartans believed that the city-state came above the individual at all costs, and they lived as a powerful war machine. They had slaves (called HELOTS) who farmed the land while the Spartans waged wars. The city-state was an army camp, with young boys of seven years old leaving home to live in army barracks. Boys became soldiers at age twenty and stayed soldiers until sixty. Girls didn't fight, but they exercised to be strong and agile, and to produce strong offspring. The Spartans didn't travel for trade. In 431 BCE, they began fighting against the Athenians in the PELOPONNESIAN WAR, which lasted 27 years. The Athenians fell to the Spartans in 404 BCE.

The RISE of ALEXANDER

The kingdom of Macedonia was north of Greece. KING PHILIP brought the Greek philosopher Aristotle there to tutor his son ALEXANDER in Greek literature and philosophy. King Philip thought of himself as Greek too. He united Macedonia in 359 BCE and conquered the Greek city-states through bribes and threats. Philip gained control of Greece but was assassinated before he could rule his empire. Alexander took over at age twenty in 336 BCE, invading the Persian Empire and continuing the fighting into India. After eleven years, Alexander had conquered Persia, Egypt, and land beyond the Indus River. But in 323 BCE, Alexander died of a fever. (Probably not the way he thought he'd go.)

GREEK CULTURE SPREADS LIKE WILDFIRE!

Alexander's conquests spread Greek culture over a large area. He became known as ALEXANDER THE GREAT. After his death, Alexander's empire was divided into three smaller kingdoms: Greece and Macedonia formed into one kingdom, Egypt another, and Persia a third. These kingdoms were called **HELLENISTIC** kingdoms.

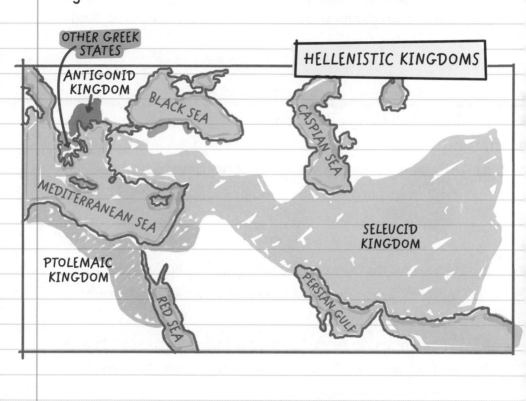

HELLENISTIC KINGDOMS

OTHER GREEK STATES

ANTIGONID KINGDOM

BLACK SEA

CASPIAN SEA

MEDITERRANEAN SEA

SELEUCID KINGDOM

PTOLEMAIC KINGDOM

RED SEA

PERSIAN GULF

CHECK YOUR KNOWLEDGE

1. Geographically, what is Greece like? How did geography affect the way its people lived?

2. What is an example of a democratic reform practiced in ancient Greece?

3. When were the Dark Ages of Greece, and what happened during these times?

4. Athens and Sparta can be described as oil and water. Explain this comparison. In what ways were these two city-states so different?

5. Who was the "king" of Greek gods? Who was the "queen"? What did the Greeks call this family of gods?

6. Philosophy can be defined as a major system of beliefs and values. Who were two famous Greek philosophers, and what were they known for?

7. What was the "golden age of Greece"? When was it and what was produced during this time?

8. What cultural contributions earned Alexander "the Great" his name?

9. What is a polis?

10. Sophocles, Euripides, and Aeschylus were three major _____.

CHECK YOUR ANSWERS

1. Greece is made up of islands and peninsulas, which made it hard for people from different islands to meet or mingle their cultures.

2. One example is how the Greek leader Pericles encouraged direct democracy. Direct democracy was a policy that said that citizens could participate in the government by giving their opinions at assemblies, electing public officials, and helping make decisions about war and foreign policy.

3. The Dark Ages lasted from the 1100s BCE to 750 BCE. It is believed that during this time, trading ended, poverty spread, and people forgot how to write. However, some epic poems were created during this time, including Homer's poems.

4. Athens was characterized by the arts and trade, while Sparta was characterized by its warring culture. Athenians wrote plays, sold goods, talked about philosophy, and were wealthy. Spartans lived for war— boys became soldiers, and girls exercised to be strong enough to produce strong offspring.

5. Zeus was the king of the Greek gods, and Hera was the queen. The family of gods was called the Olympians.

6. Pick two!
   A. Socrates taught people how to think and figure things out by asking questions (the Socratic Method).
   B. Plato taught his students about ethical living that would lead them to moral, happy lives. He wrote *The Republic* and founded an Athenian school called the Academy.
   C. Aristotle studied under Plato. Aristotle believed people's happiness was connected to their behavior; worked to define categories of logic, biology, and physics; wrote about politics; and founded his own school, the Lyceum.
7. The golden age of Greece was from 479 BCE to 431 BCE. Athens grew wealthy from silver and trade and achieved a great deal in religion, philosophy, art, and architecture.
8. Alexander earned the name "Alexander the Great" because his conquests spread Greek culture over Persia, Egypt, and lands beyond the Indus River.
9. A polis was a Greek city-state, which was usually led by aristocrats and military rulers.
10. Playwrights

Chapter 9

ANCIENT ROME

ROME WASN'T BUILT IN A DAY. This old saying means that important things take time and can't be rushed. It comes from the history of Rome, one of the world's most famous cities, which took centuries to be built, and from Rome, the name of the empire that city was the center of.

ANCIENT ROME

The ETRUSCANS came into power during the ancient period of Rome around 600 BCE and ruled as kings. The Romans rebelled against the **TYRANT** kings. Eventually, they defeated the Etruscans and formed the ROMAN REPUBLIC. In a REPUBLIC, citizens with the right to vote select their leader, who then rules as a representative of the people. The Roman Republic also had a senate to propose and vote on new laws.

> **TYRANT**
> an all-powerful, cruel ruler

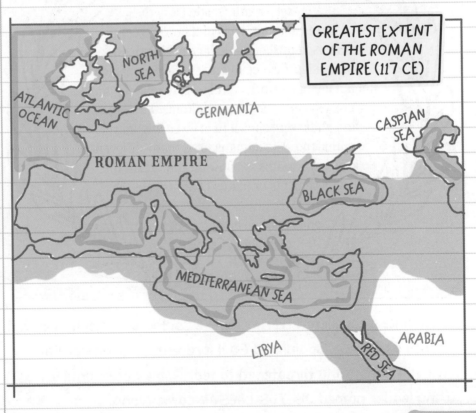

GREATEST EXTENT OF THE ROMAN EMPIRE (117 CE)

In the early republic, only PATRICIANS, or wealthy upper-class men, could sit in the senate. PLEBEIANS, or ordinary citizens, couldn't. Laws were enforced by two officials called CONSULS, who were elected by citizens. PRAETORS served as judges, who settled disputes and arguments about money and contracts.

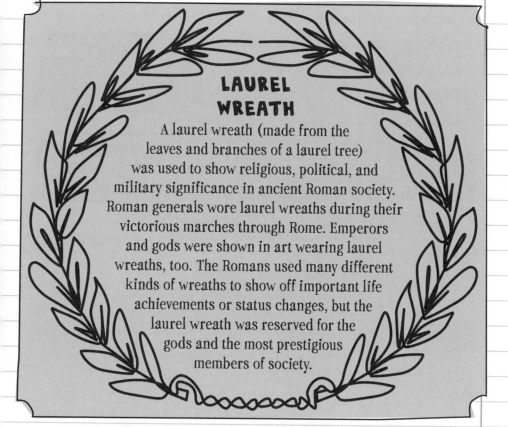

LAUREL WREATH

A laurel wreath (made from the leaves and branches of a laurel tree) was used to show religious, political, and military significance in ancient Roman society. Roman generals wore laurel wreaths during their victorious marches through Rome. Emperors and gods were shown in art wearing laurel wreaths, too. The Romans used many different kinds of wreaths to show off important life achievements or status changes, but the laurel wreath was reserved for the gods and the most prestigious members of society.

The Romans conquered territories like Carthage in North Africa, as well as Greece, Spain, and Gaul (present-day France). But civil war constantly threatened to tear Rome apart, until an army leader named JULIUS CAESAR came along.

JULIUS CAESAR

Caesar had military command in Gaul and was a powerful victor of the civil wars. He, along with two other men (Crassus and Pompey), ruled in what is known as the FIRST **TRIUMVIRATE**.

> **TRIUMVIRATE**
> a government by three people with equal power; from TRI (three) and VIRATE (of men)

Many Roman senators regretted having this new set of rulers. The senate decided Pompey should lead alone, but Caesar refused (and Crassus had been killed trying to match the military

CAESAR

CRASSUS   POMPEY

achievements of the other members of the triumvirate). In 45 BCE, Caesar defeated Pompey and took over the Roman government to create his own dictatorship. Caesar tried to fill the senate with his friends. The rest of the senate was less than thrilled. On March 15, 44 BCE (called the IDES OF MARCH), Caesar attended a meeting of the senate. The senators pulled knives from their togas and killed him. Civil war followed for thirteen years.

A SECOND TRIUMVIRATE was formed to try to restore order: MARCUS ANTONIUS (Caesar's right-hand man), OCTAVIAN (Caesar's nephew and adopted son), and a rich Roman named LEPIDUS, who mostly tried to keep his head down while Antonius and Octavian fought each other.

MARCUS ANTONIUS

LEPIDUS   OCTAVIAN

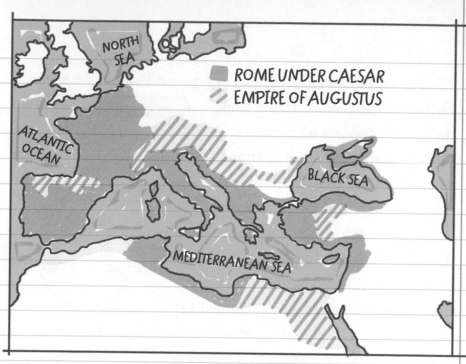

ROME UNDER CAESAR
EMPIRE OF AUGUSTUS

NORTH SEA

ATLANTIC OCEAN

BLACK SEA

MEDITERRANEAN SEA

EMPEROR AUGUSTUS

Through a lot of war and a lot of killing, Caesar's adopted son Octavian took power and was given the title of AUGUSTUS ("highly respected") by the senate in 27 BCE. The republic was over after 500 years, and now Rome had an empire, and Augustus was its first emperor.

The Roman Empire stretched from parts of Europe to Egypt at that time. Most conquered people remained free. Provinces were formed from areas of the empire, each with its own governor and army. Conquered people could become citizens (they also had to pay taxes, though). Augustus was careful to respect the senate to avoid meeting his adoptive father's fate, and he ruled until his death in 14 CE.

BUILDING ROME

The Romans were amazing builders—even if
it did take more than a day to build Rome.

IT WAS MORE
LIKE CENTURIES!

One of the most famous Roman buildings is the COLOSSEUM,
an amphitheater (stadium) where gladiatorial spectacles
were held, sometimes with people fighting animals.

The **COLOSSEUM** was as large as a football
stadium. It was used for contests between
gladiators (professional fighters), for punishing
criminals, and even for pretend sea battles.

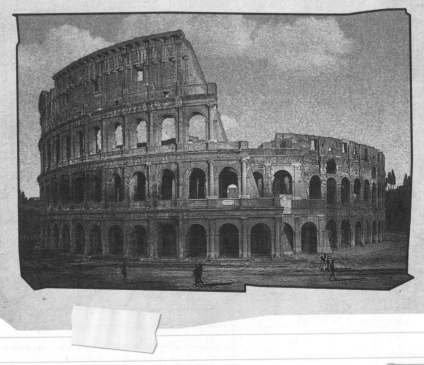

THE ROMAN FORUM

Roman cities across the empire were known for their public city centers, called FORUMS. They were places where Roman citizens would meet to trade goods, visit religious temples, vote for political leaders, celebrate military achievements, and meet up with their friends. The most important forum in Rome was called the FORUM ROMANUM.

FORUM

ROMANUM

The first Roman emperor, Augustus, wanted to make Rome the most beautiful city in the world. So, starting in 26 BCE, he built elaborate, expensive temples, basilicas, and arches in the Roman Forum. But, by 476 CE, the Roman Empire had officially fallen and the Roman people and invaders took precious stones and metal from the buildings to construct new ones. During the Middle Ages, the Romans forgot what the Roman Forum was used for and it became a cow field! They called it the *Campo Vaccino*.

In the 19th century, archeologists excavated the Roman Forum and restored much of the ruins to reflect their former glory.

The Romans also built statues and buildings with arches that allowed them to create larger indoor spaces in these new buildings. They used a crazy newfangled invention called concrete. The Romans also built roads to spread trade and to move their armies. They're also famous for their AQUEDUCTS, channels that carried water from the country to the city. They had public toilets and a lot of baths.

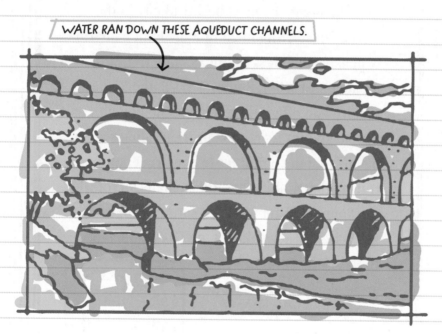

WATER RAN DOWN THESE AQUEDUCT CHANNELS.

ROMAN LAW

Many Roman laws are familiar to us now because they've been passed down through the years, like being innocent until proven guilty if you are accused of a crime.

Everything about Rome was built around families, and the government was structured to give support to them. Women, who otherwise didn't have much power, got special benefits if they had three or more kids. Unmarried men and couples with no children didn't get help from the government. Many believe this was the Roman government's way of encouraging population growth. Some also believe that this was a way to keep property in male-controlled families.

ANTONY AND CLEOPATRA

Cleopatra VII was the last independent ruler of Egypt. Julius Caesar took up with the Egyptian queen. When Caesar was assassinated, Marcus Antonius (Mark Antony) married Cleopatra after leaving his wife, Octavian's sister (so that didn't go over too well with Octavian). The Romans back in Italy thought of Cleopatra as foreign, dangerous, and way too female to be trusted. There are many plays and movies about the romance between Antonius and Cleopatra, including *ANTONY AND CLEOPATRA* by William Shakespeare.

The RISE of CHRISTIANITY

There were many religions in the Roman Empire. At first, most Romans were polytheistic (they worshipped many gods) and believed in a mix of local myths and Greek mythology. But they changed the names of the gods. For example, the Greek "Zeus" became "Jupiter" ("Zeus" + "pater," which basically means "sky father" in Latin). The Romans allowed people to worship as they wanted, for the most part, but soon Christianity began to stand out as a problem. Roman emperors began to believe that it was a dangerous cult that had broken away from Judaism.

ZEUS ⟶ JUPITER
HADES ⟶ PLUTO
POSEIDON ⟶ NEPTUNE

Christians believed in the teachings of a Jewish man named JESUS, who was also called Christ (so his followers are "Christians"). Jesus taught that there was one God (this is called monotheism), who was kind and forgiving. People had to love God and each other, show forgiveness, and lead responsible lives to have an everlasting life. Some Romans believed that the Christians assumed their God was more important than the emperor. Worried that Jesus might lead a revolt against the government, a Roman governor condemned him to death. According to the religious writings called the GOSPELS, Jesus returned to life and told his disciples to spread his teachings.

Groups of Christians gathered throughout the empire. One follower, Paul, wrote letters to groups in faraway cities and traveled to spread Jesus's teachings.

Christians grew in such numbers that the Roman government made it a crime to be Christian, and **PERSECUTION** of the Christian people followed. Many died for their religion and became **MARTYRS**. But Christianity continued to spread, and by 300 CE, nearly one in every ten Romans had become Christian.

PERSECUTE
to attack, imprison, or harass a people because of their beliefs

MARTYR
a person who is willing to undergo great suffering or die on behalf of a cause or principle

Christianity is still one of the most popular religions worldwide.

EMPEROR CONSTANTINE

The emperor CONSTANTINE also helped spread Christianity. The Roman Empire was weakening, but the Christian Church had gained more authority. Constantine, who ruled from 312 to 337 CE, converted and became the first Christian emperor. He declared freedom of worship across the empire in his EDICT OF MILAN, ending the persecution. He built churches for worship. Constantine moved the capital of the Roman Empire to Byzantium (in what is now Turkey) and called it the New Rome (later Byzantium became Constantinople, and much later it became Istanbul, which is what it's called today). The city was in a strategic location that provided protection for the eastern frontier of the empire.

DECLINE of the ROMAN EMPIRE

The emperor Commodus was eighteen when he began ruling in 180 CE, and his poor choices back then led

> **MERCENARY**
> a professional soldier hired to serve in a foreign army

to the beginning of the end for the Roman Empire. He disregarded the senate and bribed the army to stand by him. His successors also followed this pattern of bribery and poor leadership. Rome faced other problems too, like

having to pay **MERCENARY** armies who had no loyalty to the empire, battling **INFLATION** (due to making too many valueless coins), fighting off **PLAGUES**, and fighting to keep

> **INFLATION**
> an increase in prices of goods and a fall in the value of money

the land they had conquered. Eventually German invaders took over the empire in the west. Constantinople held on as the capital of the Byzantine Empire.

> **PLAGUE**
> a deadly contagious disease

CHECK YOUR KNOWLEDGE

1. Who were some of the first rulers of ancient Rome?

2. The Romans are famous for founding the first republic. So what is a republic, anyway?

3. What happened on the Ides of March?

4. Who took over after Caesar died and how was this person's fate different from Caesar's?

5. Under the Roman Empire, architecture and engineering flourished. Describe some important things the Romans created during this time.

6. Initially, were the Romans polytheistic or monotheistic? What is the difference between the two?

7. How did Christianity spread through the Roman Empire?

ANSWERS

CHECK YOUR ANSWERS

1. The Etruscans, who came to power and ruled Rome in 600 BCE

2. A republic is a form of government where citizens vote for their leader, who then represents the people. The Roman Republic had a senate to create new laws, consuls to enforce laws, and praetors to act as judges.

3. On the Ides of March, Julius Caesar was killed by a group of angry senators, and a civil war followed for thirteen years.

4. Octavian (Caesar's adopted son) took over after Caesar died. He respected the senate (to avoid getting stabbed like Caesar), and he ruled for many years.

5. One of the most famous Roman buildings is the Colosseum, an amphitheater for gladiatorial spectacles. The Romans also built statues and buildings with arches, used concrete, built roads to spread trade and move armies, and built aqueducts to move water. They also had public toilets and a lot of baths.

6. At first, most Romans were polytheistic, which means they worshipped many gods. Monotheistic means believing in a single god.

7. Disciples spread Christian teachings. Also, one follower, Paul, wrote letters about Christianity to people far away and also traveled to spread Jesus's teachings.

ANCIENT RELIGIONS and

BELIEF SYSTEM	FOUNDER	GEOGRAPHIC ORIGIN	SACRED TEXT
Christianity	Jesus	Israel	The Bible
Islam	Prophet Muhammad	Mecca	The Quran
Judaism	Prophet Abraham	Israel	The Torah
* Taoism	Laozi	China	None
* Confucianism	Confucius	China	None
Hinduism	(has no specific founder)	India	Upanishads
Buddhism	Siddhartha Gautama	India	None

PHILOSOPHIES at a GLANCE

PLACE OF WORSHIP	KEY IDEAS
Church	• Love God and live responsibly to gain everlasting life through grace. • Monotheistic
Mosque	• The Five Pillars of Islam: declaration of faith, praying five times a day, giving alms, fasting during Ramadan, and making a pilgrimage to Mecca • Monotheistic
Synagogue	• Prophets • Monotheistic
None	* Taoism is a *philosophy*, not a religion. • Living a selfless, balanced life in harmony with nature leads to happiness.
None	* Confucianism is a *philosophy*, not a religion. • Peace and order in society begin with peace and order in the individual. • Teachings later became part of training system for the Chinese government.
Temple	• Reincarnation based on karma • Polytheistic
Monastery	• One reaches enlightenment on the meaning of life through meditation.

WORLD RELIGIONS
BY PERCENTAGE
(2007 EST.)

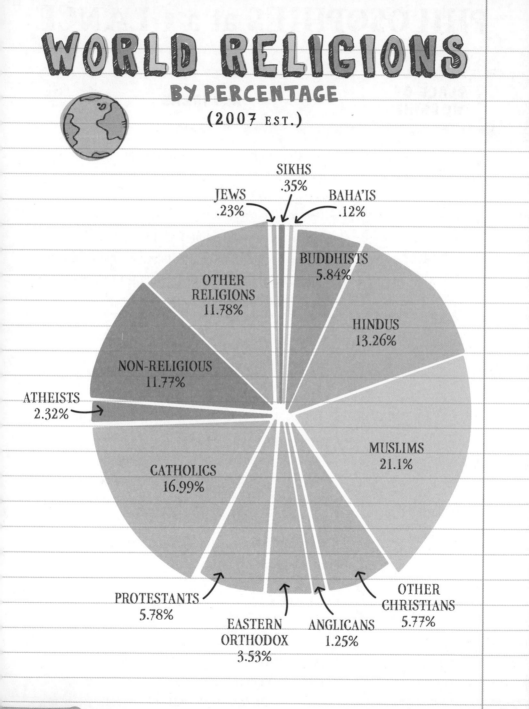

SIKHS
.35%

JEWS
.23%

BAHA'IS
.12%

BUDDHISTS
5.84%

OTHER
RELIGIONS
11.78%

HINDUS
13.26%

NON-RELIGIOUS
11.77%

ATHEISTS
2.32%

MUSLIMS
21.1%

CATHOLICS
16.99%

PROTESTANTS
5.78%

EASTERN
ORTHODOX
3.53%

ANGLICANS
1.25%

OTHER
CHRISTIANS
5.77%

unit 3

The Middle Ages
400 CE – 1500 CE

The Middle Ages are in the **MIDDLE** of how we look at history's timeline. Too late to be early, too early to be late. The Middle Ages refers to the period from 476 CE (the fall of the Roman Empire) to about 1500. It's also called the MEDIEVAL AGE. ← "MEDIEVAL": FROM LATIN, MEANS "MIDDLE AGE"

☆ Chapter 10 ☆

The BYZANTINE

★ ⭐ ☆ ⭐ ★ ☆ ⭐ ★ ☆ ⭐ ★

EMPIRE

330 CE–1400s

The BYZANTINE EMPIRE (also called the EASTERN ROMAN EMPIRE) started around 330 CE. Its capital, Constantinople, was a powerful center of trade until its fall in the 1400s.

Eventually renamed AGAIN—as Istanbul

BLACK SEA

← Byzantium
~~New Rome~~
Constantinople

ARMENIA

AEGEAN
SEA

MESOPOTAMIA

MEDITERRANEAN
SEA

JUSTINIAN

One of the greatest Byzantine emperors was JUSTINIAN, whose reign began in 527 CE. Roman laws were a mess, written and documented but shuffled around and mixed up and hard to keep track of. Justinian put a team together to sift through the ancient laws and make sense of them. Eventually, the team developed the JUSTINIAN CODE, an organized collection of Roman laws with explanations. It was basically a how-to manual on democracy and lawmaking. Most modern European countries used this code as the basis for their own legal systems!

The Byzantines preserved other traditions of Greek and Roman culture. They decorated churches with **FRESCOES**, paintings, and mosaics, and preserved ancient texts in their libraries.

> **FRESCO**
> a painting done on plaster, usually using watercolors

Justinian's accomplishments were great, but his conquests in Italy, North Africa, Palestine, and Syria (among other places) caused a lot of trouble. The Byzantine Empire became too large to protect, and threats came from all borders. With the rise of Islam around the 600s, unified Arab groups grew throughout the empire, taking over Syria and Palestine.

CHANGES in the BYZANTINE EMPIRE

By the 700s, the now-smaller Byzantine Empire, which included only the eastern Balkans and Asia Minor, was both a Greek and Christian state. The Christian Church became known as the Eastern Orthodox Church, where Greek (instead of Latin) was spoken. Around 700 CE, a Byzantine emperor outlawed praying to icons (artistic depictions—such as paintings—of holy figures or sacred events) because he thought it was a violation of God's commandments. The pope outlawed the Byzantine Empire from the church, and the split became final. Two forms of Christianity emerged: the Roman Catholic Church (in the West), and the Eastern Orthodox Church (in the Byzantine Empire).

By the twelfth century, the Byzantine Empire had expanded again and became Europe's greatest center of commerce. The Byzantines charged taxes on goods that went through Constantinople and quickly became rich.

The **CRUSADES** were military missions that lasted almost 200 years in which European Christians tried to get control of the Holy Land of Jerusalem from the Muslims. The Crusades began in the eleventh century, when Byzantine emperor Constantine asked Christian states in Europe to help fight against the Muslim Turks. The Europeans eventually lost this battle.

The **CRUSADES** and growing threats from the Turkish Ottoman Empire eventually got the best of them. In 1453, the Byzantine Empire was taken over by the Turks.

CHECK YOUR KNOWLEDGE

1. _____ was the capital of the Byzantine Empire. What is this city called today?

2. Name the approximate dates of the Middle Ages.

3. How did Constantinople become a wealthy capital?

4. Who was Justinian, and what great contribution did he make to the Byzantine Empire?

5. The fall of the Byzantine Empire in 1453 can be attributed to:
   A. attacks from the Christian crusaders
   B. attacks from the Turks
   C. both
   D. neither

6. Describe some elements, besides laws, that the Byzantine Empire retained from Greek and Roman culture.

7. Name the two forms of Christianity that emerged during this time.

ANSWERS

CHECK YOUR ANSWERS

1. Constantinople. It is called Istanbul today.
2. The Middle Ages lasted from approximately 400 to 1500 CE.
3. Constantinople became wealthy through its trade power. The Byzantines became rich by charging taxes on all goods that went through the city.
4. One of the greatest Byzantine emperors was Justinian, because he put together a team to develop the Justinian Code, which was an organized collection of laws with explanations. The laws were derived from ancient Roman laws.
5. C. both
6. The Byzantines continued Greek and Roman cultural traditions by decorating churches with frescoes, paintings, and mosaics. They also preserved ancient texts in libraries.
7. The two forms of Christianity were called the Roman Catholic Church (the Christian Church in the West) and the Eastern Orthodox Church (the Christian Church in the Byzantine Empire).

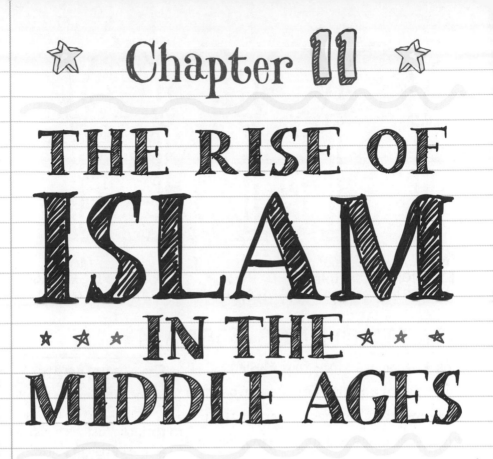

Chapter 11

THE RISE OF ISLAM
★ ★ ★ IN THE ★ ★ ★
MIDDLE AGES

Around 610 CE, Islam, a new religion, arose in the Arabian
Peninsula. According to Islamic belief, the prophet
Muhammad heard a message from God. Muhammad was
to be God's messenger and spread the teachings of Islam
among the people of the Arabian Peninsula. The holy book
of Islam, the QURAN, contained the rules of the religion.
In time, many Muslims—people who accepted Muhammad's
teachings—came to believe in the FIVE PILLARS OF ISLAM,
which formed the foundation of their religion. Muslims must:

151

MAKE A TESTIMONY OF FAITH. PRAY 5 TIMES A DAY. GIVE TO THE NEEDY. FAST FOR RAMADAN. MAKE A PILGRIMAGE TO MECCA.

The TEACHINGS of ISLAM

The five pillars state that Muslims must declare that there is one God and Muhammad is his messenger; they must pray five times a day; they must give alms to the needy; they must fast during the month of **RAMADAN**; and they must make a **HAJJ** to the city of MECCA (a center of trading and Muslim belief located in present-day Saudi Arabia).

RAMADAN
the ninth month of the Islamic year, during which Muslims fast from sunrise to sunset

HAJJ
name for the pilgrimage, or religious journey, Muslims take

Use this mnemonic to remember the five pillars of Islam:

Few **P**eople **C**rave **F**rozen **P**ickles =

Faith **P**rayer **C**harity **F**asting **P**ilgrimage

FROZEN PICKLE?

GROSS!

In 656 CE, 'UTHMĀN IBN 'AFFĀN, the third leader of the Muslim community to rule after Muhammad, was killed. His death divided the Muslim community and led to a **SCHISM** of Islam. One group of Muslims, the SHIITES, believed the next ruler should be a descendant of Muhammad. The majority of Muslims, the SUNNIS, believed that any religious Muslim man could lead the community and that Muslim scholars (not just descendants of Muhammad) could best explain the teachings of the Quran.

SCHISM
a formal split into opposing parties

ROUGHLY 85 PERCENT OF MUSLIMS TODAY ARE SUNNIS.

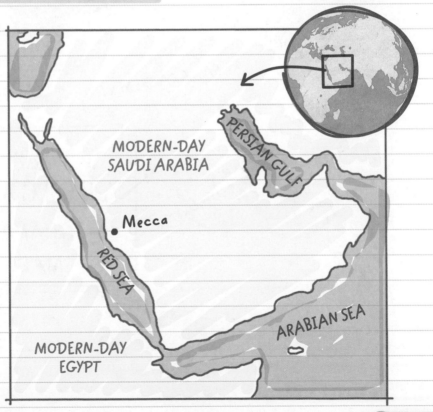

MODERN-DAY SAUDI ARABIA

PERSIAN GULF

Mecca

RED SEA

ARABIAN SEA

MODERN-DAY EGYPT

The ISLAMIC KINGDOMS of WEST AFRICA

In western Africa, two important commodities were salt and gold. Salt came from the central Sahara, and people from the rain forest in West Africa didn't have any. They wanted it for seasoning and to preserve meat, so they traded gold for salt.

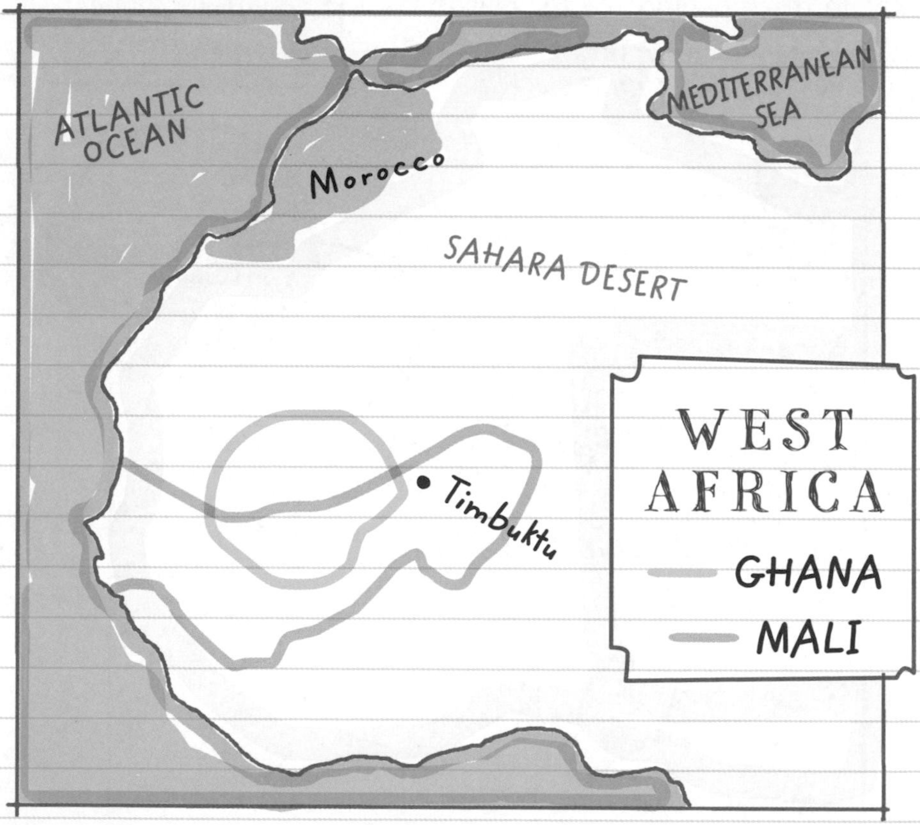

ATLANTIC OCEAN

MEDITERRANEAN SEA

Morocco

SAHARA DESERT

• Timbuktu

WEST AFRICA
— GHANA
— MALI

GHANA, a West African kingdom, grew wealthy from this gold and salt trade. This was because the people of Ghana took control of the Sahara's trade routes beginning in 400 CE. This lasted until the 1200s, when a new kingdom, MALI, took over.

Mali seized control of the salt and gold trade with the help of their leader **SUNDIATA**, ← ALSO CALLED THE LION KING. FOR REAL.
who conquered neighboring lands and helped Mali grow rich from trade. His grandnephew, MANSA MUSA, continued to expand the kingdom. Mansa Musa ruled from 1312 to 1337 and created a strong central government, dividing the kingdom into provinces ruled by governors. He taxed trade routes, and Mali grew richer. He invited scholars to teach religion, law, math, and medicine and made Mali a great center of knowledge and culture. He built mosques and libraries to make the city of TIMBUKTU not only a wealthy trading city but also a center of learning and culture. He also made Islam Mali's official religion and went on a pilgrimage to Mecca, spending so much gold on gifts for his hosts that gold lost value. Sometime after Mansa Musa's death, the kingdom's provinces began to break away, and Mali's power dissolved.

EHH...NO THANKS.

???

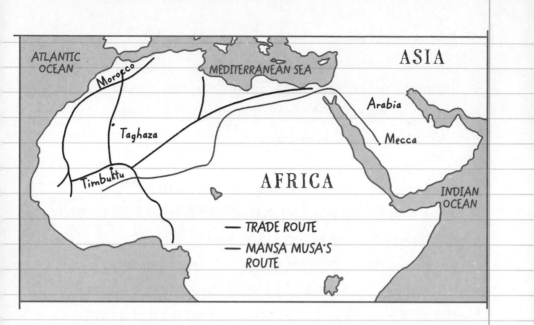

SONGHAI was one of the provinces that separated from Mali and became a major kingdom in its own right. Once a trading center within Mali, it conquered Timbuktu in 1468 and then gained control of trade in gold and salt. In less than 100 years, the Songhai Empire began to crumble. Its people fought each other, and it fell to an army from the North African nation of Morocco.

CHECK YOUR KNOWLEDGE

1. Who was Muhammad and what is he known for?

2. What is the holy scripture for the Muslim faith?

3. The Muslim house of worship is called a _____.

4. What led to the schism of Islam? What happened after that?

5. What is the main difference between the Sunnis and the Shiites?

6. Who was Mansa Musa? List some of his achievements.

7. Name the three major kingdoms of West Africa.

ANSWERS

CHECK YOUR ANSWERS

1. According to Islamic belief, Muhammad was a prophet who heard a message from God. God told him to spread the teachings of a new religion, Islam.

2. The Quran is the holy scripture for the Muslim faith.

3. Mosque

4. The killing of the Muslim community leader 'Ūthman ibn 'Affān divided the Muslim community and led to a schism of Islam. Islam divided into two groups, the Shiites and the Sunnis.

5. The main difference between the Sunnis and the Shiites is that the Sunnis believed that any religious Muslim man could lead the community. However, the Shiites believed the next ruler should be a descendant of Muhammad.

6. Mansa Musa was a ruler of Mali. He invited scholars to Mali to teach religion, law, math, and medicine. He made Islam Mali's official religion and built mosques and libraries in the city of Timbuktu. He also went on a pilgrimage to Mecca and spent so much gold on gifts for his hosts that gold lost its value.

7. Ghana, Mali, and Songhai

☆ Chapter 12 ☆

★ ★ ★ EARLY ★ ★ ★ CIVILIZATIONS of the AMERICAS

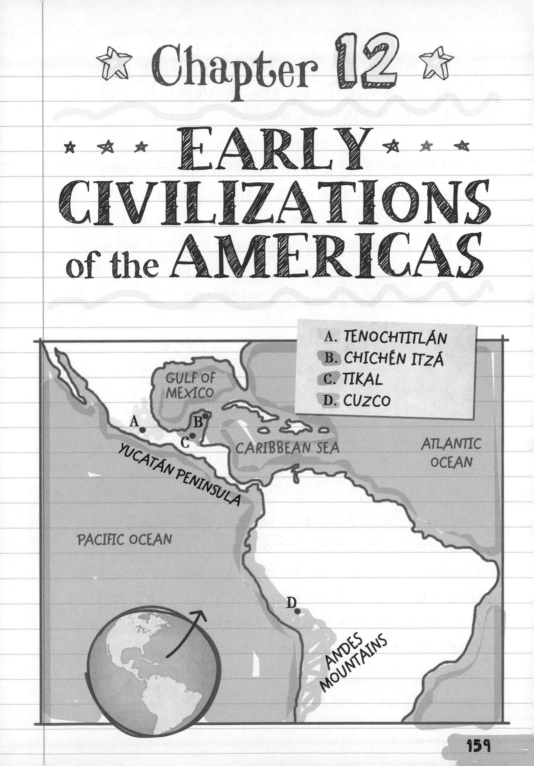

A. TENOCHTITLÁN
B. CHICHÉN ITZÁ
C. TIKAL
D. CUZCO

GULF OF MEXICO

A

B

C

CARIBBEAN SEA

ATLANTIC OCEAN

YUCATÁN PENINSULA

PACIFIC OCEAN

D

ANDES MOUNTAINS

The MAYANS: The FIRST GREAT CIVILIZATION of the AMERICAS (LASTED 2,000 YEARS)

In Central America, at the southern end of the YUCATÁN PENINSULA (the southeastern tip of Mexico), were the MAYANS. Mayan life was at its peak from about 250 to 900 CE. The Mayans farmed using a SLASH-AND-BURN technique: The "slashing" was cutting down trees; the "burning" was setting the tree stumps on fire. The ashes were used as fertilizer for new crops on the cleared land.

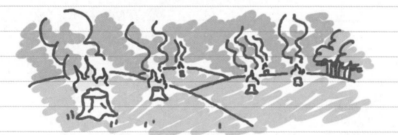

The Mayans successfully grew many crops, from beans to papayas to avocados, and most commonly MAIZE, or corn. But the slash-and-burn farming technique wore out the soil, and after a few years, farmers had to start over with a new plot of land. Some historians think this is one reason Mayan civilization began to crumble around 900. It may also have been from war, drought, disease, or any number of things.

The Mayans created large temple-pyramids in present-day Guatemala, El Salvador, Honduras, and Mexico.

They topped the pyramids with shrines to the gods and surrounded them with other temples and palaces.

> The **MAYANS, AZTECS,** and **INCAS** were all polytheistic.

The Mayans believed all life came from the hands of divine powers. They sometimes held festivals in honor of the gods and offered the gods human sacrifices. Planning religious festivities was helped by their development of a calendar based on the seasons. They also developed a system of hieroglyphics, writing in books made from the bark of trees.

> Another incredible achievement of the Mayans: the cultivation of **CHOCOLATE!** They grew cacao trees and made chocolate beverages. They even used cocoa beans as money in markets!

The AZTECS: MESOAMERICA (MEXICO and CENTRAL AMERICA)

In 1325, the AZTECS built their capital, TENOCHTITLÁN, on a swampy island in the middle of Lake Texcoco in what is now Mexico City. They chose this island based on an ancient prophecy that said that the Aztecs would find the site of a great city where an eagle perched on a cactus growing out of a rock. The Aztecs believed they were following their god's orders when they saw this occur at this site.

TENOCHTITLÁN MEANS "PLACE OF THE PRICKLY PEAR CACTUS."

The Aztecs conquered nearby lands and created an empire stretching from the Gulf of Mexico to the Pacific Ocean. Tenochtitlán was one of the largest cities of its time. This island city was connected to land by **CAUSEWAYS**. Aqueducts were built to bring in fresh water. Canals were used to transport produce to the city's marketplaces. Schools and large temples were constructed, and a yearly calendar was created. Hieroglyphics were used for record keeping.

> **CAUSEWAY**
> raised streets of hard earth

The Aztecs worshipped a sun god because they believed this god would bring good harvests—and they also believed that the sun god would rise only with the strength from human blood.

The Aztecs faithfully sacrificed
humans for the sun god. To them,
a few deaths were worth it to
protect all their people—no sun =
no crops and hungry people. The
Aztecs made it easier on themselves
by sacrificing people from other tribes.
Prisoners from battles and conquests

were the most common sacrificial offerings. However, the
constant need to capture new prisoners weakened the
empire and caused other tribes to hate the Aztecs.

In 1978—hundreds of years after Mexico City
was built—major **EXCAVATIONS**
began in Tenochtitlán, uncovering ruins like the
Templo Mayor (Tenochtitlán's main temple complex).
A number of artifacts were also discovered.

EXCAVATION
unearthing; digging

In 1519, the Spanish conquistador (or conqueror) HERNÁN
CORTÉS arrived. He and his troops fought the Aztecs with
the help of tribes that hated the Aztecs. By 1521, the battles
and the diseases the Spanish had brought made it too
hard to keep fighting. MONTEZUMA, the Aztec emperor,
surrendered, and the Spanish built Mexico City over the city
of Tenochtitlán.

The INCAS: SOUTH AMERICA

Around 1200 CE, the INCAS settled into a small village high in the Andes Mountains called CUZCO (which means "center") in what is now Peru. Two hundred years of conquering other people and their lands led to the creation of an empire that was home to as many as 12 million inhabitants and stretched 2,500 miles (4,023 kilometers) from one end of South America to the other, crossing the Andes Mountains. Cuzco would eventually become the capital of this empire.

Keeping order in an empire so populated and spread out was challenging, so the Incas developed a **CENSUS** to record who worked on which projects (such as

> **CENSUS**
> an official count of the population

mining and road building) and to make sure everyone paid taxes. The Incas kept track of things by using a QUIPU, a group of knotted strings in which each knot stood for something, like death, harvest, birth, etc. Colors were used to show different events, and knots were different sizes to show quantity. Since the Incas didn't have a written language, messages were sent by runners across the empire carrying quipus to keep the government up to date. Runners often ran up to 20 miles per day.

> The U.S. has a census too: Every 10 years, it counts and surveys each person (including YOU) to note changes in the American population and make decisions about federal funding.

The Incas are known for their mountaintop buildings, huge walls, and thousands of miles of paved roads. Many of their buildings still stand today, created with only stone hammers and bronze chisels. For example, MACHU PICCHU is a 15th century Incan estate you can even walk around in. The Incas built **TERRACES** for farming, and

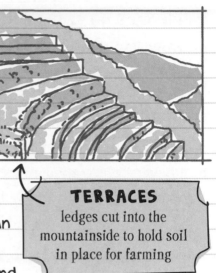

TERRACES
ledges cut into the
mountainside to hold soil
in place for farming

they built aqueducts to carry water to their farms.

STANDS 2,430 METERS
(ALMOST 8,000 FEET)
ABOVE SEA LEVEL!

MACHU PICCHU

In the 1530s, the powerful Incan Empire ended with the arrival of a Spanish conquistador named FRANCISCO PIZARRO. The Incas were just coming out of a civil war when Pizarro arrived. The Spanish had horses, iron, and weapons unlike anything the Incas had ever seen, and they brought diseases like smallpox and measles, which the Incas had never before encountered; these factors helped the Spaniards take over.

CHECK YOUR KNOWLEDGE

1. How did the Incas keep track of everyone who lived in their massive empire?

2. How was Francisco Pizarro able to conquer the Incan Empire?

3. Why did the Aztecs build their capital in the middle of a swamp?

4. In what ways were the Aztecs similar to the Mayans?

5. Imagine you are a Mayan farmer. Explain how your special farming technique works. What kind of crops do you grow?

6. How did the Mayans appease their gods?

7. What trait did the Mayans, Aztecs, and Incas have in common?
   A. They spoke the same language.
   B. They were polytheistic.
   C. All three built pyramids.
   D. B and C

8. Which civilization lasted the longest, the Mayan, Aztec, or Incan?

ANSWERS

CHECK YOUR ANSWERS

1. The Incas used a quipu, a series of knotted strings which symbolized different things they needed to keep track of, like births, deaths, and harvests.

2. Francisco Pizarro was able to conquer the Incan Empire in the 1530s with horses, iron, and weapons that the Incas had never seen. They also brought diseases that quickly made the Incas sick, which weakened them.

3. The Aztecs built their capital in the middle of a swamp because they believed they were following their god's orders, which said an eagle would perch on a cactus growing out of a rock in the place where they had to build.

4. The Mayans and Aztecs created large temples. They also offered human sacrifices to the gods, developed a calendar, and created a system of hieroglyphics.

5. As a Mayan farmer, I would use a slash-and-burn technique of cutting down trees and setting the tree stumps on fire. I would then use the ashes as fertilizer. I would grow beans, papayas, avocados, and maize.

6. The Mayans appeased gods with festivals and human sacrifices.
7. B. They were polytheistic.
8. The Mayan civilization

Chapter 13

MEDIEVAL INDIA

The DELHI SULTANATE

In 1398 CE, a brutal Turkish conqueror named TAMERLANE (also called TIMUR THE LAME) → invaded northern India, which was under the rule of the Bahmanī **SULTANATE**. Tamerlane, who had previously conquered lands in Russia and the Mediterranean, was a MONGOL, a nomad from a region north of China. The Mongols, a nomadic warrior group, captured India's capital city of DELHI and stole pearls, rubies, and diamonds. They took slaves and killed roughly 100,000 Hindu prisoners. Delhi

> **SULTANATE**
> state or country
> ruled by a sultan

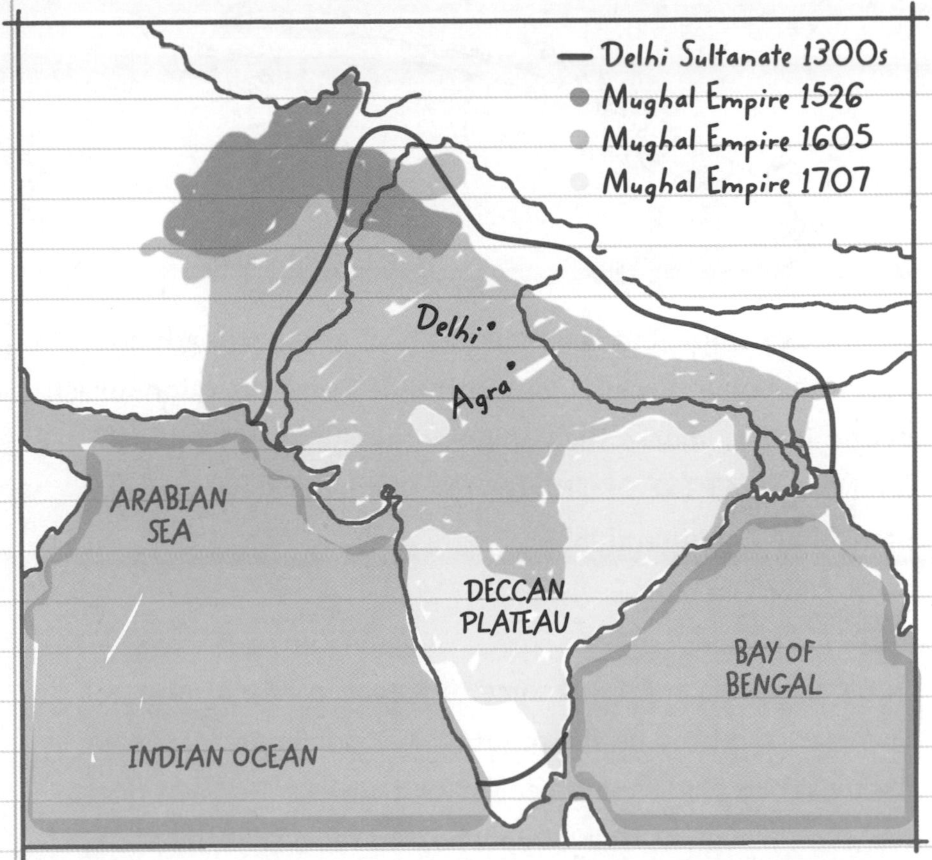

Legend:
— Delhi Sultanate 1300s
● Mughal Empire 1526
● Mughal Empire 1605
● Mughal Empire 1707

Delhi•
Agra•

ARABIAN SEA

DECCAN PLATEAU

BAY OF BENGAL

INDIAN OCEAN

was weak from the attack, and the **SULTAN**'s power was shattered. Still, sultans held on to control of parts of the country for hundreds of years. This period of time is known as the DELHI SULTANATE.

SULTANS
Muslim rulers who raided India as early as 1000 CE

BABUR

The Delhi Sultanate ended when the Mongol prince BABUR brought a small army to fight both the sultan's troops and his 100 elephants. The elephants may have seemed like a

huge advantage, but the Mongols had another weapon:
cannons. Babur quickly won control of Delhi. His reign, which
began in 1526, marks the beginning of the GREAT MUGHAL
(MONGOL) EMPIRE OF INDIA. The Mughals largely kept
control of India until 1857.

AKBAR

Babur's grandson AKBAR came to power in 1556 at age
fourteen and became the greatest Mughal leader of India.
Akbar set up studios in his court for painters. He liked poets
too, even though he didn't know how to read or write. He
invited scholars to discuss religion. Akbar was Muslim, but he
allowed the Hindu people to practice
their religion freely. This made him a
popular emperor. Also helpful: He gave
out government jobs based on merit
instead of religion or caste. Akbar
ruled peacefully for 49 years.

> Remember Akbar
> and the Mughal Empire
> with this rhyme:
> *The Mughal Empire was*
> *a powerful state*
> *under the fair rule*
> *of Akbar the Great!*

SHAH JAHAN and AURANGZEB

After Akbar died, the empire began to have some problems.
Akbar's grandson SHAH JAHAN (reigned 1628 to 1658) kept

the political system built by earlier Mughal rulers. He also expanded the empire to the Deccan Plateau and beyond.

Shah Jahan had some major money problems, though. The treasury was nearly empty when he started ruling, and building expensive, lavish structures like the **TAJ MAHAL** didn't help. Many of Jahan's subjects lived in poverty as a result of his spending.

In 1631, Shah Jahan built the **TAJ MAHAL** in the city of Agra as a tomb for his wife, Mumtaz Mahal. The tomb is considered a great work of architectural art but was so expensive to build that Shah Jahan had to raise taxes to pay for it.

After Jahan's death, his son AURANGZEB spent the empire's money on something less beautiful than the Taj Mahal: almost constant war. He tried to force Hindus to abandon their religion and convert to the Muslim religion. Following his death in 1707, the empire fractured into smaller kingdoms.

After several weak rulers, the Great Mughal Empire of India finally ended in 1857 when the remains of the empire were taken over by the British.

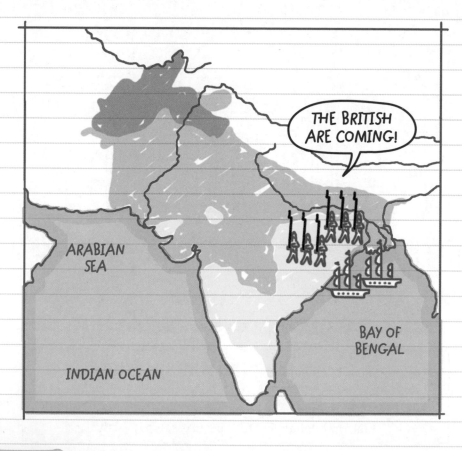

CHECK YOUR KNOWLEDGE

1. Who were the Mongols and from what land did they come?

2. Who was Tamerlane, and what is he known for?

3. How was the Delhi Sultanate eventually overthrown, and by whom?

4. Akbar is often referred to as "Akbar the Great." Why do you think he had this nickname?

5. Shah Jahan built an expensive and impressive building. What is it called, and why did he build it?

6. Why do you think the Mughal Empire flourished under Akbar but fell apart after Aurangzeb?

ANSWERS

CHECK YOUR ANSWERS

1. The Mongols were nomads from a region north of China.

2. Tamerlane was a Turkish Mongol who conquered lands in Russia and the Mediterranean and then invaded northern India. His Mongolian fighters captured Delhi, stole treasure, took slaves, and killed roughly 100,000 Hindu prisoners.

3. Mongol prince Babur brought an army and cannons to overthrow the Delhi Sultanate.

4. Akbar was called Akbar the Great because he came to power at age fourteen and ruled peacefully for 49 years. He also supported painters, poets, and scholars of different religions. He was Muslim but practiced tolerance and allowed Hindus to practice their religion freely. He also hired people for government jobs based on merit instead of religion or caste.

5. Shah Jahan built the Taj Mahal in the city of Agra as a tomb for his wife, Mumtaz Mahal.

6. The Mughal Empire fell because Aurangzeb spent the empire's money on war and he showed no tolerance of other religions and tried to force Hindus to convert to the Muslim religion.

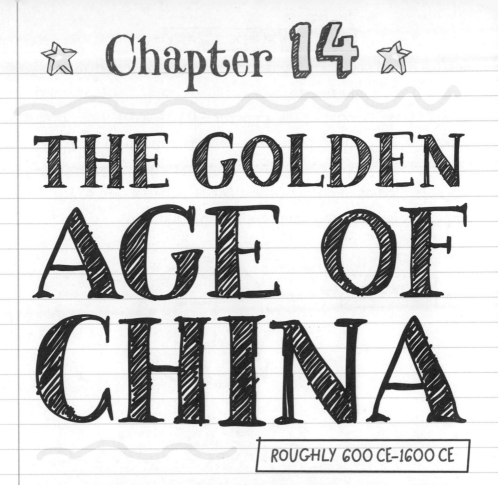

Chapter 14

THE GOLDEN AGE OF CHINA

ROUGHLY 600 CE–1600 CE

China's middle age was a highly successful one, even golden, some say. It was a period of unification, commercial and urban development, innovation, and education.

The SUI DYNASTY

After the Han dynasty ended in 220 CE, the next major dynasty in China was the SUI dynasty. The Sui ruled from 581 CE to 618 CE. In a brief 37 years they united northern and southern China for the first time in centuries. This was in part from the building of the GRAND CANAL, which connected

ALSO KNOWN AS THE YELLOW RIVER

northern and southern China through the Huang and Yangtze Rivers. The canal helped transport large supplies of rice and goods across China. But the emperor SUI YANGDI was harsh in his rule, forcing people to work on the canal and charging high taxes to support his extravagant lifestyle. Thousands of workers died building the Grand Canal. Rebellion led to the emperor's murder in a coup, ending the dynasty.

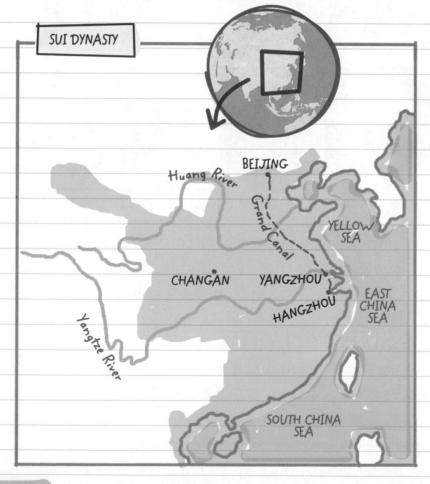

SUI DYNASTY

Huang River

BEIJING

Grand Canal

YELLOW SEA

CHANGAN   YANGZHOU

EAST CHINA SEA

HANGZHOU

Yangtze River

SOUTH CHINA SEA

The TANG DYNASTY

After the Sui, the TANG dynasty ruled for nearly 300 years (from 618 CE to 907 CE). The Tang expanded Chinese control westward into Central Asia. At the time, the capital city CHANGAN was the largest city in the entire world, with a population of about 1 million people. (That counted as a huge city during that stretch of time.)

> GUNPOWDER WAS ALSO INVENTED DURING THE TANG DYNASTY.

Under the Tang dynasty, the economy prospered. Ruler TANG TAIZONG, who rose to power in 626 CE, strengthened political peace between northern and southern China by promoting the teachings of Confucius. He hired officials trained in Confucian philosophy and gave land to the peasants who farmed it. Rice was a big crop in China.

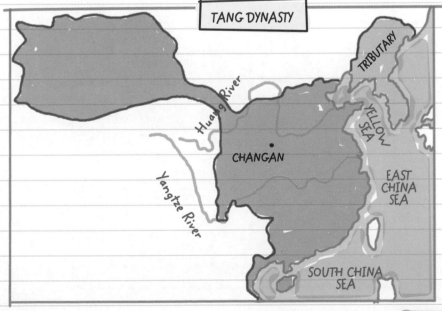

TANG DYNASTY

Huang River · Yangtze River · CHANGAN · TRIBUTARY · YELLOW SEA · EAST CHINA SEA · SOUTH CHINA SEA

The SONG DYNASTY

Fighting within the Tang leadership eventually led to its demise. The next dynasty of the golden age of China was the SONG dynasty, which ruled from 960 to 1279. It was during this dynasty that the first magnetic compass came into use.

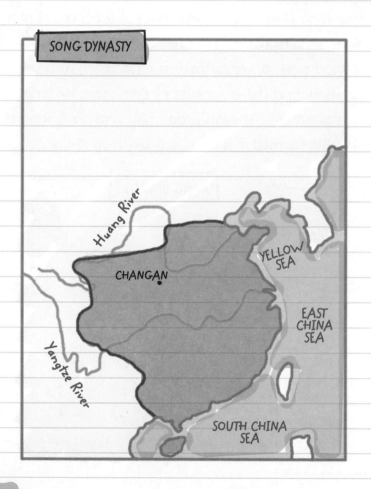

SONG DYNASTY

Huang River

YELLOW SEA

CHANGAN

EAST CHINA SEA

Yangtze River

SOUTH CHINA SEA

The Song continued to improve the Chinese system of government. Like the Mughal ruler Akbar, they hired government workers based on merit rather than family connections. Officials had to take exams to prove their aptitude (ability).

New irrigation systems and other improvements created food surpluses. This gave people more time to try new things. Music and art were encouraged, and some of the first Chinese landscape paintings were created during this time. Peaceful landscapes of water, rocks, and plants were painted on silk, another Chinese specialty. Around 1045, the Chinese invented movable type, which allowed books to be printed and distributed more easily. More people, including

women, learned to read. Poetry flourished, as well as books about medicine and religion, which helped educate the people.

The Chinese were the first to produce porcelain, a type of ceramic. This is why porcelain is sometimes referred to as "china."

The golden age of China lasted until the Mongols came to power in the late 1200s. The Mongol conqueror KUBLAI KHAN defeated the last heirs to the Song dynasty by 1279. The Mongol government lasted until 1368, when a Chinese peasant uprising ended Mongol rule.

KUBLAI KHAN

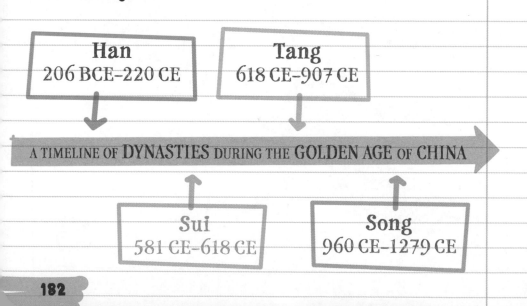

Han
206 BCE–220 CE

Tang
618 CE–907 CE

A TIMELINE OF **DYNASTIES** DURING THE **GOLDEN AGE** OF **CHINA**

Sui
581 CE–618 CE

Song
960 CE–1279 CE

CHECK YOUR KNOWLEDGE

1. The Grand Canal was a major achievement of:
   A. the Sui dynasty
   B. the Tang dynasty
   C. the Song dynasty
   D. the Huang dynasty

2. Under which dynasty did China enjoy an exceptional period of cultural achievement?

3. Under which dynasty were the teachings of Confucius used to create political peace between northern and southern China?

4. What was one way the Song improved the Chinese system of government?

5. What was so "golden" about the "golden age of China"? Why did it earn this nickname?

6. When and why did the golden age of China come to an end?

ANSWERS

CHECK YOUR ANSWERS

1. A. the Sui dynasty
2. During the Song dynasty, China had a lot of cultural achievements—the magnetic compass and movable type to print books. They also created new music and art, and landscapes painted on silk.
3. The ruler Tang Taizong of the Tang dynasty used the teachings of Confucius to strengthen political peace between northern and southern China.
4. The Song improved the government by hiring government workers based on merit and test scores instead of family connections.
5. The golden age of China was "golden" because many important inventions and advancements were made. The Song improved the government by hiring based on merit. New technology with irrigation improved food cultivation and created food surpluses. Therefore, there was leisure time and the Chinese created new music and art, and painted landscapes on silk. The Chinese invented gunpowder, the magnetic compass, and movable type to print books, which allowed more people to learn to read, including women. More books helped educate more people.
6. The golden age of China lasted until the Mongols came to power in the late 1200s and got rid of the last Song emperor by 1279.

☆ Chapter 15 ☆
MEDIEVAL
JAPAN

Unlike China, with its massive
landmass, Japan is a small country

ARCHIPELAGO
a chain of islands

formed by an **ARCHIPELAGO** off the coast of the Asian
mainland. It is located in the Pacific Ocean about 500 miles
(805 kilometers) from China and 100 miles (161 kilometers)
from Korea. Four main islands make up Japan and bring
its total land area to roughly 146,000 square miles (234,964
square kilometers). ← ABOUT THE SIZE OF THE STATE OF MONTANA

Japan's history has been greatly affected by being an island nation. Japan would face its share of outsiders trying to get into that bustling string of islands, but the islands would help it stay isolated from mainland Asia and develop its unique culture.

MEDIEVAL JAPAN

The NARA PERIOD

The NARA PERIOD of Japan's medieval history began around 710 CE, when a new capital was established in the ancient Japanese city of Nara by the EMPRESS GEMMEI.

Subsequent emperors began to use the title "Son of Heaven," but in reality held little power. **ARISTOCRATS**, wealthy land-owning families, kept taxes from their lands for themselves. The government needed tax revenue; without it, the government couldn't make useful changes and looked weak.

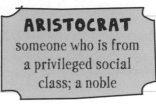

ARISTOCRAT
someone who is from a privileged social class; a noble

Many of the first national histories were written during this period, and literature thrived. Buddhism also became a fixture in society, and many great temples were built during this time—including the Great Buddha Diabatsu, which is roughly 52 feet (16 meters) high.

The HEIAN PERIOD

In 794 CE, the emperor moved the capital from Nara to HEIAN-KYO (present-day Kyoto), marking the beginning of the HEIAN PERIOD. This period lasted until 1185. The emperor ruled in name only; the real power belonged to the FUJIWARA clan, a powerful family that ruled the lands. Nobles with large estates hired peasants to work for them in a system called **FEUDALISM**. For protection, nobles hired their own armies, made up of warriors called SAMURAI. Samurai took an oath to follow a strict set of rules and a code of honor called BUSHIDO. Honor was more important than wealth or even life itself. Samurai were expected to be fearless in the face of the enemy and to commit ritual suicide rather than ever surrender.

> ### FEUDALISM
> a social system in which nobility held land for the royalty in exchange for loyalty and military service; in exchange for protection, warriors were also allowed to live on these lands. Peasants also lived on these lands in exchange for their work on farms and goods.

> ### SHOGUN
> a commander-in-chief in feudal Japan; passed down military power to heirs

The samurai eventually gained power and formed their own clans. In 1192, the emperor chose one clan leader, MINAMOTO YORITOMO, as the new **SHOGUN**, or supreme military leader, of all

Japan. Yoritomo set up the KAMAKURA SHOGUNATE, a series
of military dynasties that would rule Japan from 1192 to 1333.
Paper, porcelain, and iron markets grew, along with foreign
trade with Korea and China.

The TOKUGAWA PERIOD

The Japanese defeated the Mongol invaders in the 1200s, and
it was another 300 years before foreigners got anywhere
near Japan. In the mid-1500s, the Japanese began trading
with the West, but European influence didn't last long. Under
TOKUGAWA IEYASU, the founder and first shogun of the
TOKUGAWA shogunate, Japan outlawed Christianity and
trade with foreigners—he worried that Europeans would
monopolize its trade routes. As a result, Japan was cut off
from the outside world for over 200 years.

RELIGION IN EARLY AND MEDIEVAL JAPAN

According to the ancient Japanese **SHINTO** religion, ancestor and
nature spirits are always near. The early Japanese people believed
in mountain, river, and tree spirits called **KAMI**. They believed
their ancestors' spirits blew in the air around them. Shinto
became tied to the sacredness of Japan and its emperor.

Another religion that became popular in Japan is **BUDDHISM**.
Buddhist monks had come from China to Japan around 500 CE.
One type of Buddhism, **ZEN**, became popular with Japanese
aristocrats. Zen Buddhism's beliefs about self-discipline were
even integrated into the bushido of the samurai.

SHINTO MEANS "THE WAY OF THE GODS."

A **HAIKU** is a three-line poem that developed during the Tokugawa shogunate in Japan. The first and last lines are each five syllables long, and the middle line is seven syllables long, like this:

Medieval Japan
So many brave samurai
Firm in their beliefs

Nara PERIOD
710 CE–794 CE

Kamakura Shogunate PERIOD
1192 CE–1333 CE

A TIMELINE OF MEDIEVAL JAPAN

Heian PERIOD
794 CE–1192 CE

Tokugawa PERIOD
1600 CE–1868 CE

CHECK YOUR KNOWLEDGE

1. Describe Japan's geography. What in particular affected the country's history?

2. Who held the *real* political power during the Nara period?

3. How did feudalism work in Japan?

4. What was the code of the bushido?

5. Between 1192 and 1333, the Japanese military leader with greater power than the emperor was called the:
   A. shogun
   B. samurai
   C. bushido
   D. nara

6. What are the Shinto religion's main beliefs?

7. Who outlawed Christianity and trade with foreigners in Japan? Why?

ANSWERS

CHECK YOUR ANSWERS

1. Japan is a small country formed by an archipelago—a chain of islands—which helped to keep it isolated from outside influences.

2. Aristocrats held most of the real power and kept all the tax revenue during the Nara period.

3. Feudalism in Japan was a system where powerful families of nobles hired peasants to work on their large estates. Also, nobles hired their own armies of samurai warriors for protection.

4. The code of the bushido was a set of rules that samurai took an oath to follow. Samurai were expected to act honorably, follow the code, be fearless in the face of the enemy, and to commit suicide instead of ever surrendering.

5. A. shogun

6. According to the Shinto religion, spirits of nature and ancestors are always near.

7. Tokugawa Ieyasu outlawed Christianity and trade with foreigners because he was worried that Europeans would take over Japanese trade routes.

☆ Chapter 16 ☆

EUROPE
✷ ✷ ✷ IN THE ✷ ✷ ✷
MIDDLE
AGES

476 CE TO THE 13TH, 14TH, OR 15TH CENTURY CE
DEPENDING ON WHOM YOU ASK WHEN THE RENAISSANCE BEGAN

The Middle Ages in Europe includes the Age of Chivalry (the 1200s to 1400s). This was a time of knights and ladies-in-waiting, of nobles and kings. But it was also a time of hardship for peasants and farmers, and a time of struggle between church and state.

CHARLEMAGNE

The Middle Ages began when the Roman Empire collapsed in 476 CE, after several groups, including the FRANKS, invaded it. The king of the Franks, CHARLEMAGNE, took control of Western Europe in 768 CE and united it for the next 50 years. In 800 CE, Charlemagne was crowned emperor of the Romans—the Holy Roman Emperor—by the pope, and the "kingdom of Europe" he created combined Roman, Christian, and German elements. He was a powerful Christian ruler.

> A GERMANIC-SPEAKING PEOPLE THAT DOMINATED MODERN-DAY NORTHERN FRANCE, BELGIUM, AND WESTERN GERMANY

After Charlemagne's death in 814 CE, small kingdoms formed throughout Western Europe. These kingdoms were attacked by the VIKINGS, explorers and warriors from Northern Europe in what is now called Scandinavia. The Vikings destroyed towns and attacked local armies. A new system was needed to bring about order. What resulted was a European brand of feudalism.

RAWR! HELP!

KINGS

The FEUDAL SYSTEM

The feudal system was a way of organizing economic, political, and military needs. Kings and NOBLES (LORDS) owned land but gave shares (called **FIEFS**) to their **VASSALS** (lesser nobles). The FEUDAL CONTRACT was a set of unwritten rules between a lord and his vassal. Vassals were expected to follow the landowner's rules and fight for him (many vassals were knights). Feudal society was built around warfare.

By 1000 CE, feudalism had taken over Western Europe.

NOBLES

VASSALS

INCLUDING

KNIGHTS

SERFS

> **FIEF**
> in the feudal system, a grant of land to a vassal

> **VASSAL**
> in the feudal system, a tenant of the lord; the lord protects the vassal, and the vassal promises loyalty and military service in return

FEUDAL SYSTEM

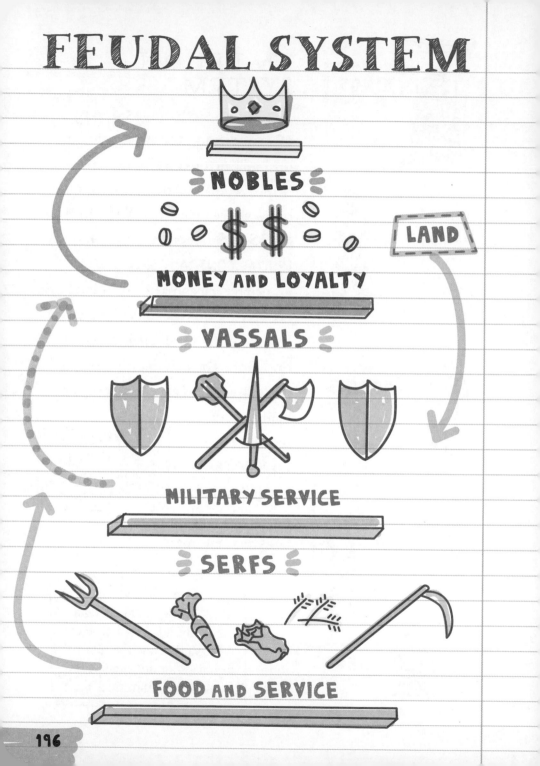

NOBLES

$ $

MONEY AND LOYALTY

LAND

VASSALS

MILITARY SERVICE

SERFS

FOOD AND SERVICE

MANORIALISM

MANORS were large, self-sufficient estates with farmland and sometimes whole villages. They were ruled by lords who collected taxes and harvests from peasants who farmed the land. Many peasants were SERFS who were bound to the manor. Serfs couldn't even get married without permission of the lord. They could only leave the manor if they saved enough money to buy their freedom and some land—or if they escaped and survived a year and a day without getting caught.

The DEVELOPMENT of TOWNS

Feudalism declined after the 1200s, as towns and trade expanded. Kings hired armies to protect towns and became more powerful than, say, a group of nobles banding together against the king. A middle class of merchants, traders, and craft workers grew. They formed **GUILDS** to set prices and keep a high standard of quality for their goods. There were guilds for shoemakers, weavers, and other craftspeople.

> **GUILD**
> an organization of people with common interests or goals

The Crusades also weakened the power of nobles and feudalism. Many nobles went off to fight in the Crusades (and maybe didn't come back) and gave their land to the king.

NATION BUILDING

By the 1100s, the empire initially ruled by Charlemagne was called the HOLY ROMAN EMPIRE. The unification of kingdoms throughout the empire led to the idea of NATION BUILDING, or uniting a community of people under a single government.

All over Europe, larger kingdoms turned into nations with national identities and national governments. In Spain, a royal marriage united two powerful kingdoms, and in France, a long line of kings consolidated royal power.
In England, the process of unification had begun early: During the NORMAN CONQUEST, William of Normandy, a duke from France also known as WILLIAM THE CONQUEROR, became king of England after his victory at the Battle of Hastings in 1066. William refined the system of taxation and royal courts that earlier Anglo-Saxon kings had begun. He gave land to Norman knights and took a census of people, manors, and animals.

> GOT ITS NAME FROM THE FRANKS!

Around the year 1200, a successor to King William, King John, heavily taxed the English people and tried to block the pope's choice for bishop. His poor decisions led nobles to create the MAGNA CARTA, a **CHARTER** that limited the king's power. The king now had to consult a lawmaking council that later became the English PARLIAMENT.

> **CHARTER**
> an agreement on rights or authority

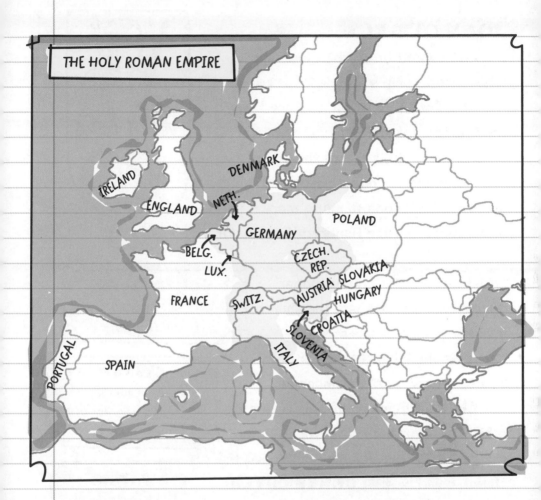

THE HOLY ROMAN EMPIRE

IRELAND
ENGLAND
DENMARK
NETH.
BELG.
LUX.
GERMANY
POLAND
CZECH. REP.
AUSTRIA
SLOVAKIA
HUNGARY
FRANCE
SWITZ.
CROATIA
SLOVENIA
PORTUGAL
SPAIN
ITALY

More than a century later, the HUNDRED YEARS' WAR
between France and England solidified each nation's
boundaries and identities. The war, beginning in 1337 and
fought over an area of land in France called the Duchy of
Gascony, resulted in French victory in 1453 (people lived their
whole lives at war, as did their kids and their kids' kids, etc.).

JOAN OF ARC was a young French peasant girl turned warrior whose leadership in battle inspired her French **COMPATRIOTS**. Captured by the English, Joan of Arc was tried for witchcraft and burned at the stake. Her death made Joan a martyr and inspired the French to many more victories during the Hundred Years' War.

Christianity grew even stronger during the Middle Ages. The church had the power to collect taxes and was the largest landowner in Europe. There was a member of the **CLERGY** in every village: a priest, a bishop, or an archbishop, or, in Rome, the **PAPACY**. People who didn't obey the church could be **EXCOMMUNICATED**. People were afraid they wouldn't go to heaven after death if they were excommunicated; that threat kept people in line.

> **COMPATRIOT**
> a fellow countryman or countrywoman

> **CLERGY**
> religious leaders, such as priests, who perform religious services

> **PAPACY**
> the government of the church as led by the pope

> **EXCOMMUNICATED**
> cut off from church life

THE PLAGUE

Between 1347 and 1351, one-third of Europe's population died from the **BUBONIC PLAGUE**, also known as the **BLACK DEATH**. It was initially spread by a bacterium carried by fleas living on rats. The plague arrived in Europe when Italian merchants returned from the Black Sea in October 1347. By the end of the year, Italy and France had been hit by the plague. It spread to Germany, the Netherlands, England, and Scandinavia by 1349.

By 1351, Eastern Europe and Russia were affected. Entire villages disappeared.

With more than 25 million people dead, normal life was challenging. The labor shortage led the workers who survived the plague to ask for higher wages. Farmers looked for projects that would require fewer workers, like grazing sheep instead of growing crops. A smaller population caused a decrease in demand for food. Peasants bargained with their lords and were freed from serfdom, agreeing to pay rent instead. The feudal system was greatly weakened.

Many people believed God was punishing them. Some accused Jews of poisoning wells and causing the plague; these **ANTI-SEMITIC** beliefs led to attacks on Jews, especially in Germany. Many Jews fled Germany for Poland, where the king protected them.

ANTI-SEMITIC
prejudiced against Jews

In art and literature, death became a common topic;
historians study paintings and poems from the
mid-thirteenth century to learn more about the plague.

1. How did the Middle Ages begin? What king reigned in Western Europe at the time?

2. What was the purpose of the feudal system? How did it work?

3. Guilds were used for:

    A. controlling serfs on the manor

    B. setting a standard of prices among craft workers

    C. voting on local political issues

    D. establishing centers of religion in small towns

4. What was the Norman Conquest?

5. The Magna Carta resulted in:

    A. an increase in the king's power, granting him more independent rule than before

    B. a decrease in the king's power, limited by a lawmaking council

    C. a decrease in both the power of the king and the power of Parliament

    D. no change to the balance of power in lawmaking

6. What happened to people who openly disobeyed the church?

7. How did the plague arrive in Europe?

ANSWERS

CHECK YOUR ANSWERS

1. The Middle Ages began when the Roman Empire collapsed and the King of the Franks, Charlemagne, took control of Western Europe. He was crowned Holy Roman Emperor of the "kingdom of Europe."

2. The purpose of the feudal system was to organize the economy, politics, and military. Kings and nobles owned land but gave pieces to the lesser nobles (vassals). In turn, vassals had to follow the landowner's rules and fight for him. Serfs farmed the land and lived on a lord's manor.

3. B. setting a standard of prices among craft workers

4. The Norman Conquest was the period when William of Normandy became king of England after his victory at the Battle of Hastings.

5. B. a decrease in the king's power, limited by a lawmaking council

6. People who didn't obey the church could be excommunicated. People believed that meant they wouldn't go to heaven when they died.

7. The plague arrived in Europe when Italian merchants returned from the Black Sea. The ships carried rats that had fleas that carried the deadly bacterium.

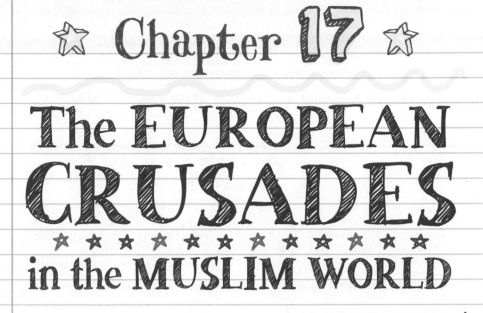

Chapter 17

The EUROPEAN CRUSADES

★ ★ ★ ★ ★ ★ ★ ★ ★ ★ ★ ★ ★

in the MUSLIM WORLD

ROUGHLY LATE 11TH CENTURY TO 13TH CENTURY

The CRUSADES were a series of military expeditions in which Europeans tried to gain control of the Holy Land of Jerusalem from the Muslims. They began in the eleventh century, when the Byzantine emperor in Constantinople asked Christian states in Europe to help fight against the Muslim SELJUK TURKS, and lasted almost 200 years.

POPE URBAN II

At the Council of Clermont in 1095, POPE URBAN II called for Christians to help free Jerusalem. He declared that those who died in the holy war would be immediately **ABSOLVED** of their sins. People were convinced that fighting

ABSOLVE
to free from blame or guilt

this war was the will of God. The pope hoped the Crusades
would stop Christians from fighting among themselves.
The Seljuk Turks posed a particular threat to the Christian

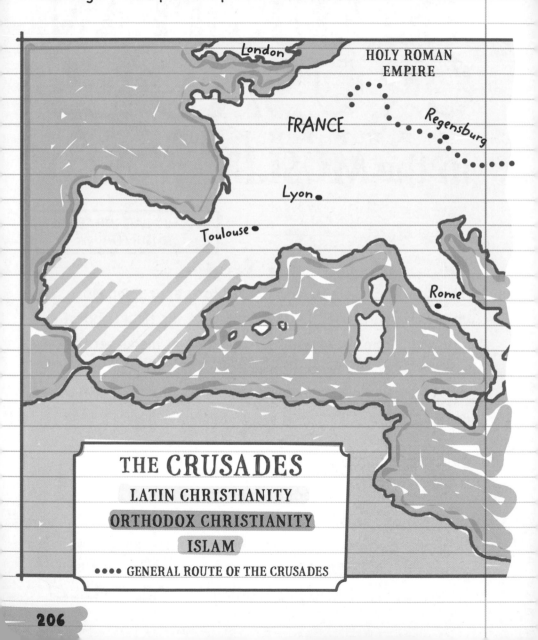

HOLY ROMAN EMPIRE

London

FRANCE

Regensburg

Lyon

Toulouse

Rome

THE CRUSADES

LATIN CHRISTIANITY

ORTHODOX CHRISTIANITY

ISLAM

•••• GENERAL ROUTE OF THE CRUSADES

religion: They had risen to power in Jerusalem and attacked European Christians making pilgrimages into the city. The pope also wanted power for himself and the church.

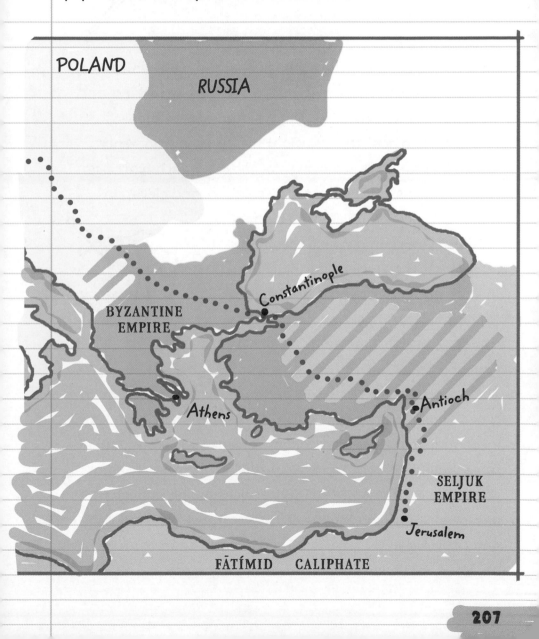

The FIRST CRUSADE

In the summer of 1096, 12,000 French peasants, along with two armies from Germany, marched through Europe in the PEOPLE'S CRUSADE. They lost one-third of their people before they reached Constantinople. Untrained, in rags, and with no money, they wandered, attacking and stealing from villages. The emperor gave them supplies and ships and sent them to fight the Turks in Asia Minor. In 1097, great lords led armies of mostly French warriors, along with vassals, wives, cooks, children, and clerks, in the NOBLES' CRUSADE. These knights fought for religion but also sought adventure. They welcomed the chance to fight and possibly gain wealth or a fancy title. Many poor people saw the military as a way to rise in social class.

The French warriors reached and took Jerusalem in 1099 in a deadly massacre of the city's Muslim, Christian, and Jewish inhabitants alike. Most crusaders returned to Europe, but some stayed and organized four crusader states. Italian port cities like Genoa, Pisa, and Venice saw an opportunity and began trading with the crusader states, growing rich and powerful in the process. The Muslims began to strike back, but the crusaders fought them once more.

LATER CRUSADES

The **SECOND CRUSADE** was less successful than the first. King Louis VII of France and Emperor Conrad III of Germany failed in their fight against the Muslims in the 1140s. A **THIRD CRUSADE**, in 1187, was fought against the Muslim sultan **SALADIN**, who had regained control of Jerusalem. Led by German Emperor Frederick Barbarossa, English King Richard I (**RICHARD THE LIONHEART**), and French King Philip II (Philip Augustus), the conquest was doomed. Frederick drowned early in the fight. The French and English, who had arrived by sea, struggled to make it inland. Philip headed back home to France, leaving King Richard I to negotiate a settlement with Saladin. The agreement allowed Christian pilgrims access to Jerusalem once more.

KING RICHARD I

is known as one of the greatest English kings of the Middle Ages, while his younger brother John is considered one of the worst. Richard's courage on the battlefield earned him the nickname "Richard the Lionheart." According to English legend, he and Robin Hood lived at the same time.

Six years after Saladin's death, **POPE INNOCENT III** called for another crusade, the **FOURTH CRUSADE**. The army sacked Constantinople in 1204. This increased the division between the Eastern Orthodox Church and the Roman Catholic Church.

There were nine crusades in all, some failures, some gaining successes through diplomacy—but eventually defeats led to the end of the Crusades.

EFFECTS of the CRUSADES

The Crusades helped Italian port cities prosper and increased trade with the East. Rugs, jewelry, glass, and spices became big commodities. The Crusades also brought new ideas to Western Europe and the Middle East. Advances made by the Arab dynasties in mathematics, technology, and medicine boosted European knowledge in these areas, and Europeans learned to make better maps and ships.

The Crusades helped break down feudalism. Many vassals sold their land to pay the rising war taxes and freed their serfs to fight in the Crusades. This allowed kings to claim the land of the nobles and form stronger central governments. Kings gained new wealth through trade with the East, which helped them develop nation-states.

Unfortunately, the Crusades also caused the deaths of untold numbers over centuries of warfare. It bred religious intolerance, including attacks on the Jews. The split between Eastern and Western Christianity became permanent.

CHECK YOUR KNOWLEDGE

1. What were the Crusades?

2. How did the Crusades affect the division of power in medieval society?

3. What did the agreement signed between Richard the Lionheart and Saladin state?

4. The treaty between King Richard and Saladin was signed during the:
   A. First Crusade, in 1099
   B. Second Crusade, in the 1140s
   C. Third Crusade, in 1187
   D. Fourth Crusade, in 1204

5. What was the effect of the Crusades in terms of trade?

6. What is the importance of the city of Jerusalem?

7. How did the Crusades positively affect life in Europe? How did they negatively affect life in Europe?

ANSWERS

CHECK YOUR ANSWERS

1. The Crusades were a series of military expeditions that lasted more than 150 years in which Europeans tried to get control of the Holy Land of Jerusalem.

2. The Crusades helped break down feudalism because many vassals sold their land to pay war taxes and freed their serfs to fight in the Crusades. Kings also created stronger central governments by amassing new wealth through the claimed land of the nobles and trade with the East.

3. The agreement between Richard the Lionheart and Saladin stated that Christian pilgrims could visit Jerusalem.

4. C. Third Crusade, in 1187

5. The Crusades helped Italian port cities prosper and increased trade with the East, which introduced new types of goods, like rugs, jewelry, glass, and spices.

6. Jerusalem was (and is) called the Holy City. It was (and is) valued by Jews, Christians, and Muslims.

7. The Crusades brought new trade with, and advances in mathematics, technology, and medicine from, the Arabs. Europeans learned to make better maps and ships. However, the Crusades also caused the deaths of many, bred religious intolerance, and created a permanent split between Eastern and Western Christianity.

Unit 4

Renaissance and Reformation 1350–1650

The RENAISSANCE began a time of cultural change that originated in Italy in the 1300s and spread through Europe over the next two centuries. "Renaissance" literally means "rebirth," and it was a time of rebirth of ancient Greek and Roman culture.

REMEMBER US?

Chapter 18

The RENAISSANCE
BEGINS

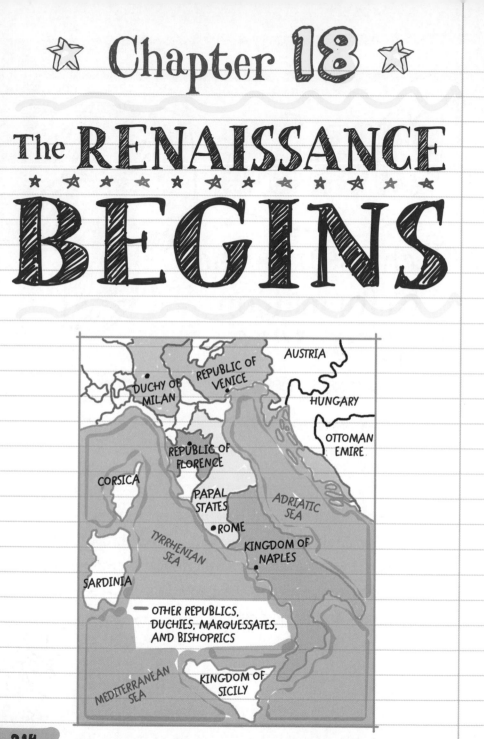

AUSTRIA

HUNGARY

OTTOMAN
EMIRE

REPUBLIC OF
VENICE

DUCHY OF
MILAN

REPUBLIC OF
FLORENCE

CORSICA

PAPAL
STATES

ADRIATIC
SEA

●ROME

TYRRHENIAN
SEA

KINGDOM OF
NAPLES

SARDINIA

— OTHER REPUBLICS,
DUCHIES, MARQUESSATES,
AND BISHOPRICS

MEDITERRANEAN
SEA

KINGDOM OF
SICILY

The Renaissance emphasized the importance of the individual as well as **SECULARISM**. The interest in humans apart from religion was called **HUMANISM**. It grew in part from the Crusades, when Europeans and Muslims interacted. The rise of the middle class introduced new points of view and led to the belief that humans are unique individuals capable of great things.

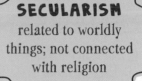

SECULARISM
related to worldly things; not connected with religion

HUMANISM
system of thought that focuses on humans rather than divine matters

ORIGINS of the RENAISSANCE

The Renaissance began in Italy, where powerful port cities had become city-states independent of the control of a king or even the church. Wealthy Italian leaders borrowed and loaned money without regard for the church's

regulations against **USURY**. Some of the wealthiest families, like that of COSIMO DE' MEDICI, became **PATRONS** of the arts and promoted the study of classical (ancient) literature.

USURY
the practice of lending money at a very high interest rate

PATRON
a person who supports artists, writers, or creative institutions with money, gifts, or social or political influence

RENAISSANCE LITERATURE

In Renaissance literature, the focus was less on religion and the church and more on Greek and Roman ideals of nature and beauty. Humanism's interest in the classics was a major part of the Renaissance. Humanists studied grammar, poetry, philosophy, history, and rhetoric—subjects that today are called "the humanities."

The first great humanist was FRANCESCO PETRARCA (known as PETRARCH), a poet whose **SONNETS** focused on a love of nature in the tradition of Roman writers. Petrarch is considered the father of Italian Renaissance humanism. He was super smart and was curious about finding Latin manuscripts to study their ideas. His searches set off other searches in **MONASTIC** libraries throughout Europe.

MONASTIC
pertaining to monasteries, or the way of life of monks and nuns

SONNET
a type of poem that originated in Italy, consisting of fourteen lines that rhyme according to a pattern. It discusses an idea in the first eight lines that's figured out (or at least the thought is completed) in the last six lines. Shakespeare's rhyme pattern is **ABAB CDCD EFEF GG**. Petrarchs's is **ABBA ABBA CDE CDE** or **ABBA ABBA CDC DCD**. (Each letter corresponds to the rhyming final words of each line.)

Another great humanist was WILLIAM SHAKESPEARE, a famous English poet and playwright. Shakespeare used plots from ancient texts rebooted in an updated way for his comedies, tragedies, and histories.

SHAKESPEARE'S WRITING EMPHASIZED HUMAN EMOTIONS THAT ARE STILL PRESENT IN OUR LIVES TODAY.

RELIGIOUS HUMANISM

There were religious humanists too. ERASMUS, a Roman Catholic priest, wanted to study and understand Christianity. He decided that the Catholic Church needed some changes and wrote "IN PRAISE OF FOLLY" (1509), mocking church practices. Much of what he wrote was considered controversial, and some people even thought Erasmus was calling for the destruction of the Catholic Church. But Erasmus only wanted to make certain reforms and leave other things unchanged. This would eventually inspire Martin Luther to call for reform within the church.

The invention of the movable-type printing press in the mid 1400s by **JOHANNES GUTENBERG** was a turning point during the Renaissance. The printing press led to the mass production of books and made new ideas available to more Europeans faster than ever before.

RENAISSANCE ART

Renaissance art also marked a return to ancient Greece and Rome. Painters and sculptors still featured religious scenes, but their central interest was imitating nature and rendering the human body in its most beautiful form. In architecture, painting, and sculpture, the focus was on the human-centered world.

LEONARDO DA VINCI

MAJOR ARTISTS

Artists like LEONARDO DA VINCI (famous for the *MONA LISA* and *THE LAST SUPPER*) studied anatomy. They worked with the laws of perspective to create realistic works of art.

MICHELANGELO's statue of the biblical hero _DAVID_ is a declaration of the perfection of the human form. Michelangelo wanted to portray the human being as a reflection of divine beauty: The more beautiful the body, the more godlike the figure. His fresco on the ceiling of the SISTINE CHAPEL features ideal bodies in perfect proportions.

The **SISTINE CHAPEL** is a chapel in the Apostolic Palace, which is the official residence of the pope. It's famous for its architecture and frescoes and is located in Vatican City.

The sculptor DONATELLO studied Greek and Roman statues and sculpted figures such as the famous Christian figure _SAINT GEORGE_.

Architect FILIPPO BRUNELLESCHI studied the buildings of classical Rome and designed churches with classical columns and rounded arches as an alternative to **GOTHIC** cathedrals.

GOTHIC
a style of architecture used in Western Europe from roughly the 1200s through the 1400s and characterized by pointed arches and vaulting and the use of detailed woodwork and stonework

FLEMISH
people of the Flanders region—an area now divided among Belgium, France, and the Netherlands

Outside of Italy, **FLEMISH** artist JAN VAN EYCK, for example, imitated nature by painting on wooden panels. By experimenting with oil paints, he was able to capture true-to-life details.

CHECK YOUR KNOWLEDGE

1. What does the term "Renaissance" refer to? Why was it used to describe this time?

2. What is secularism?

3. How did secularism contribute to the emergence of the Renaissance in Italy?

4. Who was Cosimo de' Medici?
   A. the leader of an important Italian guild
   B. a patron of the arts
   C. a strong supporter of the pope
   D. a famous Italian artist

5. Define "humanism." How did it change educational approaches?

6. Erasmus believed that:
   A. the Catholic Church should be destroyed.
   B. the Catholic Church should be reformed.
   C. the Catholic Church was perfect just the way it was.

7. Name two important Renaissance artists and describe their achievements.

ANSWERS

CHECK YOUR ANSWERS

1. "Renaissance" literally means "rebirth." "Renaissance" was used to describe this time because there was a rebirth of ancient Greek and Roman culture.

2. Secularism is an attention to things and ideas not connected with religion.

3. Secularism allowed people to study humans (humanism) and things apart from religion. It introduced new points of view and led to the belief that humans are unique and capable of great things.

4. B. a patron of the arts

5. Humanism is the study of people. It changed education by dividing the world into subjects that today are called "the humanities," such as grammar, poetry, philosophy, history, and rhetoric.

6. B. the Catholic Church should be reformed.

7. Any two of the following:

   → **LEONARDO DA VINCI:** famous for *The Last Supper* and the *Mona Lisa*; studied anatomy; worked with the laws of perspective to create realistic works of art

   → **MICHELANGELO:** famous for his fresco on the ceiling of the Sistine Chapel and his statue of the biblical hero *David*, a testament to the perfection of the human form

→ **DONATELLO**: a sculptor who studied Greek and Roman statues and created statues such as one of *Saint George*

→ **FILIPPO BRUNELLESCHI**: an architect who studied the buildings of classical Rome and designed churches with classical columns and rounded arches as an alternative to Gothic cathedrals

→ **JAN VAN EYCK**: a Flemish artist who imitated nature by painting on wooden panels and captured true-to-life details by experimenting with oil paints

Chapter 19

★ THE ★
REFORMATION

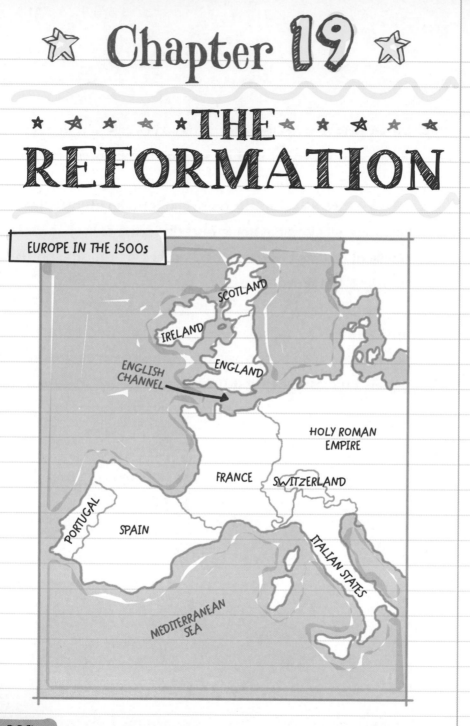

EUROPE IN THE 1500s

SCOTLAND

IRELAND

ENGLAND

ENGLISH
CHANNEL

HOLY ROMAN
EMPIRE

FRANCE   SWITZERLAND

PORTUGAL

SPAIN

ITALIAN STATES

MEDITERRANEAN
SEA

The REFORMATION is the reform, or change, that established **PROTESTANTISM** as a branch of Christianity. Humanists like Erasmus believed that the Roman Catholic Church needed to reform its ways and focus more on inner piety and less on external displays of religion like pilgrimages and **RELICS**.

> **PROTESTANT**
> a Christian who does not adhere to the Catholic, Anglican, or Eastern Churches; also, one who protests

> **RELIC**
> an object from the past, usually associated with a saint or martyr

CORRUPTION in the CHURCH

In the early 1500s, the church had a big problem with corruption. From 1450 to 1520, a series of popes called "the Renaissance popes" were more interested in politics than religion. The church became a place where some people tried to advance their careers and increase their wealth, and where some priests were illiterate and unfamiliar with the Bible.

Ordinary folks were just trying to figure out how to get into heaven. The church began to sell them **INDULGENCES**, which you could buy to get out of punishment for sin.

> **INDULGENCES**
> pardons, sometimes sold along with relics to sinners, who were expected to venerate (show respect to) the relics

MARTIN LUTHER

In 1517, a monk named MARTIN LUTHER took his criticism to the church in his 95 THESES, a list of grievances (complaints) against the church. He posted his list on a church door, and it was printed and spread all over Germany. It appealed to both nobles who resented the pope's power and

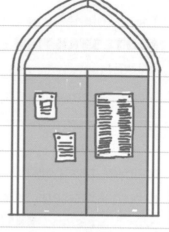

peasants who believed in Luther's message of equality. Luther held that it was faith alone—not doing a lot of good acts (GOOD WORKS)—that brought about **SALVATION**. He especially criticized the selling of indulgences.

> **SALVATION**
> the act of being saved or protected from sin

Pope Leo X didn't take Luther seriously, but Luther kept on. Luther wanted to establish a reformed German church with a new system of **SACRAMENTS**.

> **SACRAMENT**
> a religious symbol or ceremony in the Christian church

The Catholic Church finally excommunicated Luther in 1521. The emperor of the Holy Roman Empire, CHARLES V, declared Luther an outlaw in his EDICT OF WORMS, forcing Luther into hiding.

> AS IN THE PLACE—NOT THE ANIMAL. EWW!

Luther gained the support of many German rulers, who took control of the Catholic churches in their territories and formed government-supervised state churches. Luther's beliefs became the first Protestant faith, LUTHERANISM. In 1555, under the PEACE OF AUGSBURG, Lutherans won the right to practice their religion. German states were free to choose between Catholicism and Lutheranism, and the Roman Catholic Church was no longer such a powerful political body.

CALVINISM

There were divisions within Protestantism. JOHN CALVIN (1509-1564), a French Protestant, agreed with Luther that faith alone was enough for salvation. He talked about the "power, grace, and glory of God." He believed that God **PREDESTINED** certain people to be saved (THE ELECT), and others to be damned (the **REPROBATES**). Followers of Calvin were called CALVINISTS, and they spread their faith to others as missionaries, emphasizing salvation through grace and good works.

PREDESTINE
to predetermine or choose in advance

REPROBATE
wicked or unprincipled person beyond the hope of salvation

CONSISTORY
a court for enforcing moral discipline

Calvinism was based in Geneva, Switzerland, where Calvin set up a **CONSISTORY**. Genevan citizens could be punished for "crimes" like dancing, swearing, drinking, and playing cards. Calvinism spread to parts of France, Scotland, and the Netherlands. By the mid-sixteenth century, it had become the most prominent form of Protestantism.

CHANGES in the ENGLISH CHURCH

The call for religious reform spread to other parts of Europe. In 1534, KING HENRY VIII had Parliament formally separate the Catholic Church in England from the pope in Rome (though many believe it was because he wanted more personal control and, mainly, the right to divorce his wives).

HENRY VIII

HENRY VIII wanted to divorce his wife Catherine because she had given birth to a girl and Henry needed a male heir for the throne. He asked the pope to ANNUL (cancel) his marriage so he could marry ANNE BOLEYN instead. The pope was taking too long, so Henry VIII turned to the English church courts instead. In 1533, the archbishop of the highest church court in England, THOMAS CRANMER, ruled that the king's marriage to Catherine was null and void. Henry married Anne, but she had a baby girl too. Henry tried again and ended up having six wives. Still, his daughter with Anne went on to become QUEEN ELIZABETH I.

The ACT OF SUPREMACY in 1534 made the king the supreme head of the CHURCH OF ENGLAND, which was also called the ANGLICAN CHURCH. Henry VIII chose whom to appoint to important church positions. People who opposed these changes were often beheaded.

After Henry VIII's death, the Church of England became more and more Protestant, especially during EDWARD VI's reign. (Edward was Henry's nine-year-old son, so he didn't have much of a say in the matter.) His half sister, QUEEN MARY, was called "Bloody Mary" when she tried to restore the church to its Roman Catholic roots by having 300 Protestants burned at the stake. (Queen Mary's reign lasted from 1553 to 1558, and she was pretty much despised by the end of it.) After Mary's death, QUEEN ELIZABETH I restored Protestantism to England.

The Catholic Church needed to change or it would continue to split apart. The COUNTERREFORMATION (also known as the CATHOLIC REFORMATION) brought about three changes (THREE PILLARS) in the Catholic Church:

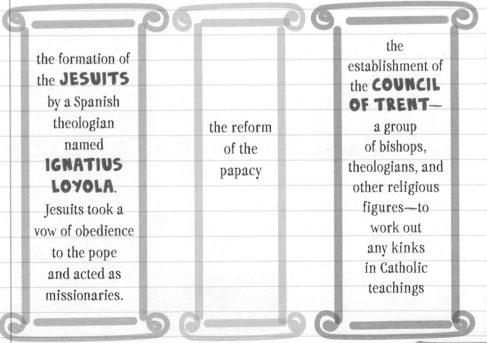

the formation of the **JESUITS** by a Spanish theologian named **IGNATIUS LOYOLA**. Jesuits took a vow of obedience to the pope and acted as missionaries.

the reform of the papacy

the establishment of the **COUNCIL OF TRENT**— a group of bishops, theologians, and other religious figures—to work out any kinks in Catholic teachings

The SPANISH ARMADA

Catholicism was strong in Spain under KING PHILIP II. From his father, Charles V (former Holy Roman Emperor, King of Spain, and Archduke of Austria), Philip inherited kingdoms in Italy, the Netherlands, and what Europeans called the New World (the Americas). He insisted that his entire empire conform to Catholicism. England was under the reign of Elizabeth I. In 1588, Philip II sent his impressive SPANISH **ARMADA** to overthrow Protestantism there (as well as the queen). Spain's navy was worn down from a century of voyages over the Atlantic Ocean to protect their colonies

> **ARMADA**
> a fleet of warships

230

in the New World. The English ships were fast and destroyed the Spanish fleet. The failed invasion left Spain bankrupt. The balance of power shifted out of Spain's favor and into the hands of England and France.

The REFORMATION in FRANCE

By the early 1560s, HUGUENOTS, French Protestants, made up only a small part of the total French population but nearly half of the French nobility. The tension between Catholics and Huguenots resulted in the WARS OF RELIGION, a series of civil wars (1562–1598). In 1589, a Huguenot leader named HENRY OF NAVARRE became KING HENRY IV, and later helped end the war. He converted to Catholicism so he'd be accepted by the mostly Catholic French. In 1598, he created the EDICT OF NANTES, which declared Catholicism to be France's official religion but allowed Huguenots to worship freely and hold public office.

RELIGIONS IN EUROPE

- ● ROMAN CATHOLIC
- ● LUTHERAN
- CALVINIST
- ● CHRISTIAN MIX
- ● ANGLICAN
- ● ISLAM
- ● ANABAPTIST (a radical Protestant movement)
- ○ EASTERN ORTHODOX

CHECK YOUR KNOWLEDGE

1. What does "The Reformation" refer to?

2. What one practice of the church put Martin Luther over the edge?

3. Explain why Martin Luther's teachings may have been so appealing to peasants.

4. Who were the "elect" and "reprobates" in Calvin's view?

5. What do many believe was Henry VIII's primary motivation in breaking with the Roman Catholic Church?
   A. to separate church and state
   B. to promote his religious views
   C. to marry Anne Boleyn
   D. to gain power over the pope

6. Who were the Huguenots?

7. What was the Spanish Armada, and why was it used to attack England?

ANSWERS

CHECK YOUR ANSWERS

1. The Reformation refers to the change where Protestantism branched off of the Roman Catholic Church.

2. Martin Luther criticized the church's sale of indulgences. He didn't think it was right that people could pay their way out of punishment for sin.

3. Martin Luther's teachings were appealing to peasants because he taught about equality. He thought that faith alone—not doing a lot of good works or paying for indulgences—could bring about a person's salvation.

4. In Calvin's view, the "elect" were people predestined to be saved, and the "reprobates" were predestined to be damned.

5. C. to marry Anne Boleyn

6. The Huguenots were French Protestants who made up a small part of the French population but nearly half of the French nobility.

7. The Spanish Armada was King Philip II's fleet of ships. He sent the Spanish Armada to overthrow Protestantism (and the queen) in England, but the English ships destroyed the Spanish fleet.

Unit 5

The Age of Exploration
1400–1800

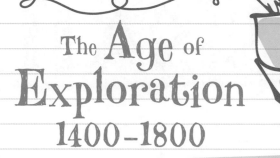

Europeans set sail and spread around the world. They started new systems of trade with profitable new goods. They also spread religion and the African slave trade, and they wiped out much of the Native American population.

☆ Chapter 20 ☆
EUROPE
★ ★ ★ ★ ★ ★ ★ ★ ★ ★ ★ ★ ★ ★
SETS SAIL

WHY EUROPEANS EXPLORED: GOLD, GLORY, and GOD

Trade and the Crusades got Europeans excited about foreign goods like silk and spices, which were unavailable in Europe. Merchants wanted to expand beyond the shores of Europe and find direct routes to the goods. Rulers across Europe sought fame, power, and glory, believing that conquering distant lands would bring them what they wanted, often in the name of God. Europeans had heard of Marco Polo's journey to the East and wanted to gain riches in far-off lands.

PORTUGUESE EXPLORERS

In 1415, young PRINCE HENRY THE NAVIGATOR of Portugal
helped take over CEUTA, a rich Muslim trading city in North
Africa. From Ceuta, the Portuguese gained access to expert
maps of North Africa. Although Prince Henry never explored
distant lands, Portuguese sailors trained in his navigation
school in Lisbon and sailed down the western coast of Africa
on his ships. Wherever they went, the Portuguese established
trading posts. They also returned to Portugal with African
captives who could be traded as slaves—the beginning of the
European slave trade.

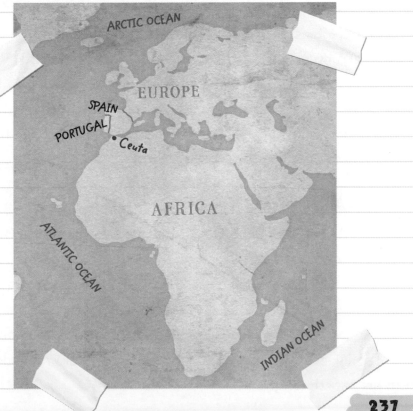

WEST AFRICA in the 1400s was no longer made up of major kingdoms. Instead, it consisted of more than 100 independent kingdoms that constantly went to war over land and trade. Even before these wars took place, enslaving captured enemies was an established practice in West Africa. The winning kingdom received free labor from the defeated kingdom. In addition, the victor would often sell the slaves to traders. (Arab Muslim traders included slaves with their shipments of salt and gold as early as the 600s CE.) By the last half of the 1400s, two of the more successful kingdoms, the **KONGO** (on the Zaire River) and the **NDONGO** (to its south), had dominated their neighbors and sold their enemies into slavery. By the time the Europeans arrived in the 1480s, the African slave trade was already big business.

BARTOLOMEU DIAS, a Portuguese explorer, sailed to the southern tip of Africa in 1488. Nine years later, in 1497, VASCO DA GAMA sailed around the southern tip of Africa into the Indian Ocean. He reached Calicut, India, and returned many times for spices. With their expert seamanship, the Portuguese opened the seas for Europe's age of exploration.

The ADVENTURES of SPAIN

CHRISTOPHER COLUMBUS had three ships (the NIÑA, the PINTA, and the SANTA MARÍA). He wanted to reach India and the East by traveling west around the earth. Though he was from Italy, QUEEN ISABELLA of Spain paid for his voyage. Queen Isabella was a leader who saw Columbus's potential, even though many kings in Europe did not believe in his expedition plans.

In 1492, Columbus sailed the ocean blue. Columbus thought he had reached India but was really in the Americas. This is why the Caribbean islands are sometimes called the West Indies and why Native Americans are sometimes called Indians. Columbus returned three more times to the region in search of gold. He explored Hispaniola (the island of present-day Haiti and the Dominican Republic), Cuba, Jamaica, and the coasts of Central and South America. Though many of the people who already lived in those areas were friendly to Columbus and his men when they arrived, the European settlers were more interested in gold than in friendship and, in general, treated the native people cruelly.

In 1519, the Spanish conquistador HERNÁN CORTÉS reached Tenochtitlán, in modern-day Mexico, which was home to the Aztec Empire. Legend has it that MONTEZUMA, leader of the Aztecs, welcomed the Spaniards because the Aztecs had never seen armor and horses, and they believed that Cortés was QUETZALCÓATL, a pale-skinned god. With advantages such as superior weapons (guns) and the help of other tribes who disliked the Aztecs for taking so many prisoners, Cortés eventually destroyed the city (in 1521) and the Aztec Empire.

FRANCISCO PIZARRO embarked on a conquest in the Incan Empire, located in modern-day Peru. He arrived in 1532 and captured the Inca king ATAHUALPA. Pizarro promised to spare the king if he filled a room with gold. After Atahualpa

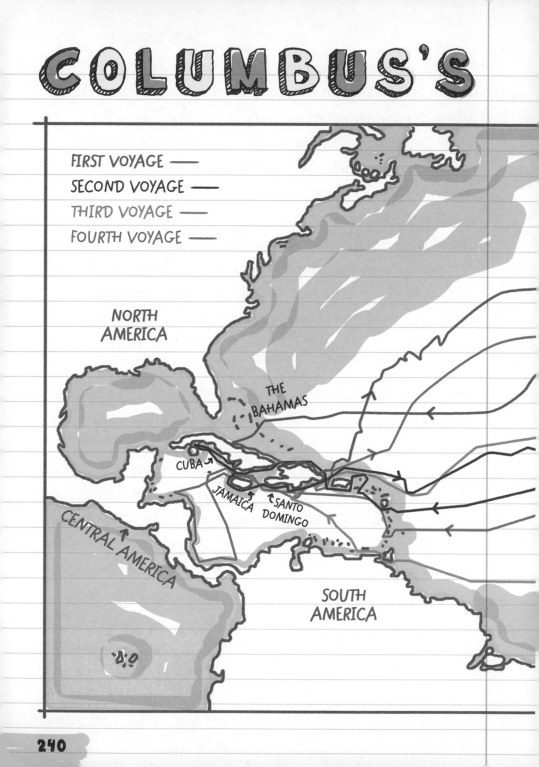

COLUMBUS'S

FIRST VOYAGE ——
SECOND VOYAGE ——
THIRD VOYAGE ——
FOURTH VOYAGE ——

NORTH
AMERICA

THE
BAHAMAS

CUBA

JAMAICA
SANTO
DOMINGO

CENTRAL AMERICA

SOUTH
AMERICA

VOYAGES

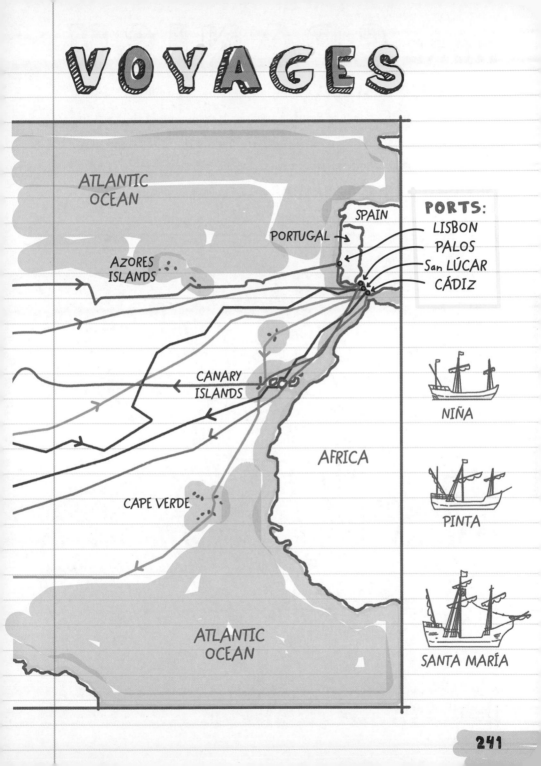

ATLANTIC
OCEAN

PORTUGAL →

SPAIN

PORTS:
LISBON
PALOS
San LÚCAR
CÁDIZ

AZORES
ISLANDS

CANARY
ISLANDS

AFRICA

CAPE VERDE

ATLANTIC
OCEAN

NIÑA

PINTA

SANTA MARÍA

MORE SPANISH

1502: AMERIGO VESPUCCI, an Italian who made voyages for Spain, sailed along the coast of South America. He was one of the first to realize he wasn't in Asia, so a German mapmaker labeled the new land "America" in his honor.

1513: VASCO NÚÑEZ DE BALBOA hiked across Panama and was the first European to see the Pacific Ocean by heading west.

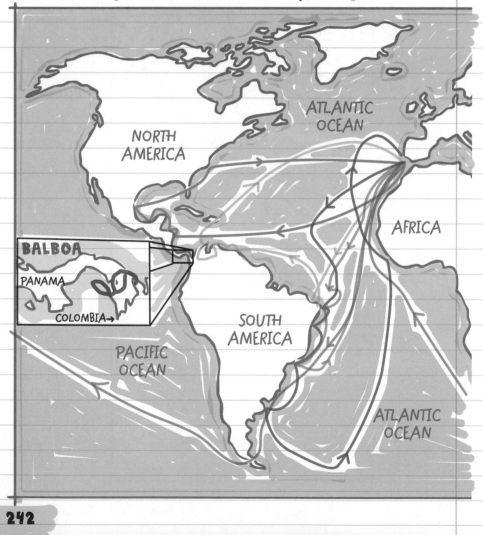

EXPLORERS

1520: FERDINAND MAGELLAN, a Portuguese man sailing on
behalf of Spain, reached the tip of South America. He died
on the trip, but his ships returned in 1522 as the first crew
to **CIRCUMNAVIGATE**
the earth.

> **CIRCUMNAVIGATE**
> sail around ("circum-"—
> think, "circle")

EUROPE

ASIA

PACIFIC
OCEAN

INDIAN
OCEAN

MAGELLAN

AUSTRALIA

VESPUCCI: FIRST VOYAGE → SECOND VOYAGE →
THIRD VOYAGE → FOURTH VOYAGE →

had his subjects bring enough gold to fill the room, Pizarro killed him anyway. The Spanish army used guns and horses to defeat the Incas. Diseases brought from Europe helped both Dias and Pizarro destroy these empires by killing off huge numbers of the population.

THE COLUMBIAN EXCHANGE

There had been no mixing of plants and animals between the Americas and the rest of the world for over ten thousand years. Things like corn, tobacco, cocoa, and potatoes didn't exist elsewhere until they were brought back from the Americas. In return, Europeans brought wheat, barley, grapes, and onions, as well as cattle, pigs, and horses, to the Americas. The plants changed the diets of people all over the world, and the animals changed the way land was used in the Americas.

The humans hadn't been exposed to any of each other's germs either. Diseases such as smallpox, measles, and the flu were common in Europe, but Native Americans didn't have **IMMUNITY**. About 20 million people died from disease in a 100-year span in Central America alone. This mixing of plants, animals, viruses, and bacteria is known as the COLUMBIAN EXCHANGE or the GREAT BIOLOGICAL EXCHANGE.

IMMUNITY
resistance to a disease or sickness, particularly due to previous exposure to the germs

CHECK YOUR KNOWLEDGE

1. What prompted the Europeans to pick up and set sail?

2. Describe the beginnings of the European slave trade. How did it start?

3. Bartolomeu Dias, Vasco da Gama, and Prince Henry the Navigator are often cited as three of Portugal's most important explorers. Who claimed what?

4. How was the Aztec Empire conquered?

5. Who funded Columbus's infamous journey west? Where did Columbus wind up?

6. The Spanish conquerors of America were called:
   A. emperors
   B. conquistadors
   C. governor-generals
   D. expatriates

7. Who was Quetzalcóatl?

ANSWERS ⟩ 245

CHECK YOUR ANSWERS

1. Short answer: "Gold, Glory, and God."
   After the Crusades, Europeans were more
   interested in foreign goods, and merchants
   wanted to find more profitable trade routes. Rulers
   across Europe also sought fame, power, and glory,
   often claiming new lands in the name of God.

2. The European slave trade began when the
   Portuguese returned from their explorations with
   African captives.

3. Bartolomeu Dias claimed the southern tip of Africa.
   Vasco da Gama sailed around the southern tip of
   Africa into the Indian Ocean and reached Calicut,
   India. Prince Henry never actually claimed anything
   himself, but sailors on his ships explored the western
   coast of Africa.

4. Spanish conquistador Hernán Cortés and his men
   conquered the Aztec Empire by using guns and with
   the help of the people who had been dominated
   by the Aztecs. European diseases probably also
   weakened the Aztec people.

5. Queen Isabella of Spain funded Christopher Columbus's voyages. Columbus ended up in the Americas. He explored Hispaniola (present-day Haiti and the Dominican Republic), Cuba, Jamaica, and the coasts of Central and South America.
6. B. conquistadors
7. Quetzalcóatl was an Aztec god. According to legend, Montezuma believed that Cortés was the return of Quetzalcóatl.

Chapter 21

EUROPE EXPLORES ASIA

(OR TRIES TO)

Europeans were fascinated with Asian products, like silk, jade, and porcelain. Trade posts were set up in India and Southeast Asia in the 1500s, but trading with China and Japan wasn't as easy.

EUROPEAN TRADE IN ASIA

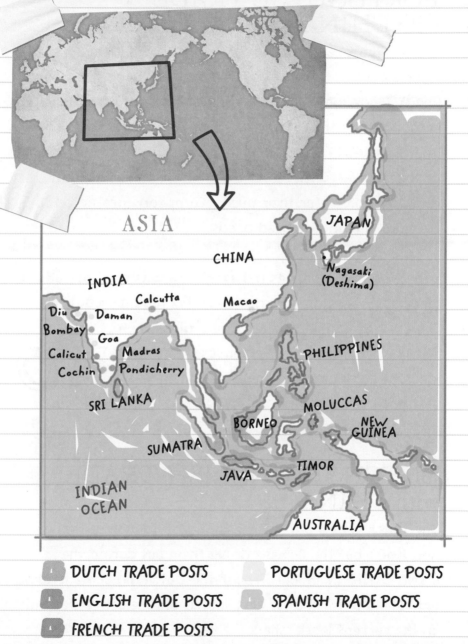

ASIA

JAPAN

CHINA

INDIA

Calcutta

Nagasaki
(Deshima)

Diu
Bombay
Daman

Goa

Calicut

Cochin

Madras

Pondicherry

Macao

PHILIPPINES

SRI LANKA

MOLUCCAS

BORNEO

NEW
GUINEA

SUMATRA

TIMOR

JAVA

INDIAN
OCEAN

AUSTRALIA

DUTCH TRADE POSTS   PORTUGUESE TRADE POSTS

ENGLISH TRADE POSTS   SPANISH TRADE POSTS

FRENCH TRADE POSTS

PORTUGUESE TRADE
with CHINA

The Portuguese set up a post in MACAO, China, but it was China's way or the highway (the highway being the Silk Road). Trade was strictly controlled and not formally recognized by the Chinese government. During the MING DYNASTY (1368-1644), the Chinese were at the height of their power. They didn't trade much. When they did, they requested silver for their goods. Europeans preferred to trade with manufactured goods.

What the two countries did exchange was a lot of cultural ideas. Christian missionaries from Portugal brought the Chinese people things like reading glasses. The Chinese taught the Portuguese the ideas of Confucius and impressed them with their architecture and the wide availability of books.

DUTCH and ENGLISH TRADE
with CHINA

The Dutch seized part of the island of Taiwan in the 1630s and 1640s, but the Chinese drove them out during the QING DYNASTY in 1661. Though the Dutch did some trading with China after that, it was limited and selective depending on the current leadership.

About a century after the Chinese pushed out the Dutch, the Qing set up a trading post on a small island but limited trade to October through March. The British followed China's **STIPULATIONS** but ended up importing way more than they exported and got into debt. The Chinese rejected a British request for better trade policies, resulting in a worse trade conflict years later.

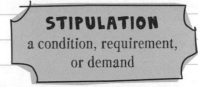

STIPULATION
a condition, requirement, or demand

DUTCH TRADE with JAPAN

Trade with Japan was similarly limited. The Portuguese had landed there in the 1540s by chance after being blown off course. Problems arose between the Portuguese and the Japanese over religion and European missionaries. When trade with Taiwan didn't work for the Dutch, they became trading partners with the Japanese. Under strict surveillance, Japan allowed the Dutch to establish a trading post on an island called Deshima, close to Nagasaki. The Dutch remained the only major European trading power in Japan until the 1800s.

KEY ECONOMIC DEVELOPMENTS DURING EUROPE'S AGE OF EXPLORATION:

THE BEGINNINGS OF CAPITALISM: The start of an economic system in which people invest in trading and goods for profit. Goods were no longer **BARTERED** (traded for other products) but were instead traded for money. Silver and gold coins were used, and new banking systems and trading companies were created to manage the sale of goods.

MERCANTILISM: Capitalism was largely based on the theory of **mercantilism**, the major economic theory of the sixteenth, seventeenth, and eighteenth centuries. This theory said that a nation's worth was based on its supply of gold and silver. It also stressed the importance of having an excess of exports over imports to maintain a favorable balance of trade.

BALANCE OF TRADE: Nations wanted a favorable **balance of trade**, meaning that the goods they exported would be worth more than those imported. They could make money by selling high-priced products to other nations and spend less money buying less-expensive products from other nations. Colonies played a major role in providing both raw materials and markets for finished goods.

All this led to the development of a market economy, a market driven by the supply and demand of slaves and goods, like sugar. It also led to the rise of the new middle class.

CHECK YOUR KNOWLEDGE

1. What did the Chinese typically accept when trading their goods?

2. Until the 1800s, how many trading partners did Japan have? Who were they?

3. What was the main factor that caused distrust between Japanese rulers and the Portuguese?

4. The only major trading post in Japan before the 1800s was located in a place called:

    A. Nagasaki   C. Kyoto

    B. Deshima   D. Tokyo

5. Define "capitalism."

6. According to mercantilism, what does a nation's wealth depend on?

7. What class grew in response to the new market economy?

    A. the middle class   C. the lower class

    B. the upper class   D. slaves

ANSWERS

CHECK YOUR ANSWERS

1. The Chinese accepted silver when trading.
2. There was only one main trading power in Japan until the 1800s—the Dutch.
3. Distrust between the Portuguese and Japanese was over religion and the presence of Christian missionaries.
4. B. Deshima
5. Capitalism is an economic system in which people invest in trading and goods for profit.
6. Mercantilism said that a nation's wealth is based on its supply of gold and silver.
7. A. the middle class

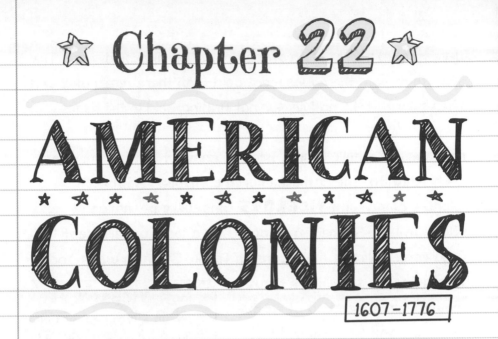

☆ Chapter 22 ☆
AMERICAN
★ ★ ★ ★ ★ ★ ★ ★ ★ ★ ★ ★ ★
COLONIES
1607–1776

European colonies grew in North America, South America, and Central America. The Spanish controlled land all the way from the present-day U.S. to southern South America. One part of South America wasn't under Spanish rule: Brazil was claimed by Portuguese explorer PEDRO ALVAREZ CABRAL, and Portuguese is spoken there to this day.

The ENCOMIENDA SYSTEM and VICEROYS

The Spanish relied on enslaved Africans to work for them, and they used an **ENCOMIENDA** SYSTEM that gave them royal permission to force Native Americans to work. Native Americans were supposed to receive food and other care in return but

> **ENCOMIENDAS**
> small areas of land where native peoples were enslaved to farm or dig in mines

255

were treated poorly. Much of the population died of disease. The Spanish thought there was more gold than there really was and often punished the natives for not finding gold in the mines.

The Roman Catholic Church tried to convert Native Americans to Christianity. The Catholic Church controlled Spain's colonies, along with **VICEROYS**, who were in charge of VICEROYALTIES. The clergy acted as a local government. They forced Native Americans to follow Spanish ways and beliefs, though sometimes they allowed for a blending of Native American and Spanish cultures.

> **VICEROY**
> a person who rules a section of land called a viceroyalty in the name of a king or queen

BRITISH and DUTCH SETTLEMENTS

The first permanent British settlement in what was to become the United States was JAMESTOWN, settled in 1607 in Virginia. Jamestown flourished once CAPTAIN JOHN SMITH developed relations with the Native Americans, who taught the settlers how to grow maize and helped them cultivate tobacco.

JAMESTOWN

Another British settlement was PLYMOUTH, started in 1620 by the PILGRIMS, who were called that because of their journey, or pilgrimage, to seek religious freedom.

The Dutch established a **COLONY** named New Netherland in 1624, and then the city of New Amsterdam, along with colonies in the Caribbean. The British took over New Netherland in 1664 and renamed it New York.

ME

VT

NH

NY

MA

CT

RI

Plymouth

ATLANTIC OCEAN

New York (New Amsterdam)

PA

NJ

OH

MD

DE

WV

VA

Jamestown

NC

BRITISH AND DUTCH SETTLEMENTS
- BRITISH COLONIES
- DUTCH COLONIES
- PRESENT-DAY STATES

Numerous English colonies sprang up on the East Coast of North America. These colonies expanded and pushed the Native American population westward. As before, Europeans brought diseases that ravaged the native populations.

FRENCH SETTLEMENTS

In 1608, SAMUEL DE CHAMPLAIN established a French settlement in what is today the Canadian province of Quebec.

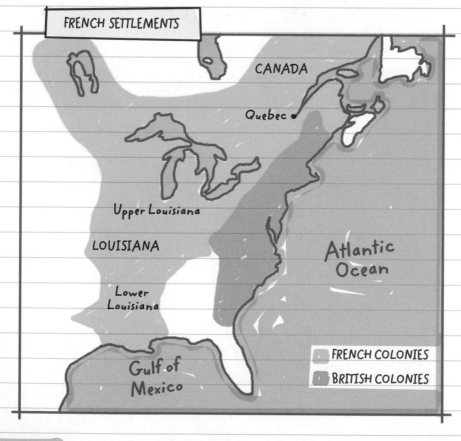

FRENCH SETTLEMENTS

CANADA

Quebec •

Upper Louisiana

LOUISIANA

Lower Louisiana

Atlantic Ocean

Gulf of Mexico

FRENCH COLONIES
BRITISH COLONIES

The French traded fur with the help of Native Americans and eventually claimed land from the Great Lakes to Louisiana. The French colonies were only thinly populated, unlike the British North American colonies, which were home to over one million people by 1750.

The SEVEN YEARS' WAR

The French and the English had become the major COLONIZERS of North America. In 1756, they fought over the

COLONIES DURING SEVEN YEARS' WAR

Hudson Bay

CANADA

Gulf of St. Lawrence

BOTH THE FRENCH AND THE ENGLISH WANTED CONTROL OF THESE AREAS.

Ohio River

Atlantic Ocean

FRENCH COLONIES

OHIO RIVER VALLEY

BRITISH COLONIES

land in the FRENCH AND INDIAN WAR, also known as the SEVEN YEARS' WAR. Both the French and the English wanted to control the fur trade and waterways of the Gulf of St. Lawrence and the Ohio River Valley. French trade activity was preventing the British from expanding.

The Europeans and their Native American trading partners joined together to fight their common enemy. The French learned **GUERRILLA WARFARE** from the Huron tribe, and the Iroquois helped the English because of their hatred for the French explorers like Samuel de Champlain, who had slaughtered many Iroquois chiefs. George Washington fought for the English in the French and Indian War, but learned the French could be beat using guerrilla tactics. The English colonists also had help from Britain's PRIME MINISTER,

GUERRILLA WARFARE
using small raids to disrupt army supply lines and engage in surprise attacks when the terrain is to one's advantage

WILLIAM PITT THE ELDER, who heavily funded the British navy for the war. The French were eventually defeated. Under the terms of the TREATY OF PARIS, the French surrendered control of Canada and the lands east of the Mississippi River to England.

IROQUOIS LONGHOUSE

CHECK YOUR KNOWLEDGE

1. Name the explorer who colonized the South American country of Brazil.

2. How did this explorer's influence in Brazil differentiate the country from the rest of South America?

3. Spanish and Portuguese settlements in Central and South America generally formed along coastlines. Why do you think this might have been?

4. What was the encomienda system and how did the Spaniards benefit from it?

5. Match the colonizer to the colony:
   A. Dutch   1. Jamestown
   B. French   2. New Netherland
   C. British   3. Quebec

6. It's pretty obvious how long the Seven Years' War lasted. What factors led up to it? Who were the key players, and what were they fighting for?

7. Samuel de Champlain established which of the following settlements?
   A. Plymouth
   B. Louisiana
   C. Quebec
   D. Montreal

8. What did the French learn from the Hurons?

ANSWERS ➤ 263

CHECK YOUR ANSWERS

1. Pedro Alvarez Cabral
2. Because Cabral was Portuguese, Brazil was controlled by Portugal, so Portuguese was spoken there (and is spoken there today)—unlike other South American countries where Spanish is spoken.
3. Coastlines were easy entrances for ships and allowed for trading between colonies and their rulers overseas.
4. The encomienda system allowed Spaniards to force Native Americans to work on Spanish-held plantations. Native Americans were supposed to get food and other care for their work but were treated poorly. The Spaniards profited greatly from the free labor.
5. A. Dutch: 2. New Netherland
   B. French: 3. Quebec
   C. British: 1. Jamestown
6. The Seven Years' War happened because both the French and the English wanted to control fur trade and the waterways of the Gulf of St. Lawrence and the Ohio River Valley. Also, French trade activity was holding back the British from expanding.
7. C. Quebec
8. Guerrilla warfare

Unit 6

Revolution and Enlightenment
1500-1865

Revolutions meant new types of governments, which meant new thoughts about the role of these governments in economics, politics, and society. New concepts in thought and science, and lots of change, were the theme for these three hundred years.

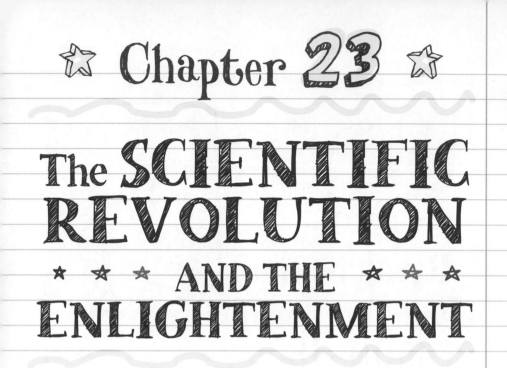

Chapter 23 ☆

The SCIENTIFIC REVOLUTION

★ ★ ★ AND THE ★ ★ ★ ENLIGHTENMENT

New ideas inspired by humanism and Luther's Reformation spread into the realm of science.

The SCIENTIFIC METHOD

The SCIENTIFIC METHOD means using a step-by-step process to conduct experiments. Everyone should get the same results from an experiment if they follow the same set of rules, which, in turn, would prove that the results are correct. FRANCIS BACON, who developed the scientific method around 1620, was an English philosopher. Bacon believed scientists needed to

use systematic reasoning to understand nature, so he developed a set of instructions for how people should collect and analyze evidence. Many other scientific and mathematical developments were made during this SCIENTIFIC REVOLUTION (approximately 1500–1700).

The SCIENTIFIC REVOLUTION

Some ancient scientists believed the earth moved around the sun. However, in general, people believed that Earth was the center of the universe, based on the ideas of the astronomer PTOLEMY, who lived in the 100s CE. His **GEOCENTRIC** theory made Earth the motionless core in a universe of spheres rotating around it. That put humans at the center of the universe, and God and the Heavens in the outermost sphere, which was the "prime mover" that moves all other spheres. The Roman Catholic Church accepted Ptolemy's theory.

GEOCENTRIC
Earth-centered

In 1543, the Polish mathematician and Catholic priest NICOLAUS COPERNICUS revived the proposition that the solar system was HELIOCENTRIC—that the sun was at the center—which was originally conceived by the ancient Greek

Sun · Mercury · Venus · Earth · Mars · Jupiter · Saturn · Uranus · Neptune

astronomer and philosopher ARISTARCHUS. Copernicus found that while planets revolved around the sun, the moon revolved around the earth. Astronomer JOHANNES KEPLER agreed, and he calculated that planetary orbits are **ELLIPTICAL**, an oval rather than circular shape.

These findings made the Catholic Church nervous, but when the mathematician GALILEO GALILEI confirmed with a telescope that Ptolemy's theories were wrong,

SATURN · JUPITER · MARS · SUN · EARTH · MOON · MERCURY · VENUS

the church got really upset. Galileo's telescope showed that the planets had mountains and moons, just like Earth. They weren't heavenly bodies made of pure spheres of light. Galileo published his findings in *STARRY MESSENGER* in 1610—and the church sentenced him to life imprisonment. Other scientists were also jailed for proposing theories that opposed the teachings of the Catholic Church.

Remember Galileo with this rhyme:
Galileo said, "The Earth revolves around the Sun."
So the Catholic Church imprisoned him,
and his teaching days were done.

DISCOVERIES in MATH and PHYSICS

In the 1630s, RENÉ DESCARTES proposed a system of geometry using letters in math. Descartes's work became the basis of analytic geometry.

"I THINK, THEREFORE I AM"
Descartes was a philosopher who also wrote about doubt and uncertainty, and about casting aside everything he had ever learned and starting from scratch. The only thing he believed he could truly know to be true, beyond a doubt, was that he himself existed. That's where "I think, therefore I am" comes from—that was Descartes.

THE SCIENTIFIC

1507–1542:
Nicolaus Copernicus publishes two books about how the solar system is heliocentric, which places the sun at its center.

1616:
The Catholic Church bans Copernicus's books.

1610:
Galileo uses a telescope to look at the planets and the moon. He publishes his discoveries in *Starry Messenger*.

1628:
William Harvey publishes a book on anatomy and shows that the human heart is what pumps blood through the body.

REVOLUTION

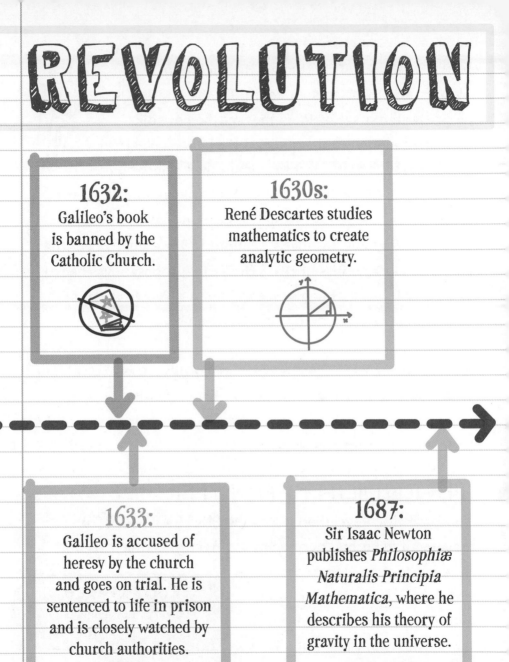

1632:
Galileo's book is banned by the Catholic Church.

1630s:
René Descartes studies mathematics to create analytic geometry.

1633:
Galileo is accused of heresy by the church and goes on trial. He is sentenced to life in prison and is closely watched by church authorities.

1687:
Sir Isaac Newton publishes *Philosophiæ Naturalis Principia Mathematica*, where he describes his theory of gravity in the universe.

SIR ISAAC NEWTON studied the motion of planets and of objects on Earth. In the late 1600s, he presented a set of laws that mathematically explained motion and explained that every object in the universe is attracted to every other object by a force called GRAVITY (or: why stuff falls down). Newton's ideas led people to see the universe as a massive machine with specific laws. His ideas dominated the view of how the universe works until ALBERT EINSTEIN proposed his theory of relativity in the twentieth century (a different way of explaining the finer details of how the universe works).

MY LAWS RULE!

English doctor WILLIAM HARVEY made advances in anatomy when he discovered that the human heart (not the arteries, as previously thought) pumps blood in a circuit throughout the body. He published a book on his findings in 1628.

The ENLIGHTENMENT

The Scientific Revolution led to the ENLIGHTENMENT, a movement in Europe during the eighteenth century. People believed that science, reason, and natural laws of behavior would help them better understand the world and bring them to a more

> **ENLIGHTENED**
> to be very knowledgeable or aware; freed from ignorance

ENLIGHTENED state. Also called the AGE OF REASON, the Enlightenment affected thinking in politics, literature, art, religion, and, of course, science.

The ENLIGHTENMENT and INDIVIDUAL RIGHTS

The Enlightenment brought about new theories on how the government should be run. Many ideas were based on the rights of individuals. Descartes thought that anyone with a good education could reason and make good decisions, and people could govern themselves.

JOHN LOCKE had ideas about an individual's rights. He disagreed with the idea of the divine right of kings and believed that all people had NATURAL RIGHTS to LIFE, LIBERTY, AND PROPERTY. His book *TWO TREATISES OF GOVERNMENT* (1690) argued that people, not the king, should hold the power of the government. According to Locke, the government needed to follow the natural laws of the people and protect their rights. If it failed to do so, the people should have the government overthrown. The American Declaration of Independence used many of Locke's ideas.

> Use this repetition to remember John Locke:
> John **LOCKE** was against the divine right of kings—
> he didn't want to get **LOCKED** into someone else's
> rules, but instead pursue his own rights.
> Life, Liberty, and Property = Locke approved!

According to JEAN-JACQUES ROUSSEAU, people in a society both depend on each other and compete with each other.

They need a SOCIAL CONTRACT in which everyone agrees to be governed by the general will of society as a whole, and that'll be what's best for everyone. Rousseau wrote about this idea in *THE SOCIAL CONTRACT*, published in 1762.

The ENLIGHTENMENT and ECONOMIC THOUGHT

ADAM SMITH, a Scottish philosopher, supported the idea of **LAISSEZ-FAIRE** in his work *AN INQUIRY INTO THE NATURE AND CAUSES OF THE WEALTH OF NATIONS* (1776).

> **LAISSEZ-FAIRE**
> a French term that means "to let people do what they want" or let the economy develop naturally

↖ OFTEN ABBREVIATED AS "THE WEALTH OF NATIONS"

A laissez-faire government protects citizens from invasions, defends them from injustice, and takes care of public works needed for trade (like keeping roads in good shape).

A laissez-faire government does NOT interrupt the development of the economy, regulate it, or interfere. Smith believed that if individuals pursue their own economic self-interests, everyone benefits. He is considered the father of **CAPITALISM**.

> **CAPITALISM**
> an economic system in which the production and distribution of goods is controlled by individuals and corporations, not the state

↗
THE ECONOMIC SYSTEM OF THE U.S.

CHECK YOUR KNOWLEDGE

1. Who developed the scientific method, and what is it?

2. What theory did Galileo prove to be right?

3. What sorts of ideas did Sir Isaac Newton come up with?

4. What was the principal idea of the Enlightenment?

5. Who is considered to be the father of capitalism?
   A. John Locke
   B. Adam Smith
   C. Jean-Jacques Rousseau
   D. René Descartes

6. What is a laissez-faire government?

7. Who said, "I think, therefore I am"?
   A. Locke
   B. Smith
   C. Voltaire
   D. Descartes

ANSWERS

CHECK YOUR ANSWERS

1. Francis Bacon developed the scientific method, which is a set of instructions for how people should collect and analyze evidence. The scientific method means using a step-by-step process to conduct experiments.

2. Galileo Galilei confirmed that the heliocentric theory (that the earth moves around the sun) is right and that the geocentric theory (the earth is the center of the universe) was wrong.

3. Sir Isaac Newton presented a set of laws that mathematically explained motion and explained that every object in the universe is attracted to every other object by a force called gravity.

4. The principal idea of the Enlightenment was that science, reason, and natural laws of behavior would help people better understand the world and bring them to a more enlightened state.

5. B. Adam Smith

6. A laissez-faire government does not interrupt economic development or regulate the economy, but it does protect and defend citizens as well as take care of public works necessary for trade.

7. D. Descartes

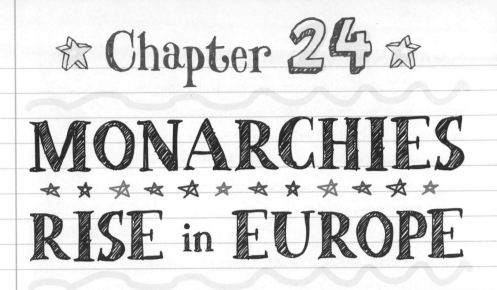

☆ Chapter 24 ☆

MONARCHIES
✶ ✰ ✶ ✰ ✶ ✰ ✶ ✰ ✶ ✰ ✶ ✰ ✶
RISE in EUROPE

Monarchies arose as a form of government all across Europe. Some monarchs improved conditions in their nations. Others took advantage of their power, prompting revolt.

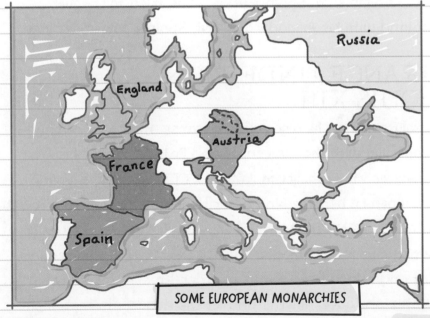

Russia

England

Austria

France

Spain

SOME EUROPEAN MONARCHIES

SPANISH MONARCHS

CHARLES I of Spain inherited the Holy Roman Empire and became CHARLES V (the guy who outlawed Martin Luther). When Charles gave up his throne in 1550, his brother Ferdinand took over the Holy Roman Empire, and Charles V's son PHILIP II became king of Spain.

CHARLES V

PHILIP II

Philip II had ABSOLUTE RULE, meaning that he wielded ultimate control over the government and its people. He had the authority to lead an **INQUISITION** to hold trials for people accused of "false" religious beliefs, and he removed many Protestants, Jews,

> **INQUISITION**
> an official investigation

and Muslims from Spain. But after he tried to conquer England with his Armada and lost, Spain's power declined.

FRANCE UNDER KING LOUIS XIII

Absolute monarchs also ruled in France. Henry IV reigned peacefully with the Huguenots and Catholics after his conversion to Catholicism. LOUIS XIII was only a young boy when he became king after Henry, so ARMAND JEAN DU PLESSIS DE RICHELIEU ← HE LATER BECAME CARDINAL ARMAND RICHELIEU.

helped him and his mother MARIE DE' MEDICI (the regent) rule and helped keep things in order. He built relations with Protestant governments and let the Huguenots keep their religious rights. But he took away their political and military rights to prevent them from growing too powerful. Paranoid

* Blah Blah, Richelieu, Blah Blah...*

about losing power, Richelieu set up a network of spies to uncover secret plots by discontented nobles. He crushed conspiracies and executed the conspirators.

This was the time of *The Three Musketeers*! It is a popular adventure novel about an elite fighting force in France.

FRANCE'S "SUN KING"

LOUIS XIV was only four when he inherited the monarchy in 1643. He got help from chief minister CARDINAL MAZARIN, who took control of the government. Like Richelieu, Mazarin crushed any opposition from nobles.

Eventually, Louis XIV grew old enough to rule on his own and became an absolute monarch for over half a century. Altogether he reigned for over 72 years. He stripped power from nobles, local officials, and others and created an elaborate and decadent royal court at VERSAILLES. Every decision had to be approved by him. Louis XIV gained complete authority over foreign policy, the church, and taxes.

VERSAILLES

He called himself the SUN KING—the source of light for all his people. His rule was based on the divine right of kings; a rebellion against a king was a rebellion against God.

Louis XIV waged four wars between 1667 and 1713. The cost of Louis's courts, palaces, and wars grew too great for France's budget. When he died in 1715, France faced enormous debt and a legion of enemies.

Louis XIV tried to convert the Huguenots to Catholicism by destroying Huguenot churches and closing their schools. Nearly 200,000 Huguenots fled to England, the German states, and elsewhere in order to escape the king's **PERSECUTION**.

RUSSIAN MONARCHS

Russian monarchs were called CZARS (derived from "Caesar").
PETER I ruled from 1682 to 1725 and loved Western Europe.
He wanted Russia to adopt customs and manners from
Western Europe and be more like it. He ordered Russian men
to shave their beards to look more like Western Europeans.
If they didn't, they were taxed! Peter I built a strong navy,
enlarged Russia, and built the great city of St. Petersburg,
which earned him the nickname PETER THE GREAT. More
than three decades after his death, CATHERINE THE GREAT
ruled from 1762 to 1796. She expanded Russia, encouraged
education, and modernized farming.

AUSTRIAN MONARCHS

In Austria, MARIA THERESA became ruler
of the immense HAPSBURG EMPIRE in
1740 after the death of her father, Charles
VI. She was the only woman ever to rule
the 650-year-old dynasty. When Maria
Theresa took the throne in 1740, Prussia's
KING FREDERICK THE GREAT invaded, declaring that he
didn't accept Maria Theresa as the legitimate ruler of the
empire. The war grew when France joined Prussia against
Austria and Great Britain came to Austria's defense, in what
became known as the WAR OF THE AUSTRIAN SUCCESSION
(1740-1748). The war ended with the signing of the Treaty of
Aix-la-Chapelle in 1748.

Maria Theresa built a strong government, created a fair justice system, united the Hapsburg Empire, and improved conditions for serfs, all while having sixteen children.

The BEGINNINGS of the STUART MONARCHY in ENGLAND

England didn't have an absolute monarchy; it had a LIMITED MONARCHY. England's government was in part controlled by Parliament.

After Elizabeth I's death in 1603, the TUDOR dynasty came to an end. Elizabeth's cousin JAMES I (king of Scotland) took the throne as the first in the line of many STUART dynasty leaders. James refused to work with Parliament. He believed it was his divine right to rule. This attitude led to the growing discontent of the PURITANS, a group of Protestants in England inspired by Calvinist ideas. Many Puritans who were part of the House of Commons (the lower house of Parliament) didn't support the king's strong alliance with the Church of England and wanted to separate the church from the king.

James's son CHARLES I ruled next, and his distaste for Parliament was even stronger than his father's. In 1628, he ordered Parliament to stop meeting and didn't let them meet for twelve years! Civil war followed. Parliament's supporters (called ROUNDHEADS because of their short

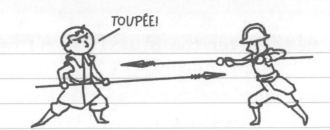

TOUPÉE!

haircuts) went to battle in 1642 against the king's supporters, the CAVALIERS, or ROYALISTS. By 1646, the Roundheads had won, and Charles I was taken captive.

ENGLAND during the PROTECTORATE

OLIVER CROMWELL, one of the military leaders behind the Roundheads, worked to protect people's rights against absolute power. Cromwell dismissed members of Parliament who weren't on his side. The Parliament that remained, the so-called RUMP PARLIAMENT, ordered Charles I to be executed for **TREASON** in 1649. Parliament overthrew the monarchy and the House of Lords and declared England a new kind of republic,

> **TREASON**
> a betrayal, especially of one's country or sovereign (leader)

> **COMMONWEALTH**
> term for the English government beginning when the monarchy ended in 1649 and lasting until the Restoration in 1660

a **COMMONWEALTH**. Then Cromwell formed a military dictatorship and ruled as a different kind of absolute ruler, not as king but as LORD PROTECTOR of England 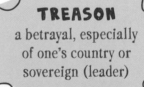 ↰ *THIS IS IRONY!* during the period known as the PROTECTORATE (1653-1659).

ENGLAND after the RESTORATION of the STUART MONARCHY

When Cromwell died in 1658, Charles I's son CHARLES II took the throne and restored the monarchy. But things were different. During the English RESTORATION (beginning in 1660), Charles II suspended laws that Parliament had passed earlier that discriminated against Catholics and Puritans, and Parliament in turn said that only Anglicans could hold military and civil offices. More religious and political disagreement followed. Just before his death, Charles II converted to Catholicism, leaving his brother JAMES II to follow his reign. James II was also Catholic, and problems with Parliament worsened.

Parliament asked WILLIAM III (also known as WILLIAM OF ORANGE), the captain general of Holland, to rule England. James left London, and in 1689 William III and MARY II—James II's son-in-law and daughter—were declared king and queen of England during the GLORIOUS REVOLUTION (so-called because it involved very little bloodshed and the time period that followed was peaceful). The pair accepted Parliament's offer to take up the throne and signed the English BILL OF RIGHTS, which set forth Parliament's right to make laws and LEVY (impose) taxes. It also said the monarchy could raise an army only with Parliament's consent, and it helped create a system of government based on a limited monarchy.

CHECK YOUR KNOWLEDGE

1. What does it mean for a leader to use absolute rule? Give an example of using this power.

2. During the 1600s, a popular nickname for Cardinal Richelieu was "the Iron Cardinal." Who was Cardinal Richelieu, and why might the people have called him that?

3. Who was the "Sun King"?

4. "Czar" is the Russian way of saying _ _ _ _ _ _.

5. What advancements did Peter and Catherine of Russia make to earn "the Great" after their names?

6. Who were the Puritans?

7. The Glorious Revolution was led by _ _ _ _ _ _ _ _ _ _ and _ _ _ _ _ _ in 1689.

CHECK YOUR ANSWERS

1. Absolute rule means the leader has complete and ultimate control over the government and its people. Philip II of Spain used absolute rule to hold trials for people accused of "false" religious beliefs and remove many Protestants, Jews, and Muslims from Spain.

2. Cardinal Richelieu helped Louis XIII rule France. He formed relationships with Protestant governments and let the Huguenots keep their religious rights. However, he might have been called the Iron Cardinal because he took away the Huguenots' political and military rights, created a network of spies, crushed conspiracies, and executed conspirators.

3. Louis XIV called himself the Sun King.

4. Caesar

5. Peter earned his name by building a strong Russian navy, enlarging Russia, and building the city of St. Petersburg. Catherine earned her name by expanding Russia, encouraging education, and modernizing farming.

6. The Puritans were a group of Protestants in England inspired by Calvinist ideas. Many Puritans were part of the House of Commons and wanted to distance the Church of England from the king.

7. William III (or William of Orange) and Mary II

☆ Chapter 25 ☆

The AMERICAN
★ ☆ ★ ☆ ★ ☆ ★ ☆ ★ ☆ ★
REVOLUTION

1775–1783

In 1776, America formally declared independence from the British. How did it happen?

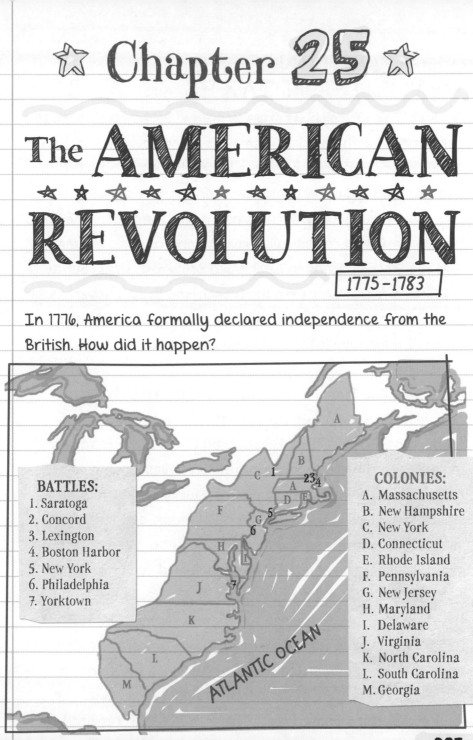

BATTLES:
1. Saratoga
2. Concord
3. Lexington
4. Boston Harbor
5. New York
6. Philadelphia
7. Yorktown

COLONIES:
A. Massachusetts
B. New Hampshire
C. New York
D. Connecticut
E. Rhode Island
F. Pennsylvania
G. New Jersey
H. Maryland
I. Delaware
J. Virginia
K. North Carolina
L. South Carolina
M. Georgia

ATLANTIC OCEAN

The BEGINNINGS of the REVOLUTION: TAXES

Back in 1607, 105 colonists from Britain established their first permanent North American homes in Jamestown. A hundred or so years later, what has been estimated as up to 1,700,000 people of European descent were living in British North America. Many of these settlers had never even been to Europe. Britain profited economically from having colonies in America and required all goods to be shipped on British ships. But after the Seven Years' War with the French, the British government was suddenly in debt. The colonists were upset that they had to leave their families to fight England's war.

Since the war took place in America, the British believed the colonists should help pay off the debt, so they taxed them. The SUGAR ACT of 1764 actually LOWERED taxes on molasses that were brought into the colonies, hoping to minimize SMUGGLING. Because they were trying to stop smugglers, ships were searched by customs officers. Any suspected contraband could be taken away, even before the smuggler was convicted. Colonists believed that the Sugar Act violated their legal rights as British citizens by denying the right to trial—and some went even further: JAMES OTIS, a lawyer in Boston, argued that Parliament didn't have a right to tax the colonists at all, since the colonists didn't have representatives there to debate the taxes. In 1765, Parliament passed the STAMP ACT, which required that

all printed materials be produced on British
paper and bear a stamp for which taxes
needed to be paid.

The colonists were upset—they already
paid taxes to Great Britain, and they didn't feel they had
the same rights as other English citizens. They had no choice
in electing governors or anyone in Parliament.
It was TAXATION WITHOUT REPRESENTATION.
When Parliament taxed the colonists under
laws called the TOWNSHEND ACTS, the
colonists refused to pay.

"NO TAXATION
WITHOUT
REPRESENTATION"
WAS A PHRASE
USED BY THE
COLONISTS IN
PROTEST.

STAMP AGENTS WERE TARRED AND FEATHERED,
AND MOBS PREVENTED STAMP DISTRIBUTIONS. ➡️ NOOOO!

In response, England's KING GEORGE III
sent troops to Boston. In March 1770,
an argument between a British soldier
(a REDCOAT) and a **CIVILIAN** attracted a
crowd and grew violent. The Redcoats killed
five colonists in the BOSTON MASSACRE.

CIVILIAN
a person who is
not on active duty
with the armed
services or a
police force

Parliament passed the TEA ACT in 1773, which allowed the
British to sell tea to the colonists at a reduced rate but
destroyed the businesses of local tea merchants.

On December 16, 1773, protestors threw British tea overboard into the Boston harbor in the BOSTON TEA PARTY.

WAR and the STRUGGLE for INDEPENDENCE

The colonists organized themselves, creating the FIRST CONTINENTAL CONGRESS in Philadelphia in 1774. The colonists were encouraged to take arms and get ready. When King George III sent more Redcoats to the colonies, PAUL REVERE took his famous midnight ride on April 18, 1775, to warn the colonists. British troops marched to CONCORD and LEXINGTON, Massachusetts; the colonists fought back and the AMERICAN REVOLUTIONARY WAR officially began.

Colonists who supported independence were called **PATRIOTS**, while those who remained loyal to Britain were called **LOYALISTS**. Many Loyalists fled the colonies, often heading to Canada.

At the SECOND CONTINENTAL CONGRESS, GEORGE WASHINGTON became commander in chief of the colonists' army, called the CONTINENTAL ARMY.

A number of battles between the Continental Army and the British followed. The colonists tried to make peace with King George III by sending him the OLIVE BRANCH PETITION, which stated that the colonists still wanted to be loyal to England as long as their rights were protected, but King George III ignored it and sent more British troops to the colonies.

Initially most Native Americans didn't take sides in the Revolutionary War, but the majority of those who fought supported the British. The British convinced many tribes to fight against colonists settling in frontier regions.

The Second Continental Congress debated what to do, and on July 4, 1776, the colonies declared their independence from the British in the DECLARATION OF INDEPENDENCE. THOMAS JEFFERSON wrote it, stating that the people had the right to overthrow their government if the government did not take care of them. It gave people the right to "LIFE, LIBERTY, AND THE PURSUIT OF HAPPINESS," which are also called INALIENABLE rights. Jefferson's ideas were influenced by the French Enlightenment thinkers and John Locke.

The committee to draft the Declaration of Independence also included John Adams and Benjamin Franklin.

INALIENABLE
absolute; not capable of being surrendered or transferred

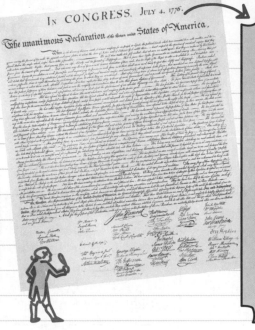

The DECLARATION ❦ of ❦ INDEPENDENCE in 40 WORDS

Government is a social contract. If the ruler doesn't protect the people and their natural rights, the contract is broken and the people can overthrow him. King George III broke the contract, so now the U.S. is its own nation.

The FIGHTING GOES ON

Although the colonists had declared their independence, the war wasn't over yet. The Continental Army soon got help from the French, which led to a victory in the BATTLE OF SARATOGA in 1777. After that, the French supplied more arms and money to the colonists as a way of getting back at the British after their losses during the Seven Years' War of 1756. Some French officers, such as the MARQUIS DE LAFAYETTE, even served in Washington's army. The colonists and the French used guerrilla warfare tactics that they learned from the Native Americans to ambush the English in the forests.

292

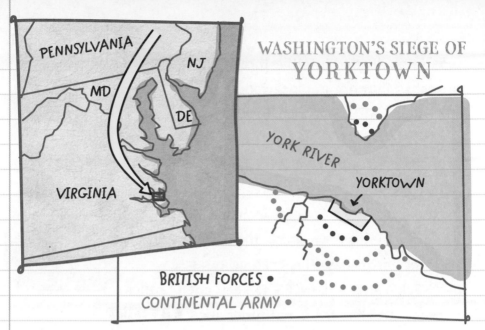

YORKTOWN

PENNSYLVANIA

NJ

MD

DE

VIRGINIA

YORK RIVER

YORKTOWN

BRITISH FORCES •
CONTINENTAL ARMY •

Other countries were also eager to get back at the British and help tear down the empire the British had built. Spain and the Dutch Republic (present-day Netherlands) entered the war against the British. Under the leadership of George Washington, the colonists defeated the British army at the BATTLE OF YORKTOWN in 1781, which ended the fighting. In 1783, both sides signed the TREATY OF PARIS, which formally recognized the colonists' independence from the British.

INDEPENDENCE at LAST

The colonies wrote the ARTICLES OF CONFEDERATION in 1777 to govern the new country, but it granted too much power to the states and not enough power to the federal government to enforce laws. In 1787, a new document, the CONSTITUTION, outlined a set of rules in which national and state governments would share power. The national government was to be divided into the three branches that are in place today: the LEGISLATIVE branch (which creates the laws), the EXECUTIVE branch (which carries out the laws), and the JUDICIAL branch (which interprets and explains the laws). Each branch has the power to restrain, or check, the acts of the other branches. This created a system of CHECKS AND BALANCES to keep each branch in order. In 1790, the Constitution was **RATIFIED** by all thirteen United States.

RATIFY
to formally approve

Congress proposed some changes, ten of which were approved as **AMENDMENTS** to the Constitution and became known as the BILL OF RIGHTS. Ratified in 1791, they guaranteed:

AMENDMENT
changes, additions, or modifications

> the right of free speech
> freedom of the press and of religion
> trial by jury
> the right to bear arms
> the protection of property rights, and more

Rights for women, African Americans, and Native Americans were still not secure, but the United States of America had begun.

CHECK YOUR KNOWLEDGE

1. What does "no taxation without representation" mean?

2. What happened after the colonists decided not to pay taxes?

3. Who wrote the Declaration of Independence?

4. The Declaration of Independence calls for three inalienable rights. What are they? Who influenced the writing of the Declaration?

5. How many constitutional amendments are in the Bill of Rights?

6. Whose rights were not included in the Bill of Rights?

7. Why was the Battle of Saratoga such a decisive one?
   A. It was the first battle of the American Revolution.
   B. It led to British victory over New York and Philadelphia.
   C. It prompted French participation and the support of the colonists.
   D. It marked the decisive victory of the colonists over the British.

8. American independence came through which 1783 Treaty?

ANSWERS 295

CHECK YOUR ANSWERS

1. "No taxation without representation" was a phrase that colonists used to protest the fact that they had no choice in electing governors or any of the people in Parliament yet still had to pay taxes to Great Britain.

2. When the colonists refused to pay taxes, King George III sent troops to Boston and there was a confrontation called the Boston Massacre in which Redcoats killed five colonists.

3. The Declaration of Independence was written by Thomas Jefferson.

4. The three inalienable rights are "life, liberty, and the pursuit of happiness." The Declaration was influenced by the French Enlightenment thinkers and John Locke.

5. There are ten amendments in the Bill of Rights.

6. The Bill of Rights didn't include rights for women, African Americans, or Native Americans.

7. C. It prompted French participation and the support of the colonists.

8. The Treaty of Paris in 1783 formally recognized the American colonists' independence from the British.

☆ Chapter 26 ☆
The FRENCH
REVOLUTION
1789–1799

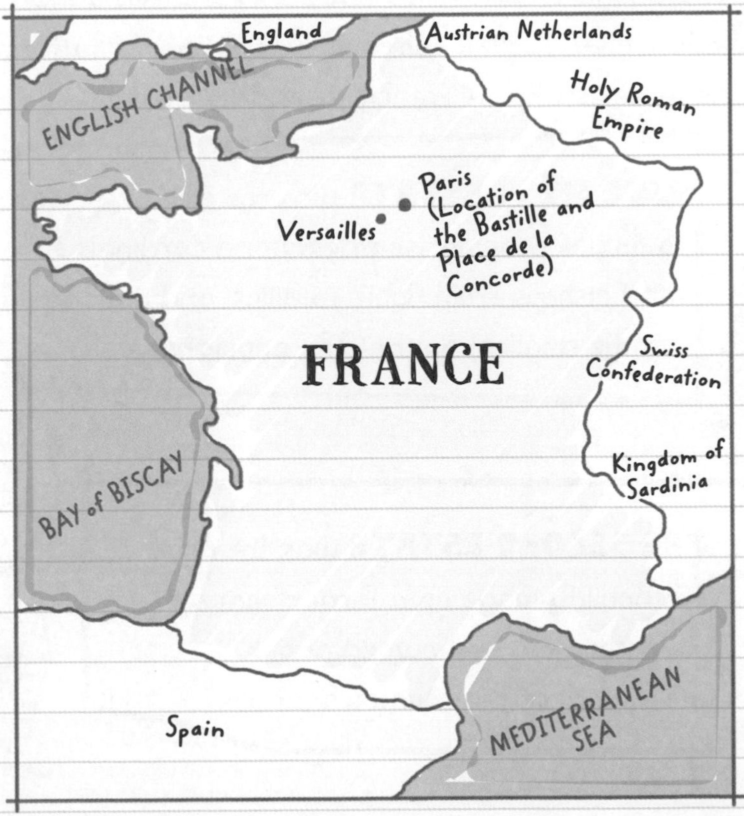

England

Austrian Netherlands

Holy Roman Empire

ENGLISH CHANNEL

Paris
(Location of
the Bastille and
Place de la
Concorde)

Versailles

FRANCE

Swiss
Confederation

Kingdom of
Sardinia

BAY of BISCAY

Spain

MEDITERRANEAN
SEA

Like the Americans, the French wanted to overthrow their royal government. They were tired of the injustice of the class system in France. The first shot in the Battles of Lexington and Concord in the American Revolution was called "the shot heard 'round the world" in part because it showed people of other countries that they could replace monarchy with democracy.

DISCONTENT RISES in FRANCE

France, like England, had to repay war debt. To figure out how, in May 1789, French KING LOUIS XVI called a meeting of the ESTATES-GENERAL, which included representatives from the three estates of French society:

THE FIRST ESTATE was the clergy. It was a mix of poor parish priests and cardinals and bishops from noble families, and it made up the smallest part of the population.

THE SECOND ESTATE was the nobility. The nobility made up a larger share of the population and owned about one-fourth of the country's land.

THE THIRD ESTATE was peasants, craft workers, and middle-class members of society, who formed about seventy percent of the French population but owned very little land compared to the other estates. Many of them didn't have any land to live on at all.

Members of the Third Estate resented the privileges granted to the nobles. Neither the First nor the Second Estates were required to pay the French tax on land, called TAILLE. Only the poorest paid it.

> The middle class in France was also called the **BOURGEOISIE**, when the term denoted someone who lived in a walled town.

Bad harvests in 1787 and 1788 led to food shortages, rising food prices, and unemployment. The king continued spending his wealth on fancy entertainment and elaborate dinners. The people were starving, and there was his wife, MARIE ANTOINETTE, throwing another party!

The PEOPLE TAKE ACTION

Fed up with the monarchy's system of ruling and desperate for change, in June 1789, members of the Third Estate declared themselves the NATIONAL ASSEMBLY, a new governing body for France. The National Assembly had to meet in an indoor tennis court because they were locked out of the meeting hall in Versailles;

they believed the king was trying to get them to disband. In what is known as the TENNIS COURT OATH, they swore to continue meeting until a new constitution was written.

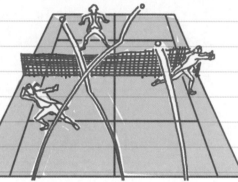

Louis XVI encouraged nobles and clergy to join this new assembly while at the same time mobilizing troops to dissolve it. On July 14, 1789, French citizens in Paris stormed the city's prison—the BASTILLE—in search of weapons and ammunition to defend themselves, but no ammunition was found. The angry crowd destroyed the Bastille one brick at a time. Revolts spread across the country.

> JULY 14TH IS NOW KNOWN AS BASTILLE DAY AND CELEBRATES FRENCH INDEPENDENCE. IT'S LIKE FRANCE'S JULY 4TH!

MORE CHANGES
in the GOVERNMENT

The National Assembly took over to create a government based on the new American democracy. The French wrote a document called the DECLARATION OF THE RIGHTS OF MAN AND OF THE CITIZEN. Approved in August 1789, it granted basic rights to individuals, such as "liberty, property, security, and resistance to oppression."

Many noblemen and clergy left France and convinced countries like Prussia and Austria to invade. The French government arrested the king for supposedly supporting these armies. A new constitution was set up in 1791, calling for a limited monarchy; there was still a king, but he was limited by the power of a LEGISLATIVE ASSEMBLY, which would make laws. However, this new government allowed only men who paid certain taxes and who were over twenty-five to vote, which was still not equality for all.

PROBLEMS in
FRANCE ESCALATE

On top of all this, the people of France were still hungry. Mobs in Paris became violent. The PARIS COMMUNE, a group of radicals, called for universal male **SUFFRAGE** and for the Legislative Assembly to suspend the monarchy.

SUFFRAGE
the right to vote

In 1792, a new NATIONAL CONVENTION began meeting. They drafted a new constitution and abolished the monarchy to form a REPUBLIC, but it was unstable. Leaders struggled for power, and the National Assembly became divided. Various political clubs had formed during the revolution, each with its own ideas about how the republic should work.

A group led by MAXIMILIEN ROBESPIERRE, called the JACOBINS, declared a "policy of terror" to control their opponents, arresting

DECREE
a formal order having the force of law

people left and right for supporting the king or disagreeing with their **DECREES**. During the REIGN OF TERROR (1793–1794), thousands of people were **GUILLOTINED** at a public square in Paris that is now called PLACE DE LA CONCORDE, including Marie Antoinette. (Louis XVI was executed a few months before the Reign of Terror began.) Robespierre and the Jacobins ruled as dictators under the title of the COMMITTEE OF PUBLIC SAFETY. They kept an army of over a million men to push back invaders in the FRENCH REVOLUTIONARY WARS (1792–1802). In July of 1794, Robespierre was arrested and accused of being a tyrant; he was executed the next day.

GUILLOTINE
a device designed to cut the head off of a person

A NEW LEADER COMES to POWER

With Robespierre's death, the Reign of Terror came to an end. A new government, the DIRECTORY, took over. But they were weak. People did not know the best way to rule the country.

A national army hero named NAPOLEON BONAPARTE abolished the Directory and set up a new government in 1799, finally ending the French Revolution. Five years later, he declared himself EMPEROR NAPOLEON I.

By 1812, Napoleon had expanded France's empire to include present-day Italy, Germany, Switzerland, and other European countries (but not Britain).

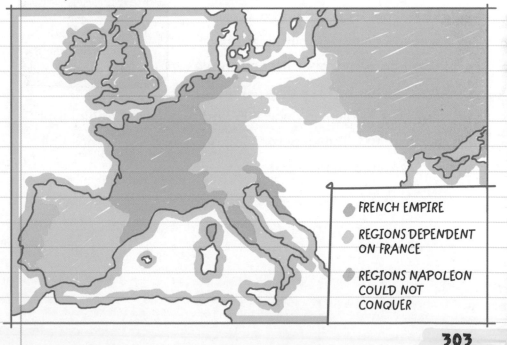

FRENCH EMPIRE

REGIONS DEPENDENT ON FRANCE

REGIONS NAPOLEON COULD NOT CONQUER

British viscount Horatio Nelson defeated Napoleon's fleet at the BATTLE OF TRAFALGAR in 1805. Napoleon was a famous war leader who expanded France, but he made the mistake of expanding too much by invading Russia. His troops froze and fled. He also created the NAPOLEONIC CODE in 1804 to protect individual liberty, property rights, the right to work, and the right to one's own opinions. All citizens were equal before the law. On the NEGATIVE side: He censored nearly all of France's newspapers and books to protect his image. He had mail opened by the government police. Liberty was replaced by **DESPOTISM**.

> **DESPOTISM**
> system of government in which the ruler has absolute, unlimited power

Eventually, Napoleon was **EXILED** from France by an alliance of European countries, but he escaped and went back to France. Napoleon was defeated at the BATTLE OF WATERLOO in

> **EXILE**
> forced or voluntary absence from one's country or homeland

present-day Belgium in June 1815 and was exiled again until his death in 1821. The emperor was gone, and the French still hadn't created a democracy.

CHECK YOUR KNOWLEDGE

1. What impact did the American Revolution have on French allies across the ocean?

2. French society was divided into three classes prior to the Revolution. What were they called and who was in each class?

3. What happened on July 14, 1789?

4. What was the French version of the Declaration of Independence called? What did it say?

5. What group did Maximilien Robespierre lead during the Reign of Terror?

6. Which of the following is one of the principles of the Napoleonic code?
   A. All citizens are equal before the law.
   B. Women's rights are recognized.
   C. Rights of the military are most important.
   D. Individual liberty is not allowed.

7. What happened to Napoleon at the Battle of Waterloo?

ANSWERS

CHECK YOUR ANSWERS

1. The American Revolution showed the people of other countries, including France, that they could replace monarchy with democracy, which is why they call the first shot in the Battles of Lexington and Concord "the shot heard 'round the world."

2. The First Estate was made up of the clergy. The Second Estate were the nobility. The Third Estate were peasants, craft workers, and middle-class people.

3. On July 14, 1789, French citizens stormed the Bastille, the prison in Paris, in search of weapons and ammunition and destroyed the prison one brick at a time.

4. The French version of the Declaration of Independence was called the Declaration of the Rights of Man and of the Citizen. It granted basic rights to individuals, such as "liberty, property, security, and resistance to oppression."

5. Maximilien Robespierre led the Jacobins. They ruled as dictators and called themselves the Committee of Public Safety.

6. A. All citizens are equal before the law.

7. Napoleon was defeated and sent into permanent exile after the Battle of Waterloo.

Chapter 27 ☆

NATIONALISM ACROSS EUROPE
* * * * * and * * * *
INDEPENDENCE MOVEMENTS
* * * * * * in * * * * *
SOUTH AMERICA
☆ * * * and HAITI * * ☆

After Napoleon's rule ended, the many parts of Europe he had dominated were on their own. For nine months, European representatives from these countries met at the CONGRESS OF VIENNA (1814-1815). Meanwhile, in South America, several countries declared their independence.

NATIONALISM in EUROPE

The countries that took part in the Congress of Vienna (Russia, Sweden, Norway, France, the United Kingdom, Spain, Portugal, Austria, Denmark, and Prussia) tried to restore order by bringing back royal families that had been kicked out under Napoleon's rule. But **NATIONALISM** was growing in each country—the feeling that the people in each country were linked to each other through a common culture, not through loyalty to a monarch. The rise of nationalism was partly a response to Napoleon's rule: Napoleon had united the French people by encouraging national songs and holidays and promoting patriotism through flags and other symbols. This kind of national pride developed throughout Europe.

> **NATIONALISM**
> pride in one's nation; patriotic feelings, ideas, and/or actions

The 1830s REVOLUTIONS in EUROPE

Nationalism inspired people from all over Europe to fight against the kings and queens they no longer identified with. Several revolutions broke out in 1830.

After CHARLES X was appointed king of France in 1824 and tried to ignore the new French constitution, the French people staged the JULY REVOLUTION to bring in a new king, KING LOUIS-PHILIPPE, who restored power to the French people.

The Polish people revolted against the Russian rule of the czar, but they were unsuccessful.

A revolution led to the formation of the new country of Belgium.

A number of revolutions erupted in 1848 as well. Again, many of them failed, but the idea of nationalism held strong.

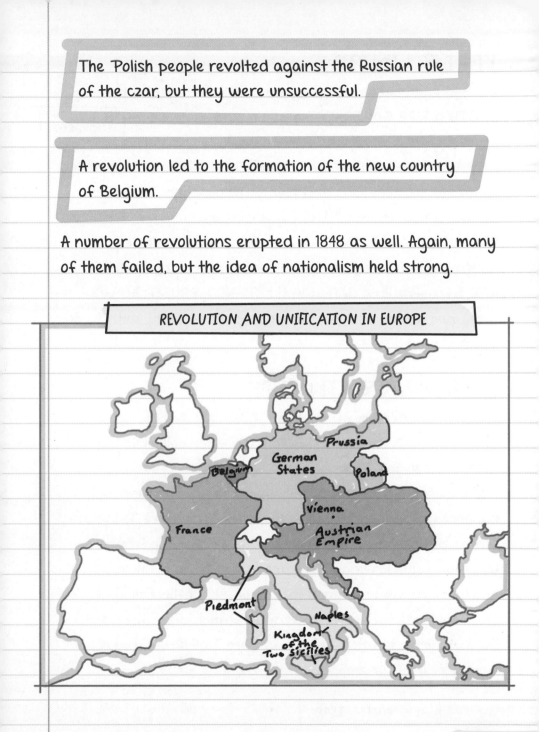

REVOLUTION AND UNIFICATION IN EUROPE

Prussia

German States

Belgium

Poland

Vienna

France

Austrian Empire

Piedmont

Naples

Kingdom of the Two Sicilies

ITALY UNITES

In 1861, Italy became an independent country with the help of GIUSEPPE GARIBALDI and his "red shirts," ← BECAUSE THEY WORE RED

who fought the Austrians for Italian independence and raised an army of 1,000 volunteers. Garibaldi took control of Sicily in 1860, and then of Naples and Piedmont. In 1861, a new state of Italy was declared under KING VICTOR EMMANUEL II. It didn't include Venice (controlled by Austria) or Rome (under France's control). In 1870, after France's defeat in the FRANCO-PRUSSIAN WAR, these two areas were finally made part of Italy, with Rome as its capital.

GERMANY UNITES

Under the leadership of Prussian KING WILHELM (WILLIAM I), PRIME MINISTER OTTO VON BISMARCK collected taxes to strengthen the Prussian army and govern Prussia without Parliament's input or approval. Bismarck went to war with the Austrians and quickly defeated them. This gave Prussia control of all of northern Germany. In 1870, in the Franco-Prussian War, Prussia won France's provinces of Alsace and Lorraine (and renamed the region Alsace-Lorraine). This convinced the southern German states to join the North German Confederation. In 1871, William I of Prussia was named KAISER, or emperor, of the German Empire.

↑
ALSO FROM "CAESAR"

HAITI DECLARES INDEPENDENCE

The small island of **HISPANIOLA** became independent in 1804. One part of Hispaniola was SAINT-DOMINGUE, a French sugar colony with a population of slaves, who were badly mistreated. Under the leadership of FRANÇOIS-DOMINIQUE TOUSSAINT-LOUVERTURE, over 100,000 of these slaves revolted and took over

Hispaniola. The Haitian slaves had made their own language so the French would not be aware of their plans and strategies. On New Year's Day in 1804, the western part of the island declared itself free. This part is called HAITI, and it was the first independent state in all of Latin America. JEAN-JACQUES DESSALINES, another leader in the Haitian revolution, became the first ruler of this new nation.

> **HISPANIOLA** is an island in the Caribbean consisting of modern-day Haiti and the Dominican Republic. It's one of the places Christopher Columbus explored during his 1492 voyage to the Americas.

CUBA

FRENCH SAINT-DOMINGUE

NORTH ATLANTIC OCEAN

CARIBBEAN SEA

HAITI

HISPANIOLA

DOMINICAN REPUBLIC

Santo Domingo

Port-au-Prince

CARIBBEAN SEA

FREEDOM for SOUTH AMERICA

South America was under the control of Spain and Portugal until the 1800s, when SIMÓN BOLÍVAR led revolutions all over the continent. Spain was weak after its wars with Napoleon, and Bolívar took advantage of this and declared Venezuela independent in 1811. Spain fought for control in Venezuela for another decade, but eventually the country was freed from Spanish control. In 1819, Bolívar declared and won (with a small army) independence for a new nation, Colombia. Bolívar was a hero all over South America, freeing countries left and right.

JOSÉ DE SAN MARTÍN fought for the independence of Argentina and Chile. He helped free Peru from Spanish rule with Bolívar's help. By the end of 1824, Uruguay, Paraguay, and Bolivia were also liberated from Spanish rule. Bolívar and San Martín supported **CREOLE** rights and led Creole armies against **PENINSULARES**.

CREOLES
Spaniards born in the New World

PENINSULARES
Spaniards in the New World born in Spain

312

CHECK YOUR KNOWLEDGE

1. Define "nationalism."

2. Who was responsible for unifying Italy?

3. Who was responsible for unifying Germany?

4. Venezuela's independence came in what year?
   A. 1824
   B. 1819
   C. 1811
   D. 1807

5. The first independent state in Latin America was _____.
   It was originally a _____ colony.

6. Which famed South American leader led Venezuela and Colombia to independence?

7. Why were the residents of Saint-Domingue unhappy? Who led them to independence?

ANSWERS 313

CHECK YOUR ANSWERS

1. Nationalism is the feeling that the people in each country are connected to each other through their common culture (not through loyalty to a king or queen). Nationalism can also mean that you're proud of your nation.

2. Giuseppe Garibaldi and the "red shirts" were responsible for liberating Italy from the Austrians. (In 1861, a new united state of Italy was declared under King Victor Emmanuel II.)

3. King Wilhelm (William I) and Prime Minister Otto von Bismarck. (Prussia took control of northern Germany and the provinces of Alsace and Lorraine—renaming the region Alsace-Lorraine—and convinced the southern German states to unite with the North German Confederation.)

4. C. 1811

5. Haiti; French

6. Simón Bolívar led Venezuela and Colombia to independence.

7. The people of Saint-Domingue were unhappy because they were enslaved. François-Dominique Toussaint-Louverture led over 100,000 slaves to revolt. (In 1804, the western part of the island declared itself free and is now called Haiti.)

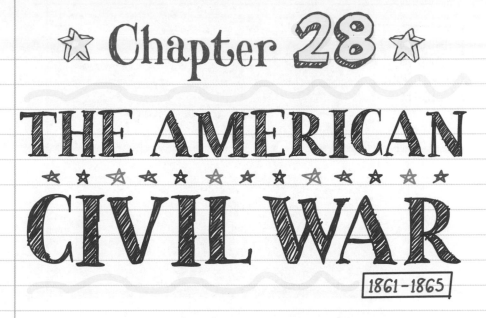

☆ Chapter 28 ☆

THE AMERICAN
CIVIL WAR

1861–1865

In the mid-1800s, nationalism was sweeping the U.S.
Northern states and Southern states had different
ideas about the balance of power between the states
and the federal government, and different ideas about
ABOLITIONISM, the movement to end slavery. The North
and South also both wanted to control the best farmland.
This led to the AMERICAN CIVIL WAR.

SLAVERY DIVIDES AMERICA

In the South, where the economy was based on tobacco and
cotton, plantation owners wanted to continue using enslaved
people. By the 1850s, over 3 million African Americans were
enslaved in the South.

Northern states had economies based on smaller farms and
manufacturing; they had little need for slave labor.

315

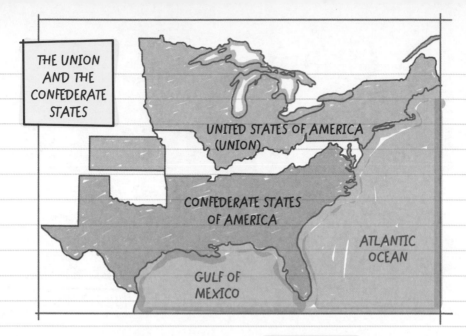

THE UNION AND THE CONFEDERATE STATES

UNITED STATES OF AMERICA (UNION)

CONFEDERATE STATES OF AMERICA

ATLANTIC OCEAN

GULF OF MEXICO

As each new state was added to **THE UNION**, there was debate on whether or not it would allow slavery. When California applied for statehood in 1850, it wanted to be a free state, but this would have upset the balance of an equal number of free and slave states. A compromise was decided: California would be a free state, and the people of each new state or territory thereafter would decide about slavery where they lived.

THE UNION
the United States; during the American Civil War, it also referred to the Northern army and Northern states

The ABOLITIONIST CAUSE

In 1855, in the territory that would later become the states of Kansas and Nebraska, citizens voted on whether or not the territory would be free. Many people already living there wanted it to be free, but thousands of people crossed the border to vote for a pro-slavery government. This fueled the abolitionist cause.

Abolitionist JOHN BROWN led riots, killing several people; hundreds more died later that summer in a period of time that became known as "BLEEDING KANSAS." Brown led a raid on an **ARSENAL** (a place where weapons are stored) in Virginia so he could arm slaves. The raid failed and Brown was sentenced to death, but he became a hero for the abolitionist cause.

FREDERICK DOUGLASS, an escaped slave, wrote several autobiographies, including *THE NARRATIVE OF THE LIFE OF FREDERICK DOUGLASS* (1845), and traveled around the nation to educate people about his harsh experiences as a slave. Douglass advised ABRAHAM LINCOLN, who was elected the sixteenth president of the United States in 1860, on the issue of slavery. Douglass also influenced President Lincoln to eventually let African American men fight in the Civil War. Many African American divisions, like the 54th regiment, helped the North win.

YOU HAVE A POINT THERE, FREDERICK.

THESE DIVISIONS WERE MADE UP OF MEN FROM BOTH FREE AND SLAVE STATES.

Lincoln thought that the divisions over slavery were dangerous to the strength of the government and its unity. He wasn't in favor of abolishing slavery altogether (not yet), but he believed that slavery shouldn't spread beyond the states where it was already practiced and that it could be encouraged to die out.

The Case of Dred Scott: DRED SCOTT was a slave who sued for his freedom. In 1857, the Supreme Court ruled that Scott was property, not a U.S. citizen, even if he was in a free state (he had spent time living in free states)—so he had no rights at all. This case further fueled the cause of abolitionism.

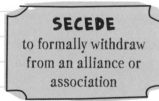

> HARRIET TUBMAN risked her life to smuggle slaves into the North through the **UNDERGROUND RAILROAD**. It was not really a railroad, but a network of secret routes and places, such as farms and houses, that helped people get to freedom.

The CONFEDERACY FORMS

In 1860, South Carolina decided to **SECEDE** from the Union to preserve its right to continue slavery. Six other states followed. In February, they formed the CONFEDERATE STATES OF AMERICA (or CONFEDERACY) and chose JEFFERSON DAVIS as president. In his inaugural address the following March, Lincoln stated that secession was illegal, but that war was not an option. In the end, though, he couldn't stop it.

> **SECEDE**
> to formally withdraw from an alliance or association

> The Union army represented the Northern states and was nicknamed the **YANKEES**. The Confederate army represented the Southern states and was nicknamed the **REBELS**.

The AMERICAN CIVIL WAR began in April 1861, when Confederate troops captured Union-controlled Fort Sumter in South Carolina. After that, Virginia, Arkansas, Tennessee, and North Carolina joined the Confederacy.

Use this rhyme to remember when the Civil War began:

In eighteen hundred sixty-one, the American Civil War had just begun.

1. South Carolina
2. Mississippi
3. Florida
4. Alabama
5. Georgia
6. Louisiana
7. Texas
8. Virginia
9. Arkansas
10. North Carolina
11. Tennessee

THIS IS THE ORDER IN WHICH THE STATES JOINED THE CONFEDERACY.

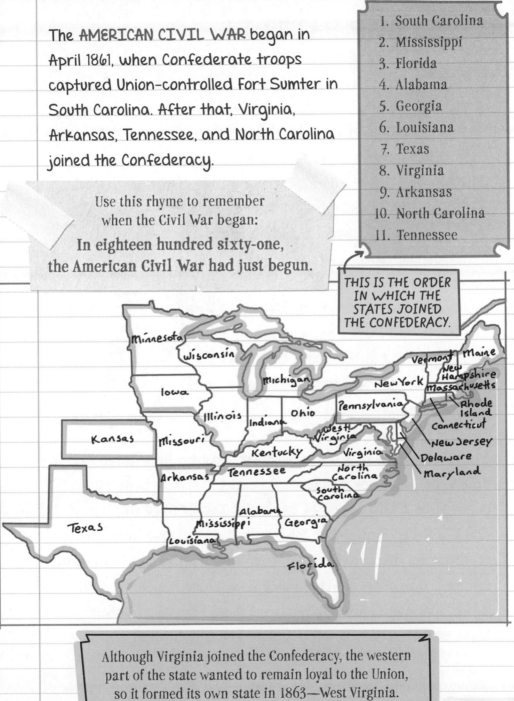

Although Virginia joined the Confederacy, the western part of the state wanted to remain loyal to the Union, so it formed its own state in 1863—West Virginia.

319

CIVIL WAR BATTLES

The first BATTLE OF BULL RUN, in Virginia in July 1861, was the first major battle of the Civil War. The Union and Confederate armies were made up mainly of volunteer soldiers, unprepared for war. The Union forces tried to capture Virginia's state capital, Richmond, but Confederate troops, led by Thomas Jackson, held their ground. Jackson got his nickname, STONEWALL JACKSON, here, when someone yelled, "There is Jackson, standing like a stone wall!" There were so many casualties that both sides realized the war would be long and difficult. The North had more people, supplies, and factories, but the South extended the war with clever generals who knew how to use guerrilla warfare.

A second Battle of Bull Run followed about a year later, and again the Union soldiers were forced to retreat, possibly because of a bad choice of generals. The BATTLE OF ANTIETAM, in September 1862, was the first Civil War battle on Union territory, in Maryland. It was the bloodiest one-day battle in U.S. history. After this battle, Lincoln warned that slaves living in Confederate states would be freed unless these states returned to the Union. The states didn't comply, and Lincoln issued the EMANCIPATION PROCLAMATION on January 1, 1863, theoretically freeing over three million people.

Lincoln did not actually have the constitutional power to end slavery, but he had the authority to seize enemy property—including slaves. So this military order could free all slaves in any area that was in rebellion. It encouraged some slaves to escape.

The BATTLE OF GETTYSBURG, in Pennsylvania in July 1863, was the turning point of the Civil War: Union troops won and gained the upper hand. General GEORGE C. MEADE, now in charge of the Union troops, decided to practice TOTAL WAR: to not only defeat the Confederate army (which was under the command of General ROBERT E. LEE) but to destroy the region's resources and morale.

SEE NEXT PAGE

THE GETTYSBURG ADDRESS

Gettysburg is also where Lincoln delivered his **GETTYSBURG ADDRESS**. On November 19, 1863, four months after the battle, Lincoln spoke at the Soldiers' National Cemetery there about how the Civil War would lead to new freedom for America and that no soldier would die in vain. The speech begins with the line **"Four score and seven years ago"**—a reference to the American Revolution—and is considered one of the greatest speeches in history.

The first line of the Gettysburg Address, "Four score and seven years ago, our fathers brought forth, upon this continent . . ." is a clue to the year in which it was delivered. A "score" is 20, so four score and seven = $4 \times 20 + 7 = 87$ years.

$1776 + 87 = 1863$.

Union general WILLIAM TECUMSEH SHERMAN led his troops from Atlanta to Savannah on a MARCH TO THE SEA in 1864, destroying railroads, plantations...everything in sight.

"TOTAL WAR" was a term coined by Union general William Sherman in 1864. Total war is a military strategy of including any and all civilians and civilian resources as military targets. It often results in many casualties. Sherman himself recognized the brutality of this tactic, but reasoned that it would destroy the Rebels and end the war faster.

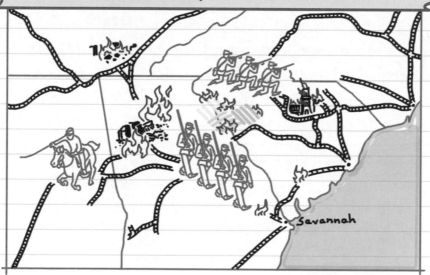

The OUTCOME and AFTERMATH

The American Civil War between the Union and Confederate armies lasted four years (1861–1865). In April 1865, at APPOMATTOX COURT HOUSE in Virginia, Lee and his Confederate army surrendered to GENERAL UYLSSES S. GRANT, ending the war. In January 1865, Congress passed the THIRTEENTH AMENDMENT, which officially abolished slavery. The Union was preserved.

CHECK YOUR KNOWLEDGE

1. What were two major issues that caused so much conflict between the Northern and Southern states?

2. What was the controversy when California wanted to join the Union?

3. Who was Frederick Douglass and what did he influence Lincoln to do?

4. The _____ army represented the Northern states, while the _____ army represented the Southern states.

5. The American Civil War began when Confederate troops bombarded:
   A. Fort McHenry
   B. Fort Sumter
   C. Fort Davis
   D. Fort Ticonderoga

6. When did the American Civil War end?

7. What amendment made the end of slavery in the U.S. official?

ANSWERS

CHECK YOUR ANSWERS

1. Slavery and states' rights divided America. (In the South, where the economy was based on tobacco and cotton, plantation owners wanted slavery. Northern states had little need for slave labor.)

2. The controversy was that California wanted to be a free state, but this would have made an unequal number of free and slave states.

3. Frederick Douglass was an escaped slave who wrote several autobiographies and traveled around the nation to educate people about his horrible experiences as a slave. He also advised President Lincoln on the issue of slavery and influenced him to let African American men fight in the Northern army.

4. Union, Confederate

5. B. Fort Sumter

6. The American Civil War ended when the Confederate army surrendered in April 1865 at Appomattox Court House in Virginia.

7. The Thirteenth Amendment officially abolished slavery.

Chapter 29

THE INDUSTRIAL REVOLUTION

1760–MID-1800s

During the **INDUSTRIAL REVOLUTION**, new technology greatly changed the way products were produced and people lived. It began in the 1760s with advances in farming, peaked with the development of factories, and lasted until about the mid-1800s.

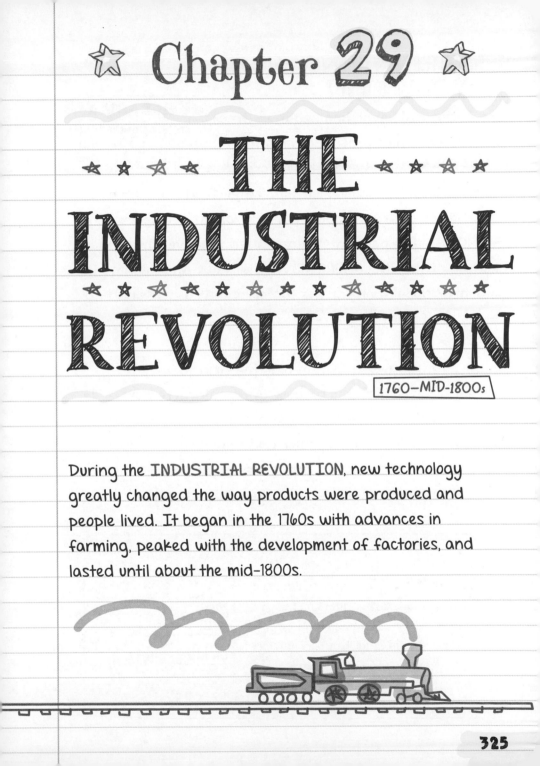

The BEGINNING of the REVOLUTION

The Industrial Revolution began in Great Britain, which had profited from an **AGRARIAN** revolution with new crops and

> **AGRARIAN**
> related to the land or farming

farming practices, which led to greater food production, which led to a larger population with longer life spans. In the 1700s, many peasants were forced to move to towns because of the ENCLOSURE MOVEMENT laws and became the new labor population for the factories that were sprouting up all over England.

Another reason Great Britain was the first to have an Industrial Revolution was because of its natural resources. It had iron for building machines and coal for running them. Its rivers provided waterpower and routes for transporting raw materials and finished goods. Britain also had a massive EMPIRE and a large market of buyers for its products.

The British Parliament passed the **ENCLOSURE ACTS**, laws that fenced off lands that peasant farmers had used in the past so that they could no longer use the common land. Land became individually owned, and some people were forced to look for jobs in cities.

The SIGNIFICANCE
of the REVOLUTION

The Industrial Revolution allowed more goods to be produced at a very fast rate. The work was largely done in factories, where workers, including men, women, and children, endured long hours and little pay. Factories relied on a DIVISION OF LABOR in which each worker did the same task over and over again to make the same product. People often worked in cramped, humid spaces with loud machines, and with their eyes and lungs full of dust. Factories were hotbeds of injuries, sickness, and disease. But people needed to work. Immigrants were brought in to work in the factories for low wages.

Larger populations and foreign markets had made industrial manufacturing profitable, particularly in terms of woven and knitted cloth. New spinning machines made textiles cheaper to produce, and textile factories took over England and Scotland.

The REVOLUTION
TAKES OFF

The Industrial Revolution also hit Belgium, France, Germany, and other countries. The governments encouraged industrialization by improving railroad and canal networks. The Japanese industrialized too, in the late 1800s.

COUGH, COUGH!

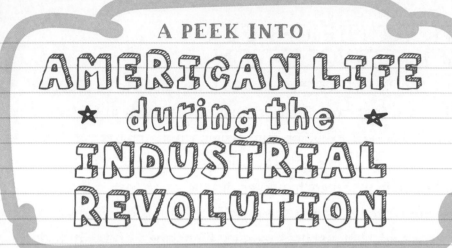

A PEEK INTO
AMERICAN LIFE
★ during the ★
INDUSTRIAL
REVOLUTION

The American Industrial Revolution is said to have begun in Rhode Island in 1793, when SAMUEL SLATER built the first American spinning mill, a factory that makes cloth. Rhode Island's geography was perfect for water-powered mills, and the War of 1812 made it tough to get imported goods, inspiring Americans to find more efficient ways to produce their own. The most famous factory was started by Francis Cabot Lowell in 1814 and mostly employed young women. It was so successful that it led to the founding of an entire town, called LOWELL, MASSACHUSETTS. The "Lowell girls" were paid well, but they worked long hours in grueling conditions.

The **INDUSTRIAL REVOLUTION** was the first time many people in America needed a clock. On a farm, you can plan your day by the movement of the sun; in a factory, not so much.

The Industrial Revolution was a time of great innovation.

NEW TECHNOLOGY
OF THE ERA INCLUDED:

INTERCHANGEABLE PARTS: First introduced by **ELI WHITNEY** (who invented the **COTTON GIN**) for muskets for the army, these pre-manufactured, identical parts created the possibility of **MASS PRODUCTION**.

The **TELEGRAPH**, invented by **SAMUEL F. B. MORSE** in 1837, improved communication. Using **MORSE CODE**, telegraphs sent short pulses of energy along a wire that were translated into letters that spelled out messages.

STEAM POWER:

The **STEAMBOAT**, perfected by **ROBERT FULTON** in 1807, improved river transportation.

The STEAM **LOCOMOTIVE**, created by **PETER COOPER** in 1830, improved land transportation and led to the development of railroads.

Once **STEAM ENGINES** were introduced in the 1830s, factories no longer had to be located near rivers.

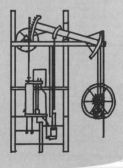

LOCOMOTIVE
a machine that moves on its own, usually powered by steam or electricity

329

New technology helped people who were headed west. They could now use better agricultural tools, like the JOHN DEERE PLOW and the McCORMICK REAPER. Wheat became a cash crop, cities such as Chicago sprang up, farms in the Midwest began to supply the factory workers in the Northeast with food, and the Northeast began to supply the Midwest with manufactured goods. Large distances seemed to become smaller, thanks to American innovation.

One of the most significant inventions was the COTTON GIN. Invented by Eli Whitney in 1793, it could clean seeds from cotton quickly. It allowed plantation owners in the South to speed up processing harvests so that workers in the North could make more cotton goods. On the flip side, however, the cotton gin also created a need for more slaves. Another invention of the Industrial Revolution was James Hargreaves's SPINNING JENNY (1764). His machine allowed several spools of yarn to be spun simultaneously and sped up the cotton production process.

The Industrial Revolution led to the growth of cities, with many workers moving from the country (where they had farmed) to the city for jobs in factories. Cities were growing, but their sanitary conditions were poor and disease was common.

CHILD LABOR

The Industrial Revolution was a time of incredible engineering and mechanical achievement but at the cost of millions of children. Child laborers were paid much less than adults, and by 1810, approximately 2 million children worked at least six 10-hour days a week for as little as 40 cents a day. The majority of child laborers were from poor immigrant families that relied on their children's wages to eat. These children worked in dark rooms or mines with polluted air and many did not go to school or play. Church groups and teachers worked hard to change child labor laws. By 1878, Great Britain and most of Europe had passed laws that improved working conditions and shortened workdays, as well as raised age requirements. The U.S. Congress wouldn't pass the Fair Labor Standards Act until 1938, and today millions of children around the world still work long hours under dangerous conditions with little access to education.

The SECOND INDUSTRIAL REVOLUTION

From the late 1800s until about World War I, a SECOND INDUSTRIAL REVOLUTION followed.

In 1855, the British made steel production less difficult and less expensive, making railroad construction easier and skyscrapers possible with the **BESSEMER STEEL PROCESS**.

1866: The first TRANSATLANTIC TELEGRAPH wire was put in place.

1867: The first commercially successful TYPEWRITER was invented by Christopher Sholes, Carlos Glidden, and Samuel W. Soule.

1876: ALEXANDER GRAHAM BELL invented the TELEPHONE, launching the telecom industry, which was started by the Bell Telephone Company.

1876: THOMAS EDISON opened a lab in Menlo Park, New Jersey, and went on to patent more than 1,000 inventions. In 1879, he invented the first electric LIGHTBULB.

1903: ORVILLE AND WILBUR WRIGHT made the first airplane flight at KITTY HAWK, NORTH CAROLINA, on December 17.

ANY THOUGHTS?

I GIVE IT A WEEK.

1908: Henry Ford devised the Model T car, created by his innovative assembly line system.

BEEP! BEEP!

ASSEMBLY LINE → If everyone on the line does one job over and over (specialization and division of labor), people working together can produce more in a shorter time. Those workers are also paid less because they have fewer skills.

CHECK YOUR KNOWLEDGE

1. What was the first Industrial Revolution? Be sure to note the time period in your answer.

2. The spinning jenny was invented in 1764 by:
   - A. Edmund Cartwright
   - B. James Watt
   - C. James Hargreaves
   - D. Eli Whitney

3. Which two natural resources contributed to the growth of the Industrial Revolution in Great Britain?
   - A. Steel and coal
   - B. Iron and coal
   - C. Cotton and steel
   - D. Wood and steel

4. Describe working conditions for many factory workers during the Industrial Revolution. Why were they so miserable?

5. How did Eli Whitney's development of interchangeable parts aid the U.S. in its quest to industrialize?

6. How did industrialization lead to the growth of cities? What were the downsides of industrialization?

7. What was the Second Industrial Revolution?

ANSWERS   335

CHECK YOUR ANSWERS

1. The first Industrial Revolution began in the 1760s and lasted until about the mid-1800s. It was a time when new technology changed the way products were made, how farming was done, and the way people lived.

2. C. James Hargreaves

3. B. Iron and coal

4. In factories, men, women, and children worked long hours for little money. Each person did the same task over and over again. People often worked in places that damaged their health—the factories were cramped, humid spaces with loud machines, and they were full of dust. There were many injuries, as well as sickness and disease, at the factories.

5. Eli Whitney's innovation allowed products with identical parts to be put together easily and mass-produced. Interchangeable parts made production much faster than before.

6. The Industrial Revolution led to the growth of cities because many workers moved from the country to the city for jobs in factories. The downside was that the cities often had poor sanitary conditions and a lot of disease, and people worked in factories under terrible conditions.

7. The Second Industrial Revolution was when steel became a mass-produced material, which helped in the creation of railroads. The telegraph, typewriter, telephone, and first electric lightbulb were also invented during the Second Industrial Revolution.

☆ Chapter 30 ☆

✶✶✶✶✶ THE ✶✶✶✶✶ WOMEN'S MOVEMENT

Women in the 1800s were expected to take care of the family and stay at home. They had little freedom and few rights. Most women in Europe and the U.S. didn't have a legal identity apart from their husbands. In the late 1700s, the first Industrial Revolution created a demand for more workers, so women began taking jobs in factories, and later on as secretaries, salesclerks, and typists. Some women became teachers and nurses. But the **FEMINIST** movement began long before then.

> **FEMINISM**
> the belief that all sexes should have equal social, political, economic, and other rights

A VINDICATION OF THE RIGHTS OF WOMAN

In 1792, a British writer named MARY WOLLSTONECRAFT argued for equal rights for men and women in her work

A VINDICATION OF THE RIGHTS OF WOMAN. Wollstonecraft stated that the power of men over women was just as wrong as the **ARBITRARY** power of monarchs over their subjects. She argued that if the Enlightenment was based on an ideal of reason in all humans, women must have reason too and were entitled to the same rights as men. Wollstonecraft sought equality in education and in economic and political life. In the 1830s, many

> **ARBITRARY**
> determined by individual preference as opposed to the law

women in Europe and the U.S. pushed for the right to divorce and own property. Women fought to go to universities. They set out to enter professions previously limited to men.

The FIGHT for SUFFRAGE

In the 1840s and 1850s, the women's rights movement began to focus on voting rights. They believed that suffrage (the right to vote) was essential. These women, called SUFFRAGISTS, campaigned in many different ways. In Britain, some suffragists went on hunger strikes and chained themselves to the prime minister's house.

In the U.S., leaders like SUSAN B. ANTHONY and ELIZABETH CADY STANTON gave lectures and spoke at rallies. At the Seneca Falls Convention,

SUSAN B. ANTHONY

held in New York in 1848, Stanton presented the DECLARATION OF RIGHTS AND SENTIMENTS she had written. Based on the Declaration of Independence, it stated

ELIZABETH CADY STANTON

that both men and women are created equal and have rights including life, liberty, and the pursuit of happiness. One hundred suffragists at the convention signed the Declaration of Rights and Sentiments to demand the right to vote. Most were women, but a few men, such as Frederick Douglass, supported women's suffrage.

Our Roll of Honor

Containing all the Signatures to the "Declarations of Sentiments" Set Forth by the First

Woman's Rights Convention,

held at

Seneca Falls, New York

July 19-20, 1848

LADIES:

Lucretia Mott	Sophronia Taylor	Rachel D. Bonnel
Harriet Cady Eaton	Cynthia Davis	Betsey Tewksbury
Margaret Pryor	Hannah Plant	Rhoda Palmer
Elizabeth Cady Stanton	Lucy Jones	Margaret Jenkins
Eunice Newton Foote	Sarah Whitney	Cynthia Fuller
Mary Ann M'Clintock	Mary H. Hallowell	Mary Martin
Margaret Schooley	Elizabeth Conklin	P. A. Culvert
Martha C. Wright	Sally Pitcher	Susan R. Doty
Jane C. Hunt	Mary Conklin	Rebecca Race
Amy Post	Susan Quinn	Sarah A. Mosher
Catherine F. Stebbins	Mary S. Mirror	Mary E. Vail
Mary Ann Frink	Phebe King	Lucy Spalding
Lydia Mount	Julia Ann Drake	Lovina Latham
Delia Mathews	Charlotte Woodward	Sarah Smith
Catherine C. Paine	Martha Underhill	Eliza Martin
Elizabeth W. M'Clintock	Dorothy Mathews	Maria E. Wilbur
Malvina Seymour	Eunice Barker	Elizabeth D. Smith
Phebe Mosher	Sarah H. Woods	Caroline Barker
Catherine Shaw	Lydia Gild	Ann Porter
Deborah Scott	Sarah Hoffman	Experience Gibbs
Sarah Hallowell	Elizabeth Leslie	Antoinette E. Segur
Mary M'Clintock	Martha Ridley	Hannah J. Latham
Mary Gilbert		Sarah Sisson

GENTLEMEN:

Richard P. Hunt	William S. Dell	Nathan J. Milliken
Samuel D. Tillman	James Mott	S. E. Woodworth
Justin Williams	William Burroughs	Edward F. Underhill
Elisha Foote	Robert Smallbridge	George W. Pryor
Frederick Douglass	Jacob Mathews	Joel Bunker
Henry W. Seymour	Charles L. Hoskins	Isaac VanTassel
Henry Seymour	Thomas M'Clintock	Thomas Dell
David Spalding	Saron Phillips	E. W. Capron
William G. Barker	Jacob P. Chamberlain	Stephen Shear
Elias J. Doty	Jonathan Metcalf	Henry Hatley
John Jones		Azaliah Schooley

In 1893, New Zealand became the first country to grant women the right to vote in national elections. In the U.S., Wyoming became the first territory to grant the right to vote to women, in 1869 (it officially became a state in 1890), but it wasn't until 1920 that women's suffrage extended nationwide, via the NINETEENTH AMENDMENT. Women over the age of twenty-one finally gained the right to vote in Britain in 1928.

Women all over the globe were fighting for their rights. In 1910, the International Feminist Congresses met for the first time, in Argentina. The second meeting was in Mexico in 1916.

CHECK YOUR KNOWLEDGE

1. In *A Vindication of the Rights of Woman* (1792), what did Mary Wollstonecraft argue for?

2. Name two leading figures in the fight for women's suffrage.

3. How might the first Industrial Revolution have led to the women's rights movement?

4. What are some examples of things suffragists did to campaign for their rights?

5. What was the first place in the U.S. to grant women the right to vote?

6. When was women's suffrage made official across America?

7. What was the first country to grant women the right to vote in national elections, and when?

ANSWERS

CHECK YOUR ANSWERS

1. Mary Wollstonecraft argued for equal rights for men and women by comparing the power of men over women to the arbitrary power of monarchs over their subjects. She also argued for equality in education and in economic and political life.

2. Two leading figures in women's rights are Susan B. Anthony and Elizabeth Cady Stanton, who gave lectures and spoke at rallies. (Frederick Douglass was also a supporter.)

3. The first Industrial Revolution created a demand for even more workers, so women began taking jobs in factories and later on as secretaries, salesclerks, and typists. Some women became teachers and nurses. Therefore, the Industrial Revolution encouraged an expanded role for women outside of the home.

4. In Britain, some suffragists went on hunger strikes and chained themselves to the prime minister's house.

5. Wyoming became the first U.S. territory to grant the right to vote to women, in 1869 (it did not officially become a state until 1890).

6. Women's suffrage was made official across America in 1920 through the Nineteenth Amendment.

7. New Zealand was the first country to grant women the right to vote in national elections. It happened in 1893.

Unit 7

The Era of Imperialism
1800–1914

The era of **IMPERIALISM** was a time of great competition among many nations worldwide and great damage for many colonized nations. For some people, imperialism meant expanding an empire and taking over new lands. For others, it meant losing their identity and resources to new rulers from a faraway place. How did imperialism work—or, in many cases, not work at all?

> **IMPERIALISM**
> the act of extending rule over a foreign country or territory and/or holding colonies

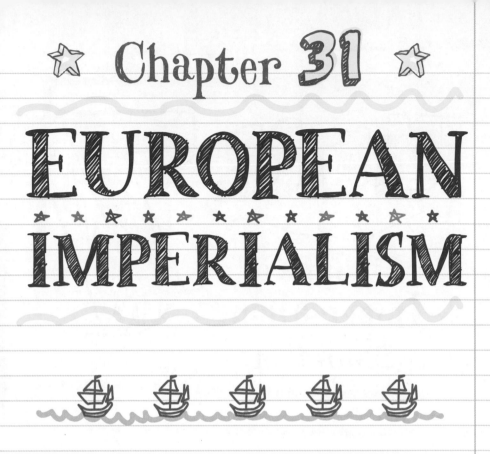

Chapter 31

EUROPEAN
IMPERIALISM

WHY EUROPEANS SOUGHT COLONIES and TERRITORIES

European explorers sought "gold, glory, and God" in their
first voyages across the sea to the East and the Americas.
In the era of imperialism, which began in the early
nineteenth century, European nations sought to conquer and
claim foreign lands. These lands were seen as resources
for raw materials that European countries needed to
industrialize.

It was a time of great competition: If one country claimed land for a certain resource (like sugarcane or rubber) it could dominate the market and make all the profit. If it could find new markets in other lands to buy its own goods, the country would be even more powerful.

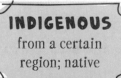

SUGAR

BECAME KNOWN AS "WHITE GOLD"

If a European country was overpopulated, it could just ship off some citizens to colonies in Asia or Africa or wherever its colonies were. Europeans were convinced that if they wanted to profit and be competitive in a growing world, imperialism was the way to go.

Many countries fell to imperial rule in the nineteenth and part of the twentieth centuries, often at the expense of people **INDIGENOUS** to the land. Just as the Mayans, Incas, Aztecs, Iroquois, and other Native Americans suffered at the hands of foreign rulers, imperialism was destructive to many cultures.

INDIGENOUS
from a certain region; native

Meanwhile, in the U.S., **MISSIONARIES** traveled west of the Mississippi River along the Oregon Trail. Their reports of the beautiful land of the West encouraged others to follow. They believed that American expansion to the Pacific coast was part of **MANIFEST DESTINY:** the idea that the U.S. was chosen by God to spread across the continent and that the expansion of the U.S. was the people's "manifest," or obvious, destiny.

MISSIONARY
someone who goes on a mission to a foreign place to spread his religion

BRITAIN ESTABLISHES TRADE with INDIA

In 1600, the British set up a monopoly on trade with India by establishing and expanding the EAST INDIA COMPANY. The opium that was sent to China was grown in India by the East India Company. The British bought spices, tea, cotton, and more from India in exchange for silver for roughly two hundred years. The French and Dutch also traded with India, but eventually control fell completely to Britain and the East India Company.

The OPIUM WAR and ITS AFTERMATH

In the beginning, China wasn't so big on foreigners and was strict about whom and what to let into the country.

BEIJING

NANJING

CHINA

EAST CHINA SEA

GUANGZHOU

HONG KONG

By the 1840s, Britain had established a trade route with China, exporting opium (an addictive, dangerous drug) that was grown in India in exchange for tea (less addictive, except for the caffeine).

The Chinese government knew the huge dangers of opium and had made it illegal to import. Chinese government official LIN ZEXU wrote an open letter to QUEEN VICTORIA of England requesting that she stop the illegal trading, but the letter was ignored, and England's shipments of opium kept hitting China's shores. The Chinese were furious, and in 1839 they dumped about 20,000 chests of the drug into the sea, beginning the OPIUM WAR (1839-1842). The Chinese blockaded the Canton (present-day Guangzhou) trading area and forced traders to surrender their opium. The British responded with equal fury and powerful warships, destroying Chinese coastal and river forts and defeating the Chinese.

In the 1842 TREATY OF NANJING, China was held responsible for the costs of the war and was forced to open five coastal ports, including Hong Kong, to British trade. British traders who lived there didn't have to follow Chinese laws, but had their own laws in a system called EXTRATERRITORIALITY.

EXTRATERRITORIALITY
being exempt, or free from, local laws

The Chinese were also forced to limit taxes on imported British goods and had to hand over the territory of Hong Kong to the British. This was a lot of punishment for trying to protect their people! And the opium trade continued.

OTHER EUROPEAN COUNTRIES TRADE with CHINA

Other Europeans traded with the Chinese. The Chinese offered the Americans the same trading deal they had with the British. Soon, all of China's ports were teeming with traders, each setting up their own SPHERES OF INFLUENCE— areas where imperial powers had the exclusive trading rights or exclusive mining and railroad-building privileges. The Chinese granted other nations these privileges in exchange for money. Britain, the U.S., France, Germany, Russia, and Japan took advantage of the deal.

Because of these new policies, the ruling QING dynasty was seen as weak and ineffective. In 1850, a group of rebels started the TAIPING REBELLION, calling for social reforms, like giving land to peasants and treating women as equals of men. The rebels seized Nanjing, killing thousands of people and continuing their massacres for years. Foreign nations took advantage of the unrest to expand their presence in China. Eventually the Europeans offered to help the Qing dynasty to get things back in order. In 1864, Chinese forces recaptured Nanjing and ended the rebellion.

The Taiping Rebellion killed 20 million people—one of the deadliest armed conflicts in history. The next year, the British and the French pressured China into giving them more trading power. China agreed to legalize the opium trade (!!!) and open up new ports. China gave more land to Britain (the Kowloon Peninsula), and other areas were seized by Britain when China resisted parts of the treaty. China's attempt to keep foreigners out had failed.

CHECK YOUR KNOWLEDGE

1. Define "imperialism."

2. How could European nations dominate a resource market? What effect did this have on their rivals?

3. What started the Opium War?

4. Explain the results of the Treaty of Nanjing.

5. Traders in an area of extraterritoriality would be likely to:
   A. follow the laws established by the Chinese government
   B. ignore Chinese law and establish their own set of laws
   C. live according to no law whatsoever

6. What city saw the start of the Taiping Rebellion of 1850?
   A. Beijing
   B. Nanjing
   C. Nagasaki
   D. Hong Kong

7. What was the East India Company?

ANSWERS 351

CHECK YOUR ANSWERS

1. Imperialism is the act of extending rule over a foreign country or territory and/or holding colonies.

2. European nations could dominate a resource market if one country claimed land for a certain resource (like sugarcane or rubber). Then it could make all the profit from selling that resource. As that nation became more powerful in that market, other countries would have less and less ability to enter that market.

3. The Opium War began because England continued to ship opium to China, even though China asked that they stop. In 1839, the Chinese dumped about 20,000 chests of opium into the sea in protest, and thus began the Opium War.

4. In the Treaty of Nanjing, China was held responsible for the costs of the Opium War and was forced to open five coastal ports to British trade. Also, the Chinese had to limit taxes on imported British goods, exempt the British traders from local laws (extraterritoriality), and give Hong Kong to the British.

5. B. ignore Chinese law and establish their own set of laws

6. B. Nanjing

7. The East India Company was a British company created in 1600 that held a monopoly on trade with India.

☆ Chapter 32 ☆

THE SCRAMBLE FOR
✶ ✶ ✶ ✶ ✶ ✶ ✶ ✶ ✶ ✶ ✶ ✶
AFRICA

1870s–1941

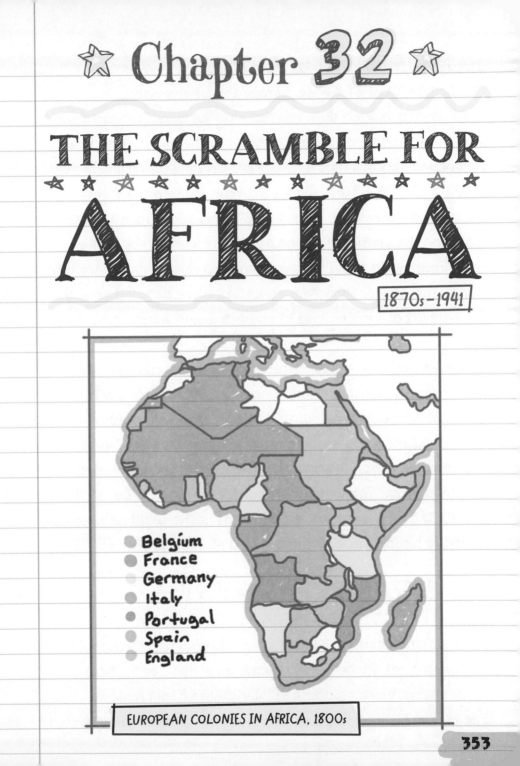

- Belgium
- France
- Germany
- Italy
- Portugal
- Spain
- England

EUROPEAN COLONIES IN AFRICA, 1800s

EUROPEANS in AFRICA

On the continent of Africa, European nations had
traditionally traded with coastal kingdoms, never venturing
far into the continent. This changed in the mid-1800s, when
Europeans began sending explorers and missionaries inward.
DAVID LIVINGSTONE was a Scottish missionary from
London who arrived in Africa in 1841 and spent thirty years
traveling the continent. Livingstone was looking for a river
route that would allow European commerce and Christianity to
"flow" into Africa. Livingstone's letters were detailed enough
for people back in England to start drawing maps from them.

When Livingstone disappeared, an American newspaper
sent a young Welsh journalist named SIR HENRY MORTON
STANLEY to track him down. Stanley found Livingstone alive
in 1871 and ended up staying in Africa a few years. Stanley
explored the Congo River and told the Brits they should set
up camp there. The British turned down the idea, but KING
LEOPOLD II of Belgium was enthusiastic. He wanted to open
Africa to his idea of civilization—and make a profit.

The SCRAMBLE for AFRICA

King Leopold II became the driving force behind
colonization in central Africa. In the late 1870s, through
Stanley, he set up Belgian settlements in the Congo. New
trade routes were established, along with new rivalries.
The French hurried to plant their flag in northern Africa.

Germany and Britain each tried to claim land in East Africa. Spain claimed western Sahara and part of Morocco, Italy took over Libya and most of Somalia, and Portugal wanted Angola and Mozambique. This rush of colonial activity and Europeans trying to grab a piece of the

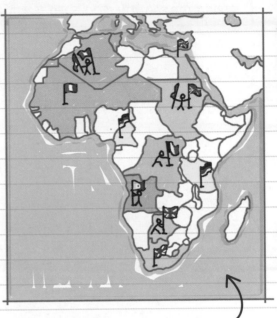

African continent is known as the SCRAMBLE FOR AFRICA.

DISAGREEMENTS AMONG the COLONIZERS ARISE

In 1884-1885, these major European nations met at the BERLIN CONFERENCE to settle disputes and formalize imperialist policies in Africa without going to war. The group agreed to **PARTITION** the continent. All this happened without the knowledge of the many different groups of people living on the continent, who would now be randomly divided (sometimes across the lines of rival nations) and put to work based on the whims of the Europeans. (No African leaders were invited to the conference.) The imposed borders bunched Africans

PARTITION
to divide a country or state into different parts, usually with different types of political rule

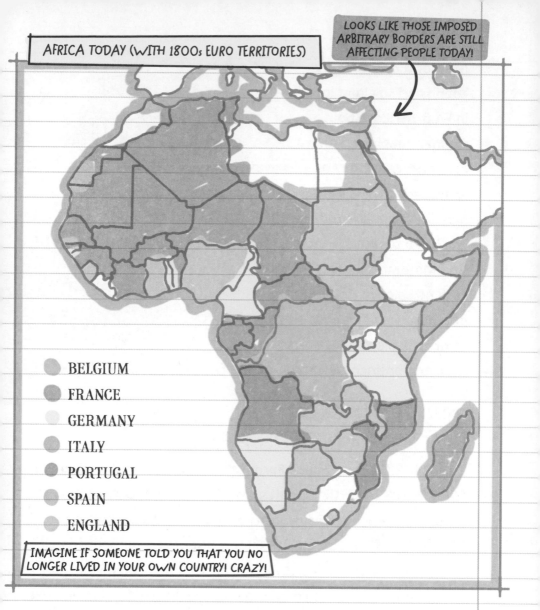

AFRICA TODAY (WITH 1800s EURO TERRITORIES)

LOOKS LIKE THOSE IMPOSED ARBITRARY BORDERS ARE STILL AFFECTING PEOPLE TODAY!

BELGIUM
FRANCE
GERMANY
ITALY
PORTUGAL
SPAIN
ENGLAND

IMAGINE IF SOMEONE TOLD YOU THAT YOU NO LONGER LIVED IN YOUR OWN COUNTRY! CRAZY!

into arbitrary groups that didn't represent their cultures or heritage and confused the ownership of local resources. (Many of these colonial borders still exist today, along with troubling effects that come with imposing borders that are arbitrary to the indigenous population.) Belgium, Spain,

Portugal, France, Great Britain, Italy, and Germany began to organize their

settlements, **EXPLOITING** the people already living there. People were forced to endure such harsh working conditions that by the early 1900s, anywhere from eight to sixteen million Africans had died.

CECIL RHODES and the BOER WAR

The Dutch were the first colonists in southern Africa, founding Capetown in the seventeenth century. In 1806, when the British took over the area (which they named CAPE COLONY), Dutch settlers (also called BOERS) decided to leave. The Dutch created two new republics, TRANSVAAL and the ORANGE FREE STATE. At the same time, the British added their own new colony, NATAL, to the east of the Boer states. The Dutch and British settlers were very different: In the British colonies, any wealthy man could vote, regardless of race; in the Boer republics, only white men could vote.

THE BOERS WANTED TO KEEP SLAVERY, BUT THE BRITISH DIDN'T, SO THE BOERS LEFT.

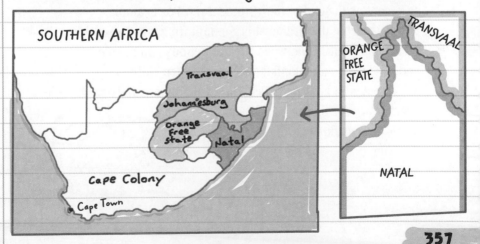

SOUTHERN AFRICA

Transvaal

Johannesburg

Orange Free State

Natal

Cape Colony

Cape Town

ORANGE FREE STATE

TRANSVAAL

NATAL

357

When the British discovered diamonds and gold in the Boer republics, they swarmed into Boer territory in the Transvaal looking to get rich quick. In 1895, the prime minister of Cape Colony, CECIL RHODES, who was also the owner of diamond and gold companies and a champion of British expansion in Africa, secretly supported a British raid on Transvaal. The JAMESON RAID was a disaster, and Rhodes was forced to resign.

But the damage was done, and the SECOND BOER WAR (they had already fought each other about twenty years earlier over control of territory and taxes—the Boers won) broke out between the British and the Dutch settlers in 1899. In 1902, the vast British army defeated the Boers. The British established a new country, the UNION OF SOUTH AFRICA, combining the Boer republics with the British Cape Colony.

Rock paintings in Africa date from prehistoric times to as recent as the end of the 19th century. For example, paintings from the Drakensberg mountain range in South Africa show battles between the indigenous San people and the European colonists, who are shown riding on horseback and holding rifles. The Drakensberg artists are also known for their three-dimensional shading.

CHECK YOUR KNOWLEDGE

1. What was trade like between Europeans and Africans before the 1800s?

2. ___ _____ _____ _____ convinced King Leopold II of Belgium to invest in Africa.

3. What led to the "scramble for Africa"?

4. What happened to African nations and groups after the Berlin Conference?

5. The Dutch created two republics in southern Africa in 1806, _____ and the _____ ____ _____.

6. The Second Boer War was fought primarily over which of two resources?
   A. silver and gold
   B. diamonds and gold
   C. emeralds and gold
   D. silver and bronze

ANSWERS 359

CHECK YOUR ANSWERS

1. European nations had mainly traded with the kingdoms on the African coasts.

2. Sir Henry Morton Stanley

3. The "scramble for Africa" was started by the new settlements in the Congo and the new trade routes through Africa that King Leopold II of Belgium set up. After Belgium began staking its claims, other countries like France, Germany, Britain, Spain, Italy, and Portugal wanted to get a piece of Africa for themselves.

4. After the Berlin Conference, African nations were divided and taken over by European nations. The preexisting African groups, tribes, and nations were arbitrarily divided, even if the divisions didn't make any sense according to the indigenous peoples' history.

5. Transvaal; Orange Free State

6. B. diamonds and gold

☆ Chapter 33 ☆

JAPAN

* * * * * * * * * * * * *

MODERNIZES

Like China, Japan had been strict about whom to let in and trade with. In 1853, an American naval officer named MATTHEW PERRY was sent by PRESIDENT MILLARD FILLMORE to ask Japan to open its ports to trade with Americans. Japan opened two ports for international trade, ending its period of isolation. Japan also entered a period of modernization.

MUTSUHITO,
EMPEROR OF THE MEIJI

The MEIJI RESTORATION

In 1868, the Tokugawa shoguns, who had outlawed trade with foreigners, were overthrown by a small group of Japanese military commanders and aristocrats, who began the MEIJI RESTORATION (1868-1912). This was a period of great growth for the Japanese, when they built

SHIPS   RAILWAYS   BANKING SYSTEMS

COAL MINES   MACHINERY   FACTORIES

COMMUNICATION SYSTEMS

The Meiji saw the importance of universal education and a common language. Education was reformed based on the American model of schools and universities. Japanese students began studying abroad, and foreign specialists were brought in to teach. In addition, Japan made changes to its military: An imperial army was formed in 1871, with new, modern weapons and compulsory military service, and every Japanese man was required to serve for three years.

JAPAN PRACTICES IMPERIALISM

Like the Europeans, the Japanese were determined to expand. They forced Korea to open its ports to Japanese trade. China was unhappy with Japan's growing influence, and in 1894

RUSSIA

MANCHURIA

SAKHALIN
ISLAND

SEA OF
JAPAN
(also called
EAST SEA)

KOREA

JAPAN

YELLOW
SEA

CHINA

PACIFIC OCEAN

TAIWAN

BOUNDARIES BEFORE THE
RUSSO-JAPANESE WAR, 1905

the two countries fought the FIRST SINO-JAPANESE WAR,
which Japan won. China handed over
TAIWAN and other lands to Japanese
control and was forced to recognize
Korea's independence as well.

"SINO" IS A PREFIX THAT
COMES FROM THE LATIN
WORD *SINAE*, WHICH
MEANS "CHINA."

Russia also wanted to extend its influence in Korea, but Japan saw Korea as a buffer between it and China and wanted to maintain its dominance there. This led to major tension between Russia and Japan, and resulted in another war.

The RUSSO-JAPANESE WAR started in 1904 with tiny Japan versus the Russians, who had proven themselves as a major power. The Japanese made a sneak attack on the Russian naval base at Port Arthur, Manchuria (in present-day northeast China). At the same time, the Japanese navy defeated the Russian fleet off the coast of Japan. With the signing of the TREATY OF PORTSMOUTH in 1905, Russia handed over control of Port Arthur and the

Russian rail system in Manchuria, giving Japan a foothold there. Japan also received part of the island of Sakhalin.

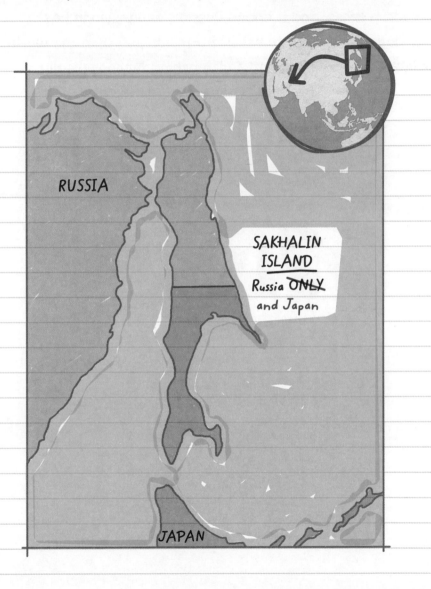

RUSSIA

SAKHALIN
ISLAND
Russia ~~ONLY~~
and Japan

JAPAN

The Japanese victory over Russia shocked the world. It was the first time an Asian nation had beaten a European power in modern times, and it ended Russia's expansion in East Asia. Japan had risen to become a major power in the world, while Russia and China had fallen behind technologically.

FLAG OF THE IMPERIAL JAPANESE NAVY

CHECK YOUR KNOWLEDGE

1. What was the Meiji Restoration? What reforms came about at this time?

2. What countries did Japan take control of and when?

3. Who was Matthew Perry?

4. What was the result of Perry's intervention?

5. Under which U.S. president did Matthew Perry's actions come about?
   A. Theodore Roosevelt   C. Millard Fillmore
   B. Woodrow Wilson   D. Herbert Hoover

6. The attack on Port Arthur began the war between which of the following nations?
   A. Japan and Korea   C. China and Japan
   B. China and Korea   D. Japan and Russia

7. What did the winner gain from the war in question 6?

ANSWERS 367

CHECK YOUR ANSWERS

1. The Meiji Restoration was a time when the Japanese built ships, railways, banking systems, coal mines, machinery, factories, and communication systems and updated the military. The Japanese also reformed the education system and modeled it after American schools and universities.

2. Japan took control of Taiwan and other lands from China after the First Sino-Japanese War in 1894. Japan later took control of parts of Manchuria and part of the island of Sakhalin in 1905.

3. Matthew Perry was an American naval officer sent in 1853 to get Japan to open its ports to trade with Americans.

4. Japan opened two ports for international trade.

5. C. Millard Fillmore

6. D. Japan and Russia

7. The winner of the Russo-Japanese War was Japan. Russia had to hand over control of Port Arthur, the Russian rail system in Manchuria, and part of the island of Sakhalin. Japan's victory also gave it a different reputation—it was now seen as a major power in the world.

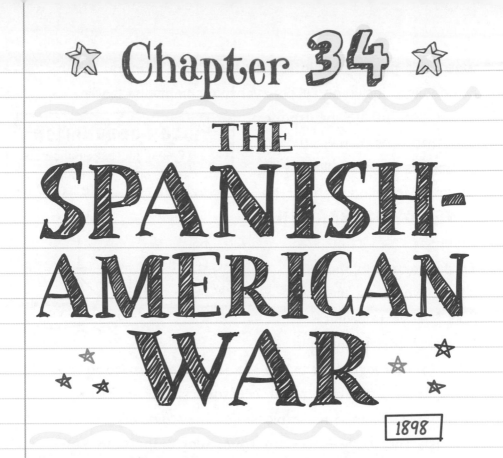

☆ Chapter 34 ☆

THE SPANISH-AMERICAN WAR

1898

The U.S. was also interested in imperial expansion. The SPANISH-AMERICAN WAR officially was fought for Cuban independence, but it allowed the U.S. to gain several new holdings.

REMEMBER the *MAINE*!

Like many other countries at the time, Cuba in the late 1800s was eager to be free from Spanish rule. In 1892, an exiled Cuban **DISSIDENT** named JOSÉ MARTÍ PÉREZ founded the Cuban Revolutionary Party to do just that, but he

> **DISSIDENT**
> one who dissents or disagrees

was killed three years later. He was a hero to many Cuban nationalists, including Cuba's eventual communist leader, FIDEL CASTRO. U.S. newspapers published sensationalized stories of Spain's mistreatment of Cubans, beginning the practice of **YELLOW JOURNALISM**.

> **YELLOW JOURNALISM**
> a type of journalism that relies on exaggeration

In January 1898, the U.S. sent a battleship, the USS MAINE, to protect American citizens living in

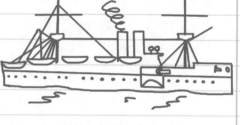

Cuba. On February 15, 1898, the Maine was mysteriously sunk in Havana Harbor, killing over 250 sailors. The American newspapers blamed the explosion of the Maine on the Spanish. This made Americans favor war with Spain. But later tests proved that the Maine likely blew up from a fire in the ammunitions cargo.

The U.S. DECLARES WAR

Assuming that Spain was to blame, the U.S. declared war on Spain in April 1898, even though PRESIDENT WILLIAM McKINLEY wanted to avoid war. Under the command of COMMODORE GEORGE DEWEY,

South China Sea

Manila

Pacific Ocean

Philippines

the U.S. naval forces headed to the Philippines, which were under Spanish rule. With the help of the locals, who also wanted freedom, the Americans defeated a Spanish fleet in Manila Bay.

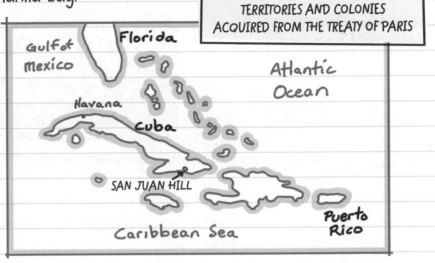

TERRITORIES AND COLONIES
ACQUIRED FROM THE TREATY OF PARIS

Gulf of Mexico

Florida

Atlantic Ocean

Havana

Cuba

SAN JUAN HILL

Caribbean Sea

Puerto Rico

Back in Cuba, a volunteer U.S. **CAVALRY** called the **ROUGH RIDERS** helped to defeat the Spanish in the BATTLE OF SAN

CAVALRY
soldiers who serve on horseback

JUAN HILL. Just four months after it began, fighting in the Spanish–American War ended in August 1898.

One of the **ROUGH RIDERS** was Theodore Roosevelt, the future president of the U.S. He was such a strong force in the cavalry that it eventually became known as "Roosevelt's Rough Riders."

The U.S. COMES OUT STRONG

With the signing of the TREATY OF PARIS (a different Treaty of Paris than the ones that ended the Seven Years' War and the Revolutionary War), Spain gave up control of Cuba, which became a PROTECTORATE of the U.S. The U.S. acquired Puerto Rico and Guam as territories, and the Philippines became an American colony. The Spanish

> **PROTECTORATE**
> a state or country that is protected by and partially controlled by a more powerful state or country

Empire was over in the Americas. Suddenly, the U.S. had a lot of new land. Colonizing the Philippines meant the U.S. was in a strong position for trade with China, keeping China out of Japan's hands and preventing Japanese imperialist expansion.

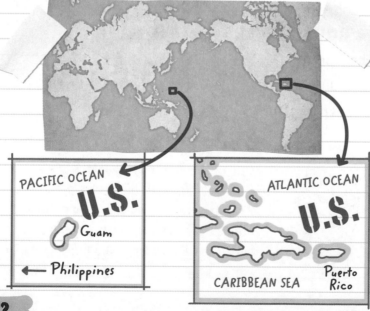

PACIFIC OCEAN

U.S.

Guam

← Philippines

ATLANTIC OCEAN

U.S.

CARIBBEAN SEA   Puerto Rico

Remember: The 1763 **TREATY OF PARIS** ended the Seven Years' War,
the 1783 **TREATY OF PARIS** ended the Revolutionary War,
and the 1898 **TREATY OF PARIS** ended the Spanish-American War.

America's desire for power and profit led to its becoming
the world's richest nation by the beginning of the twentieth
century. Less than 200 years after fighting for its own
independence, America, for better or for worse, was now
controlling its own empire.

CHECK YOUR KNOWLEDGE

1. The Spanish-American War was fought over the independence of:
   A. Guam
   B. Puerto Rico
   C. Cuba
   D. the Dominican Republic

2. Which U.S. commodore's forces defeated a Spanish fleet in 1898?

3. Which of the following did not come under American control following the Spanish-American War?
   A. Puerto Rico
   B. the Philippines
   C. Haiti
   D. Cuba

4. _____ became a protectorate of the U.S. at war's end; _____ became an American colony.
   A. Guam; Puerto Rico
   B. Cuba; Haiti
   C. the Philippines; Guam
   D. Cuba; the Philippines

5. The events in questions 1 through 4 occurred under the leadership of which U.S. president?

6. American forces came to Cuba's defense after the failure of rebellion led by ____ _____ _____.

7. Explain the relevance of America's victory over Spain in terms of trade.

ANSWERS 375

CHECK YOUR ANSWERS

1. C. Cuba
2. Commodore George Dewey
3. C. Haiti
4. D. Cuba; the Philippines
5. William McKinley
6. José Martí Pérez
7. America's victory over Spain meant that the Philippines became an American colony, so the U.S. was in a better position to trade with China. This new relationship also prevented the Japanese from expanding into China.

Chapter 35

REACTIONS

★ ★ ★ TO ★ ★ ★

COLONIZATION

LATE 19TH AND EARLY 20TH CENTURIES

Because who wants a stranger to take over their home and tell them how to live their life?

REBELLION in INDIA

In India, the SEPOY REBELLION, also called the INDIAN MUTINY, resulted from mistrust and cultural differences between the British and Indians. As the Mughal Empire declined in power, the British East India Company gained stronger control and hired Indian soldiers called SEPOYS.

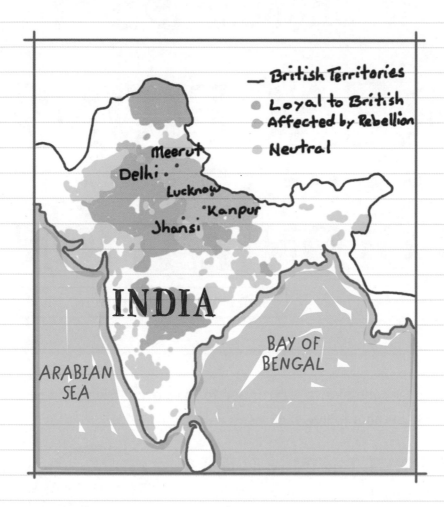

In 1857, a rumor spread in Meerut that the new rifle cartridges given to the sepoys, who followed either Hinduism or Islam, were greased with cow and pig fat. In order to load their rifles, sepoys had to bite off the end of the cartridge. The cow is considered sacred by Hindus, and the pig is taboo for Muslims. Many sepoys refused to load their rifles.

The British accused these sepoys of forming a **MUTINY** and put them in prison, and that in turn sparked a real mutiny. On April 25, 1857, the remaining sepoys freed their jailed comrades. Soon, the revolt spread to other cities in India, including Delhi,

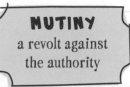

MUTINY
a revolt against
the authority

Kanpur, Lucknow, and Jhansi. But rivalries between Muslims and Hindus prevented the sepoys from waging strong battles, and some Indian troops stayed loyal to the British. The mutiny failed.

After the uprising, the British tightened their reins on India. The British government took control of India from the East India Company and established DIRECT RULE, sending officials to control certain parts of India. In other parts of the country, they set up the system of INDIRECT RULE, using local rulers to control colonies. In 1876, Queen Victoria became "Empress of India." India's people were now her colonial subjects, and India was the "jewel" in her crown. The British improved things like transportation and education in India, but they also prevented Indians from gaining political or military power in their own country.

REBELLION in CHINA

The BOXER REBELLION took place in China. The BOXERS, as Westerners referred to them, were members of a secret organization called the SOCIETY OF RIGHTEOUS AND HARMONIOUS FISTS. They practiced shadowboxing, a form of exercise where you box

> A CLEVER WAY TO DESCRIBE BOXING

with an imaginary opponent. The Boxers believed this exercise would protect them from bullets.

The Boxers weren't pleased with the recent foreign imperialist takeovers of Chinese lands. The U.S. now had a colony close to China (the Philippines) and wanted to expand trade.

The OPEN DOOR POLICY

In the second half of the 1800s, European nations and Japan convinced the weaker nation of China to grant them SPHERES OF INFLUENCE, or areas within China to control. Since the U.S. didn't have a sphere of influence there, in 1899, Secretary of State John Hay suggested an OPEN DOOR POLICY of equal access for multiple imperial powers, including the U.S., to trade with China. There wasn't any reason for the other nations to agree—until the Boxer Rebellion.

The Boxers wanted to destroy foreigners, such as Christian missionaries, who they believed threatened the Chinese way of life. Around 1900, Boxers began wandering the Chinese countryside, killing foreign missionaries, foreign businessmen, the German **ENVOY** to Beijing, and Chinese people who had converted to Christianity.

ENVOY
a diplomatic agent

Under the orders of WILHELM II, emperor of Germany, German troops entered China. William got help from Britain, France, Russia, the U.S., and Japan. The troops restored order and demanded an **INDEMNITY** from the Chinese government. The Boxer Rebellion turned out to be very costly for the Chinese.

> **INDEMNITY**
> payment for
> damages

REBELLION in AFRICA

The people of Africa also resented European domination of their people and land. Many Europeans exhibited **ETHNOCENTRIC** attitudes, believing that it

> **ETHNOCENTRICITY**
> when a group or person believes their
> culture is superior to all others

was their duty to God to colonize other countries, and that the indigenous people in the regions they took control of were meant to be under their rule.

In South Africa, the ZULU people successfully fought against Europeans. They resisted the Boers under their powerful leader SHAKA ZULU.

After Shaka's death in 1828, the Zulu people continued to remain strong under KING DINGANE, but in the ZULU WAR OF 1879, the British military defeated the Zulu, putting an end to Zulu independence.

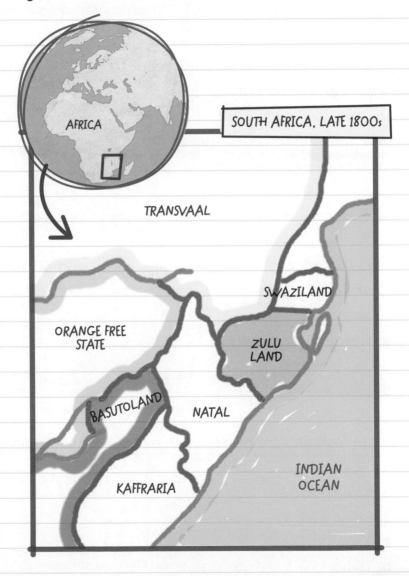

AFRICA

SOUTH AFRICA, LATE 1800s

TRANSVAAL

SWAZILAND

ORANGE FREE STATE

ZULU LAND

BASUTOLAND

NATAL

KAFFRARIA

INDIAN OCEAN

CHECK YOUR KNOWLEDGE

1. The British East India Company hired Indian soldiers called _____.

2. What event in particular caused the Indian soldiers to revolt against the British?

3. Explain the difference between direct and indirect rule in the case of Great Britain.

4. Who were the Boxers, and what did they stand for?

5. China had to pay _____ at the end of the Boxer Rebellion.
   A. an invoice
   B. foreign missionaries
   C. an indemnity
   D. an armistice

6. Queen Victoria considered which of the following colonies the "jewel" in her crown?
   A. New England
   B. South Africa
   C. Thailand
   D. India

7. The Zulu War of 1879 ended in _____.

  A. a partitioning of South Africa between the Boers and the Zulu

  B. Zulu independence from the Boers

  C. British control over the Zulu

  D. Boer independence from the Zulu

1. Sepoys

2. The revolt against the British started when some sepoys refused to load their rifles because of religious objections. When the British put these soldiers in prison, an all-out mutiny began, and the remaining sepoys freed the jailed soldiers.

3. The British government established direct rule by sending officials to control certain parts of India. In other parts of the country, they set up indirect rule, which used local leaders to control the people.

4. The Boxers were members of a secret organization that was against the foreign imperialist takeovers of Chinese lands.

5. C. an indemnity

6. D. India

7. C. British control over the Zulu

Unit 8

World Conflicts in the Early Twentieth Century: 1914–1945

The twentieth century was a period of major strife. Two world wars tore European nations apart, politically and economically. The U.S. also saw its fair share of troubles. The twentieth century was a violent one.

☆ Chapter 36 ☆

✶ WORLD WAR I ✶

WHAT THEY WERE FIGHTING ABOUT

The exact cause of World War I (WWI), initially called the Great War, is hard to pinpoint. Peace in Europe was so fragile that anything could have set off a conflict—it was a powder keg waiting for a spark from:

IMPERIALISM

➥ Especially in Africa

MILITARISM

➥ An arms race was happening.

NATIONALISM

➥ A reinvigorated sense of patriotism

➥ Countries wanted to prove their might

➥ Ethnic groups wanted to form their own nations

ALLIANCES

➥ THE TRIPLE ALLIANCE: Germany, Austria-Hungary, and Italy

➥ THE TRIPLE **ENTENTE**: Great Britain, France, and Russia

ENTENTE
an understanding or agreement

Remember the **MAIN** reasons for World War I using this mnemonic device:

MILITARISM
ALLIANCES
IMPERIALISM
NATIONALISM

The NATIONALISM overtaking Europe played a big part in the road to World War I. Each country was proud of its culture, especially newly independent countries like Greece, Romania, and Serbia, which are all in the BALKANS, a region of southeastern Europe. Bosnia wanted to break away from Austria-Hungary. The Irish in the British Empire, the Armenians in Turkey, and the Polish in the Russian Empire faced similar struggles.

The surge of IMPERIALISM throughout Europe and imperialist rivalries were also big factors. Countries fought for foreign colonies.

Increasing MILITARISM also made countries ready to do battle. Industrialization created new materials for warfare and resulted in an arms race. Many European countries were forging ALLIANCES—basically picking teams and promising to have each other's backs if things got rough. The two major European alliances in 1914 were:

389

the **TRIPLE ENTENTE:** Russia, Great Britain, and France

the **TRIPLE ALLIANCE:** Germany, Austria-Hungary, and Italy

When one country went to war, the others followed. (My team and all my team's friends versus your team and all your team's friends.)

The TRIGGER for WAR

The more immediate cause of World War I was the assassination of the ARCHDUKE FRANZ FERDINAND of Austria-Hungary and his wife, SOPHIE. On June 28, 1914, a Serbian nationalist named GAVRILO PRINCIP assassinated the heir to the Hapsburg throne and his wife in Sarajevo, Bosnia. The goal was to free Bosnia from Austria-Hungary and create a large Serbian kingdom with Russia's support. After receiving reassurance from Germany of its support, the Austro-Hungarian Empire declared war on Serbia on July 28, 1914.

MORE DECLARATIONS of WAR

With Austria-Hungary's declaration of war, Russia began to **MOBILIZE** its army, which was considered an act of war in itself. Germany then declared war on Russia and began forming its SCHLIEFFEN PLAN, which called for a two-**FRONT** war against Russia and France. To attack France, Germany needed to get through Belgium, which until then was neutral, so the Germans issued an **ULTIMATUM** demanding they be allowed to pass through Belgian territory. This demand outraged the British, who declared war on Germany the next day. The "Great War"—World War I—had begun.

> **MOBILIZATION**
> the process of assembling troops and supplies
>
> **FRONT**
> the battle line or place of conflict in a war
>
> **ULTIMATUM**
> a final command or statement of conditions

ALLIANCE RECAP

PEOPLE DEFENDED THEIR ALLIES.

Germany, an Austro-Hungarian ally, declared war on Russia, which supported Serbia.

Germany also declared war on France, a Russian ally.

When Germany invaded Belgium, a neutral country between Germany and France, Britain, an ally of France and Belgium, declared war on Germany.

By early August 1914, a full-scale war had developed in Europe. The two sides were:

The CENTRAL POWERS	The ALLIED POWERS, or the ALLIES
Austria-Hungary ⎫ PART OF	Serbia
⎬ THE TRIPLE	Russia ⎫ PART OF
Germany ⎭ ALLIANCE	France ⎬ THE TRIPLE
The Ottoman Empire	Britain ⎭ ENTENTE
Bulgaria	
	Later, Japan and Italy

AMERICAN NEUTRALITY
President **WOODROW WILSON** was determined to follow George Washington's advice to steer clear of foreign conflicts. America planned to continue trading with both the Allies and the Central Powers.

ATLANTIC
OCEAN

NORTH
SEA

NORWAY

SWEDEN

BALTIC SEA

DENMARK

GREAT BRITAIN

NETH.

BELG.

GERMANY

RUSSIA

**EUROPE
1914**

LUX.

FRANCE

SWITZ.

AUSTRIA-
HUNGARY

ITALY

ROMANIA

BLACK SEA

SERBIA

BULGARIA

PORTUGAL

SPAIN

OTTOMAN
EMPIRE

GREECE

MEDITERRANEAN SEA

The FIGHTING BEGINS

The FIRST BATTLE OF THE MARNE (September 6–12, 1914)
was the first battle of World War I and was a victory
for the Allied Powers. The French and British stopped
the Germans near the Marne River, before the Germans
were able to take Paris. Both armies used a new kind of
warfare called TRENCH WARFARE, in which the combatants'
fighting lines consisted of trenches that would shield
them from gunshots.

TRENCH WARFARE

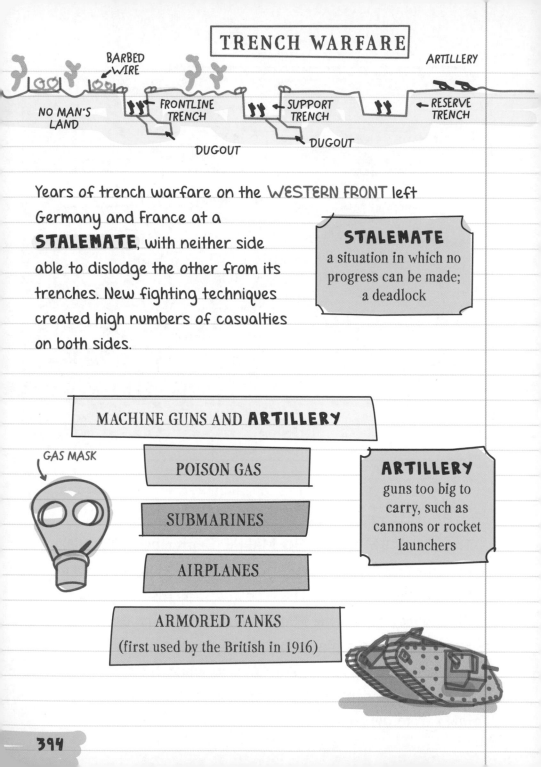

BARBED WIRE

ARTILLERY

NO MAN'S LAND

FRONTLINE TRENCH

SUPPORT TRENCH

RESERVE TRENCH

DUGOUT

DUGOUT

Years of trench warfare on the WESTERN FRONT left Germany and France at a **STALEMATE**, with neither side able to dislodge the other from its trenches. New fighting techniques created high numbers of casualties on both sides.

> **STALEMATE**
> a situation in which no progress can be made; a deadlock

MACHINE GUNS AND **ARTILLERY**

GAS MASK

POISON GAS

SUBMARINES

AIRPLANES

> **ARTILLERY**
> guns too big to carry, such as cannons or rocket launchers

ARMORED TANKS
(first used by the British in 1916)

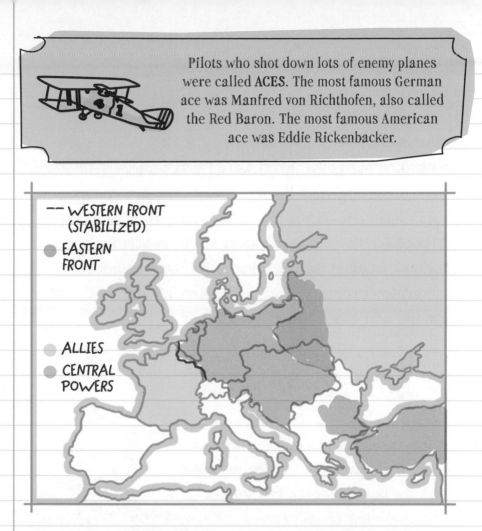

Pilots who shot down lots of enemy planes were called **ACES**. The most famous German ace was Manfred von Richthofen, also called the Red Baron. The most famous American ace was Eddie Rickenbacker.

-- WESTERN FRONT (STABILIZED)

● EASTERN FRONT

● ALLIES

● CENTRAL POWERS

On the EASTERN FRONT, the Russians were defeated by the Germans about a month into the war, but fared better against the Austro-Hungarians. Although Italy had pledged support to Germany and Austria-Hungary, the Italians stayed out of the beginning of World War I. After the Germans began using submarine warfare, Italy joined on the side of the Allied Powers (or the Allies) in May 1915.

On May 7, 1915, when a German submarine destroyed the British ship *Lusitania* and over 100 Americans (and 1,000 other passengers) were killed, anti-German sentiment sprang up in the U.S. In 1917, the discovery of the ZIMMERMAN TELEGRAM—a proposal from Germany to Mexico for the two countries to form an alliance and wage war against the U.S. (Mexico turned it down)—angered Americans. On April 2, 1917, the U.S. declared war on Germany and joined World War I.

The RUSSIAN REVOLUTION and the CLOSING of the EASTERN FRONT

The U.S. actually entered the war at the perfect time: Russia had recently bowed out of combat. In March 1917, Russia's terrible wartime conditions led to strikes and demonstrations in its capital (then called Petrograd and now called St. Petersburg). Czar Nicholas II **ABDICATED**, and his army—composed mostly of peasants—joined the side of the protestors. The czar and his whole family were later executed.

CZAR NICHOLAS II

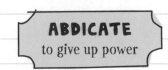

ABDICATE
to give up power

396

In October 1917, a violent revolutionary group called the BOLSHEVIKS, led by VLADIMIR LENIN, seized power and demanded a government by and for the workers and peasants. Lenin established the first COMMUNIST government in the world, based on the ideas in Karl Marx's *Communist Manifesto*. Many uppper-class citizens opposed this new communist government. The communist government replaced 300 years of czarist rule by the Romanov family. Russians needed to concentrate on the revolution happening on the home front, so Russia signed the TREATY OF BREST-LITOVSK, which ceded much of its territory to the Central Powers. This closed fighting on the eastern front, and Germany was now confident that it would win the war.

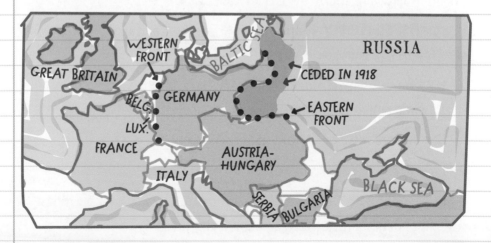

The FOURTEEN POINTS

On January 8, 1918, well before the war ended, President Wilson justified why the U.S. had gone to war and gave a set of goals. He also informed Congress that this was "the war to end all wars" and had made a plan to prevent another major war. The plan became known as the FOURTEEN POINTS, which stipulated:

1. No secret treaties/alliances

2. Freedom of navigation on the seas

3. Equality of trade

4. Smaller militaries

5. An adjustment of colonial claims

6. The evacuation and restoration of Russian territory

7. The evacuation and restoration of Belgian territory

8. The evacuation and restoration of French territory

9. A readjustment of Italian borders

10. **AUTONOMY** for the people of the former Austro-Hungarian Empire

11. The evacuation and restoration of Balkan Peninsula (Romania, Serbia, and Montenegro)

12. Autonomy for Ottoman territory

13. The establishment of an independent Poland

14. A LEAGUE OF NATIONS—an organization of countries working together to resolve disputes

AUTONOMY
self-government

OVER THERE

The arrival of American soldiers and materials stopped the Germans from advancing in the SECOND BATTLE OF THE MARNE. The MEUSE-ARGONNE OFFENSIVE, fought from September through November 1918, marked the final phase of World War I.

On November 11, 1918, following Austria-Hungary's exit from the war, the Germans agreed to sign an **ARMISTICE**.

ARMISTICE
a temporary end to hostilities between warring parties; a cease-fire agreement

The COST of WAR

The war had ravaged Europe and devastated an entire generation of European men. Historians' best guess is that 37 million were killed or wounded in four years of fighting. With no working farms or factories, the European economy was devastated as well. In 1918, a flu **PANDEMIC** called SPANISH FLU broke out. It was an extremely contagious strain of influenza that spread around the globe, killing more people than had died during the war. The world was ready for peace.

PANDEMIC
an epidemic, or widespread disease, that affects an entire country or continent, or even the entire world

3%–5% OF THE ENTIRE WORLD'S POPULATION

PEACE

In 1918, both Kaiser Wilhelm II of Germany and Emperor Karl of Austria stepped down from their thrones. And in 1919, Germany signed the TREATY OF VERSAILLES, which forced Germany to accept sole responsibility for the war, give up its foreign colonies and return Alsace-Lorraine to France, and pay heavy **REPARATIONS** to other countries. Germany was also forced to reduce the size of

REPARATIONS
compensation, usually in the form of money, to someone who has been wronged

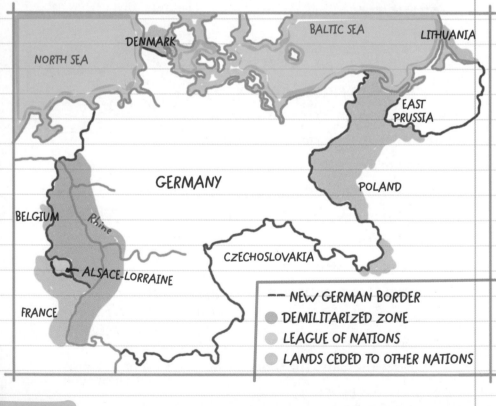

LEGEND:
- -- NEW GERMAN BORDER
- ● DEMILITARIZED ZONE
- ● LEAGUE OF NATIONS
- ● LANDS CEDED TO OTHER NATIONS

its army and navy and eliminate its air force. An area of German land along the RHINE RIVER was turned over to occupation by the Allies and declared **DEMILITARIZED** in order to prevent German aggression against France. The Germans were humiliated by the terms of the treaty but had no choice but to accept them.

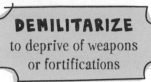

DEMILITARIZE
to deprive of weapons
or fortifications

The Treaty of Versailles also created an international organization called the League of Nations.

LIKE AN EARLY
FORM OF THE UN

It was proposed by U.S. president Woodrow Wilson in the hope of preventing future wars, promoting democracy, and keeping the peace, but it was also opposed by Congress, so the U.S. never joined. The league turned out to be mostly ineffective anyway. Starvation, poverty, and unemployment plagued Europe and set the stage for a second world war.

June 28, 1914:
Archduke Franz Ferdinand
of Austria-Hungary
and his wife Sophie are
assassinated in Bosnia
by Gavrilo Princip,
a Serbian
nationalist.

August 1914:
Through a complicated
web of alliances,
World War I begins.

July 28, 1914:
Austria-Hungary declares
War on Serbia in reaction
to the archduke's
assassination.

September 1914:
The German invasion of
France is stopped at the
First Battle of the Marne.

WAR I

October 1914:
The Triple Entente uses trench warfare to hold off the Germans in the First Battle of Ypres.

May 7, 1915:
The *Lusitania*, a British passenger ship, is torpedoed by a German U-boat (submarine). Over 1,000 people die.

April–May 1915:
During the Second Battle of Ypres, German forces successfully use poison gas on Allied troops. The death toll forces the Allied armies to withdraw.

WORLD

June–November 1916:

The Battle of the Somme claims the lives of more than 400,000 British soldiers, around 200,000 French soldiers, and anywhere from 460,000 to 650,000 German soldiers. The British are able to advance only six miles.

October 1917:

The Bolsheviks in Russia successfully take over the Russian government and withdraw from the war.

April 1917:

The U.S. declares war on Germany in reaction to Germany's declaration to use unrestricted U-boat attacks again.

November 1918:

Hungary declares independence from Austria and the Czechs take Prague to form Czechoslovakia.

WAR I

November 1918:
Both Kaiser Wilhelm II of Germany and Emperor Karl of Austria abdicate their thrones.

February 1919:
A proposed constitution for the League of Nations is announced.

November 11, 1918:
Germany signs an armistice agreement.

June 28, 1919:
Germany and the Allies sign the Treaty of Versailles. World War I on the western front is officially over.

CHECK YOUR KNOWLEDGE

1. Name the countries that belonged to the Triple Alliance and the Triple Entente.

2. Name the two major European alliances of World War I that had formed by August 1914 and the countries belonging to each side.

3. Archduke Franz Ferdinand was assassinated on:
   A. August 6, 1918
   B. June 28, 1914
   C. September 10, 1914
   D. November 11, 1918

4. The German invasion of which neutral nation spurred the British to declare war?
   A. Luxembourg
   B. the Czech Republic
   C. Belgium
   D. France

5. Italian involvement in World War I came as the result of:

    A. Japan's bombing of America

    B. Germany's submarine warfare

    C. Russia's withdrawal from World War I

    D. trench warfare between Germany and France

6. Russia pulled itself out of World War I in order to confront the _____ on its home front.

    A. Treaty of Brest-Litovsk

    B. revolution

    C. fall of communism

    D. Cold War

7. Who was the last czar of Russia and who replaced him with a communist government?

8. What was the Treaty of Versailles?

9. Who came up with the idea of the League of Nations, and what were its core goals?

ANSWERS ➤

CHECK YOUR ANSWERS

1. The Triple Alliance included Germany, Austria-Hungary, and Italy. The Triple Entente included Russia, Britain, and France.

2. The Central Powers included Austria-Hungary, Germany, the Ottoman Empire, and Bulgaria. The Allied Powers (the Allies) included Serbia, Russia, France, Britain, and later, Japan and Italy.

3. B. June 28, 1914

4. C. Belgium

5. B. Germany's submarine warfare

6. B. revolution

7. Nicholas II, Lenin

8. The Treaty of Versailles was a treaty that was signed in 1919 that forced Germany to accept full responsibility for the war, reduce its military, give up its foreign colonies, return Alsace-Lorraine to France, turn over land along the Rhine River to the Allies so it could be made into a demilitarized area, and pay a large compensation to other countries in the war.

9. U.S. president Woodrow Wilson came up with the idea for the League of Nations. Its goals were to prevent wars, promote democracy, and keep the peace.

☆ Chapter 37 ☆

The GREAT

✷ ✷ ✷ ✷ ✷ ✷ ✷ ✷ ✷ ✷ ✷ ✷

DEPRESSION

The war had left the countries involved pretty broke. By the late 1920s, the world economy had slowed down. Wages were down, sales were down, and the market for farm goods wasn't doing well.

CAUSES of the GREAT DEPRESSION in the U.S.

Britain and France had a huge debt to pay to the U.S. They wanted Germany to pay the U.S. through the reparations Germany owed Britain and France. However, Germany was out of cash too and could only pay reparations by borrowing money from the U.S. to give to Britain and France to give to the U.S. This cycle of borrowing and lending was a problem.

World War I left the U.S. in much better shape than it did Europe. The government had needed war supplies, and this created jobs. During the 1920s, Americans started investing in the stock market. They began making purchases on credit. However, the export market was down because Europeans didn't have money for American goods. When Europeans had trouble paying their debt, American banks crumbled. On October 29, 1929, the American stock market crashed, and severe unemployment followed. This economic crisis was the GREAT DEPRESSION.

BANK RUN

Many Americans ran to get money out of their banks when the stock market crashed. The banks told them sorry, but they didn't have the money! President Franklin Roosevelt made laws to ensure protection of citizens' money in banks after that.

ROOSEVELT'S NEW DEAL

Within the first hundred days of his presidency in 1933, U.S. PRESIDENT FRANKLIN D. ROOSEVELT (FDR) created a program called the NEW DEAL to combat the economic downturn, including:

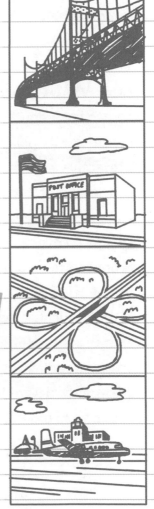

the **Federal Emergency Relief Administration (FERA):** helped the unemployed

the **Agricultural Adjustment Administration (AAA):** raised food prices to help farmers

the **Public Works Administration (PWA):** sponsored public works projects and created new jobs (building bridges, post offices, airports, and roads)

In 1935, a second New Deal established a public works program known as the WORKS PROGRESS ADMINISTRATION (WPA), which replaced FERA and created over three million jobs.

WE'RE HIRING!

The Second New Deal also created unemployment insurance and social security. FDR also improved the banking system and expanded rights for labor unions. Impressive—but three years later nearly eleven million Americans remained unemployed.

DEPRESSION AROUND the WORLD

To get back on its feet, Great Britain used traditionally conservative policies of balancing budgets and imposing protective tariffs. They also used ECONOMIC RETRENCHMENT policies, which basically meant they cut down on unnecessary expenses. Other European countries were less fortunate in facing recovery. Desperate countries turned to leaders who promised to help but who became **DESPOTS**. In Germany, ADOLF HITLER came to power as leader of the National Socialist German Workers' Party, or the NAZIS. Hitler called for a

DESPOT
a dictator

crusade against communists and Jews, whom he blamed for Germany's defeat in World War I. The Germans knew that one way to get out of debt was to attack the countries they owed money to. World War II was soon to come.

CHECK YOUR KNOWLEDGE

1. What was the major factor contributing to the decline of the world economy?

2. What happened to American banks when European countries were unable to pay off their debts?

3. What program did FDR create to combat the Great Depression?
   A. the New Deal
   B. the Open Door Policy
   C. the Works Progress Administration
   D. the League of Nations

4. Explain the details of this program.

5. How did Great Britain attempt to combat the Great Depression?

6. What major historical figure came to power in Germany during this time of economic crisis?

7. What groups of people did this figure blame for Germany's many social and economic problems during this time?

ANSWERS   413

CHECK YOUR ANSWERS

1. The major factor that harmed the world economy was World War I, because the countries that had been involved were broke by the time it ended. Overall, wages went down, sales went down, and the agricultural market went down.

2. When Europeans had trouble paying their debt, American banks fell apart, and the stock market crashed on October 29, 1929.

3. A. the New Deal

4. The New Deal set up agencies to help people through the financial crisis, such as the Federal Emergency Relief Administration (FERA) to help the unemployed, the Agricultural Adjustment Administration (AAA) to raise food prices to help farmers, and the Public Works Administration (PWA) to sponsor public works projects and create new jobs.

5. Great Britain tried to combat the Great Depression by using economic retrenchment policies, which cut down unnecessary spending and expenses. They also balanced budgets and imposed protective tariffs.

6. Adolf Hitler came to power as the leader of the National Socialist German Workers' Party (the Nazis).

7. Hitler blamed Jews and communists for Germany's problems.

☆ Chapter 38 ☆
POLITICAL SHIFTS AFTER the WAR

After World War I, some countries changed their form of leadership to **TOTALITARIANISM**. In totalitarian states, the government controls every part of a citizen's life: political, social, economic, intellectual, and cultural. They often use mass **PROPAGANDA** techniques to take over their people.

> **TOTALITARIANISM**
> a system in which the government acts as absolute ruler with complete control over every element of life

> **PROPAGANDA**
> the deliberate spreading of information, ideas, or rumors, whether true or false, to help or harm a person, institution, or cause

TOTALITARIANISM RISES in RUSSIA

In 1922, Russia (called the Russian Soviet Federative Socialist Republic after the Russian Revolution of 1917) merged with the three other Soviet republics to form a new state called the UNION OF SOVIET SOCIALIST REPUBLICS or the USSR, also known as the SOVIET UNION. Vladimir Lenin, the USSR's first leader, called for a program that he called the NEW ECONOMIC POLICY (NEP), under which peasants could sell their produce in order to end the Russian famine. Meanwhile, heavy industry, banking, and mines were in the hands of the government.

After Lenin's death in 1924, the POLITBURO, the main policy-making body of the USSR's Communist Party, had trouble deciding which way to go. LEON TROTSKY, a member of the Politboro who had helped Lenin lead the Russian Revolution, wanted to end the NEP, industrialize Russia, and spread communism abroad.

STALIN RISES to POWER

Trotsky's plans didn't really work out, and another member of the Politburo named JOSEPH STALIN started to take control. Stalin appointed his friends to political jobs in cities and towns all over the Soviet Union. In 1928, they exiled Trotsky to Siberia.

JOSEPH STALIN

416

Stalin replaced the NEP with his FIVE-YEAR PLAN to transform the USSR from an agricultural country to an industrial country, and fast. He quadrupled the production of heavy machinery and doubled oil production. He maximized production of military equipment. Rapid industrialization was matched by rapid **COLLECTIVIZATION** of agriculture.

Now the land and farming were controlled by the government. But workers were not taken care of and peasants were unhappy. Wages were low and living conditions were terrible. Stalin told the peasants that their sacrifice was for the good of the new **SOCIALIST** state.

> **COLLECTIVIZATION**
> a system that eliminates private farms and puts land in the hands of the government
>
> **SOCIALISM**
> a form of government in which property and industry are collectively owned by the society and controlled by the state

He **EXTERMINATED** anyone who resisted him or banished them to cruel forced labor camps in Siberia. Eight million army officers, intellectuals, citizens, and diplomats were eliminated in this way.

> **EXTERMINATE**
> to put to death

RUSSIA

RUSSIAN SIBERIA

ARCTIC OCEAN

NORWEGIAN SEA

NORTH
SEA

BARENTS
SEA

KARA SEA

BALTIC SEA

4
3 2 1

5

MOSCOW
*

RUSSIAN SOVIET FEDERATIVE

7   6

BLACK SEA

8

9
10

CASPIAN SEA

ARAL
SEA

11

12   13

15

14

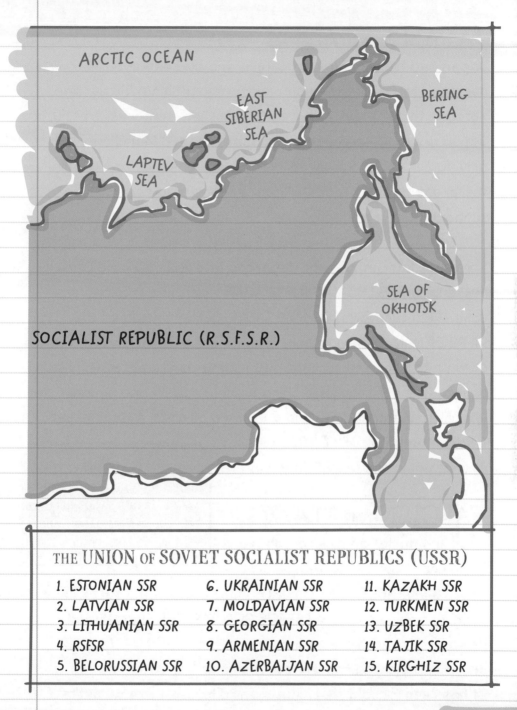

ARCTIC OCEAN

EAST SIBERIAN SEA

BERING SEA

LAPTEV SEA

SEA OF OKHOTSK

SOCIALIST REPUBLIC (R.S.F.S.R.)

THE UNION OF SOVIET SOCIALIST REPUBLICS (USSR)

1. ESTONIAN SSR
2. LATVIAN SSR
3. LITHUANIAN SSR
4. RSFSR
5. BELORUSSIAN SSR

6. UKRAINIAN SSR
7. MOLDAVIAN SSR
8. GEORGIAN SSR
9. ARMENIAN SSR
10. AZERBAIJAN SSR

11. KAZAKH SSR
12. TURKMEN SSR
13. UZBEK SSR
14. TAJIK SSR
15. KIRGHIZ SSR

JAPAN EXPANDS

Japan had become a major power and had expanded its overseas territories through wars against China, Russia, and Korea in the nineteenth and early twentieth centuries. In 1910, Japan annexed Korea. In 1931, Japan invaded Manchuria, driving out locals in order to increase the Japanese population there. Japan also needed oil (which Manchuria had) to support its new military.

Six years later, in 1937, the Japanese invaded mainland China in the second SINO-JAPANESE WAR. Japanese soldiers committed the NANJING MASSACRE, better known as the RAPE OF NANJING, massacring hundreds of thousands of Chinese soldiers and civilians and raping thousands of Chinese women. The U.S. supported China against Japan, and Japan joined Germany and Italy in a military alliance. A totalitarian leader named HIDEKI TŌJŌ was elected prime minister of Japan in 1941.

> **FASCISM**
> a form of totalitarianism with a dictator who puts the state above the people and forbids disagreement

FASCISM in ITALY

Another totalitarian dictator who rose to power after World War I was BENITO MUSSOLINI of Italy. In 1919, he founded a **FASCIST** political group called the LEAGUE OF COMBAT. Italy resented its failure to receive more land under the Treaty of Versailles, and it experienced tremendous economic loss after the war. It has been thought that since many Italians were afraid of

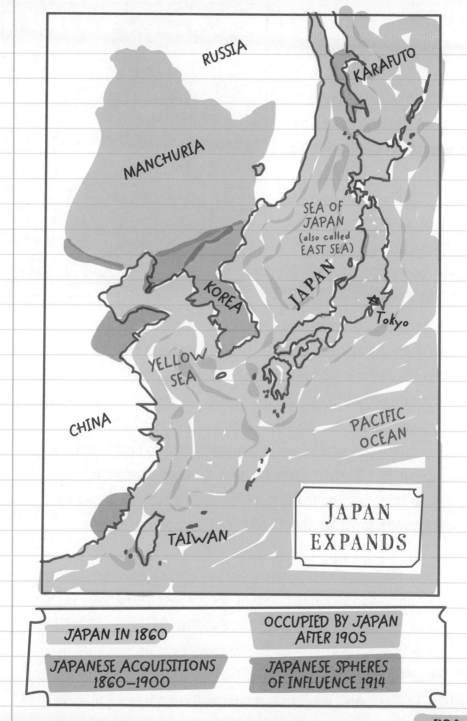

RUSSIA

KARAFUTO

MANCHURIA

SEA OF
JAPAN
(also called
EAST SEA)

JAPAN

KOREA

Tokyo

YELLOW
SEA

CHINA

PACIFIC
OCEAN

TAIWAN

JAPAN
EXPANDS

JAPAN IN 1860

OCCUPIED BY JAPAN
AFTER 1905

JAPANESE ACQUISITIONS
1860–1900

JAPANESE SPHERES
OF INFLUENCE 1914

socialism and communism, they followed the Fascist Party. Mussolini amped up Italian nationalism to get the support of the people.

In 1922, Mussolini and his group of 40,000 fascists marched on Rome. King Emmanuel III was forced to make Mussolini prime minister. Mussolini then created a dictatorship. He tried to control newspapers, radio, and film. Mussolini held the power to make laws by DECREE (just by saying it was so). He organized youth groups to spread his military and fascist values and outlawed all other political parties in 1926. He created his own secret police (called OVRA) to fight against conspiracies. (Dictators are paranoid about conspiracies against them, as they should be, since they're generally so awful that people do form conspiracies against them.)

By 1925, Mussolini had become *IL DUCE*, "The Leader" of Italy; his propaganda declared simply, "Mussolini Is Always Right." By 1936, his official title was "His Excellency Benito Mussolini, Head of Government, Duce of Fascism, and Founder of the Empire." Mussolini was definitely a powerful fascist, but Adolf Hitler in Germany would soon become even more powerful.

TOTALITARIAN EXPANSIONISM RECAP and LOOK AHEAD

Each totalitarian leader believed that his country was superior to all others and had the right to conquer.

In 1910, Japan annexes Korea.

In 1922, the USSR is formed.

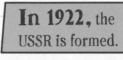
JAPAN NEEDED COLONIES WITH THEIR NATURAL RESOURCES TO EXPAND.

In 1931, Japan invades **Manchuria**; in 1937, Japan invades China, where it perpetrates the Nanjing Massacre.

In 1935, Italy conquers **Ethiopia** and leaves the League of Nations. In 1939, Italy conquers **Albania**.

In 1936, Germany annexes the **RHINELAND**, a coal-rich area that the Treaty of Versailles had declared a neutral **BUFFER ZONE**. In 1938, Germany conquers Austria.

BUFFER ZONE
an area that has the purpose of keeping two or more other areas distant from one another

GERMANY
1936
1938
Austria
Rhineland
1939
Albania
ITALY

Manchuria
1931
1937
China
JAPAN

1935
Ethiopia

CHECK YOUR KNOWLEDGE

1. What political system took hold in many countries following World War I?
   A. absolutism
   B. communism
   C. anarchism
   D. totalitarianism

2. How did these governments influence their citizens? Give an example.

3. What leaders created the Union of Soviet Socialist Republics (USSR), and when?

4. Which of the following leaders sought to end the NEP, industrialize Russia, and spread communism abroad after Lenin's death?
   A. Trotsky
   B. Stalin
   C. Politburo
   D. Mussolini

5. True or false? By 1929, Joseph Stalin had taken over the Communist Party and begun his campaign to transform Russia into an industrial society.

6. The NEP was abandoned in favor of a plan calling for rapid industrialization and rapid collectivization of agriculture. Name this plan.

7. Fascism took hold in Italy under which of the following leaders?
   A. Leon Trotsky
   B. Benito Mussolini
   C. King Emmanuel III
   D. Adolf Hitler

ANSWERS ⟶ 425

CHECK YOUR ANSWERS

1. D. totalitarianism
2. Totalitarian governments controlled all parts of their citizens' lives. For example, Mussolini controlled newspapers, radio, and film and spread only the information, ideas, and rumors he wanted people to know.
3. Vladimir Lenin and Leon Trotsky led the Russian Revolution that led to the USSR in 1922.
4. A. Trotsky
5. True
6. Stalin's plan for rapid industrialization and collectivization was called the Five-Year Plan.
7. B. Benito Mussolini

#2 has more than one correct answer.

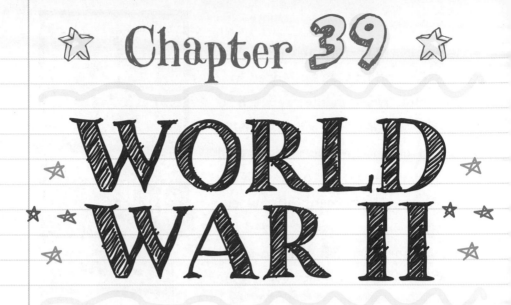

Chapter 39

WORLD WAR II

World War II started only twenty years after World War I ended, when a humiliated Germany sought to boost its image and place the blame for its situation on the Jews and communists. The Germans resented the terms of the Treaty of Versailles from World War I, so they stopped paying reparations and withdrew from the League of Nations. Extremist parties like the Nazis began to rise to power.

HITLER COMES to POWER in GERMANY

Adolf Hitler joined the German Workers' Party in 1919 after fighting in World War I. By 1921, he was in control of the party, which had been renamed the Nazi Party. In 1923, he led an armed uprising called the BEER HALL PUTSCH against the government in Munich.

Hitler's earliest uprising wasn't successful, and he was sentenced to a brief stay in prison, during which he wrote *MEIN KAMPF*, or *MY STRUGGLE*. This book outlined the basic ideas of the anti-Semitic (prejudiced against Jews), anticommunist movement Hitler would soon lead. His theory emphasized the "right" of so-called **ARYAN** nations to *LEBENSRAUM* (German for "living space").

ARYAN
a non-Jewish Caucasian

Instead of an armed uprising, this time Hitler used politics, expanding the Nazi Party until it was the largest in the German REICHSTAG (parliament). Hitler promised the people a new Germany with nationalistic and militaristic pride. Germany faced high unemployment and economic difficulties and people needed hope from any source, and the Nazi Party quickly gained power. In 1933, Germany's president, Paul von Hindenburg, declared Hitler CHANCELLOR and agreed to the creation of a new government under his lead. Hindenburg signed the ENABLING ACT of 1933, which granted Hitler the power to enact laws without the Reichstag. The Nazis dissolved other political parties and became a totalitarian ruling party. Hitler was a good speaker and used propaganda to influence the German people. In 1934, Hitler named himself **FÜHRER** and took control.

FÜHRER
German for "leader"

The THIRD REICH

Under Hitler's rule, the Nazi Party aimed to dominate Europe by creating the THIRD REICH, the "third great empire" (the first two being the Holy Roman Empire and the German Empire of 1871–1918). The Nazis set up CONCENTRATION CAMPS for Jews, communists (and other political opponents), homosexuals, Roma and a variety of ethnic groups that Nazis considered inferior (including Poles, Ukrainians, Slavs, and Serbs), and people with mental and physical disabilities. They stripped Jews of their German citizenship under the NUREMBERG LAWS of 1935. Hitler violated the Treaty of Versailles with a military draft to expand Germany's army. He made plans to create a new air force.

CONCENTRATION CAMP IDENTIFICATION BADGES

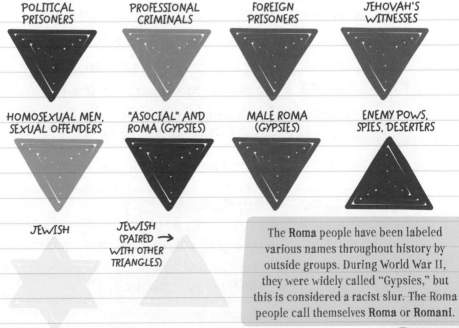

POLITICAL PRISONERS

PROFESSIONAL CRIMINALS

FOREIGN PRISONERS

JEHOVAH'S WITNESSES

HOMOSEXUAL MEN, SEXUAL OFFENDERS

"ASOCIAL" AND ROMA (GYPSIES)

MALE ROMA (GYPSIES)

ENEMY POWS, SPIES, DESERTERS

JEWISH

JEWISH (PAIRED → WITH OTHER TRIANGLES)

The **Roma** people have been labeled various names throughout history by outside groups. During World War II, they were widely called "Gypsies," but this is considered a racist slur. The Roma people call themselves **Roma** or **Romani**.

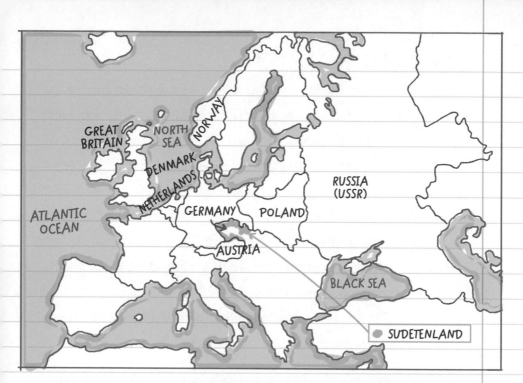

In 1936, Hitler sent troops into the Rhineland, the area of Germany that was meant to be a neutral neighbor to France. France was ready to take up arms but wouldn't without support from Great Britain, which took up a policy of **APPEASEMENT** and refused to support the use of force against Germany. Britain believed that even though Germany violated the Treaty of Versailles, it was not being unreasonable in occupying its own territory. But Hitler's

APPEASEMENT

to bring to a state of peace. In Britain at this time, appeasement was a belief that if European states satisfied the reasonable demands of dissatisfied powers, the dissatisfied powers would be content, and that would lead to stability and peace.

plans went far beyond simply occupying the Rhineland. The road to World War II was well under way.

The AXIS

With their similar philosophies, some dictators formed alliances. In 1936, Hitler and Mussolini formed the Rome-Berlin Axis, aka the AXIS. Japan joined in 1940. Russia didn't join the Axis, but signed a NONAGGRESSION PACT with Germany in which they agreed not to attack each other.

WORLD WAR II BEGINS

In 1938, Hitler declared the unification of Germany and Austria. Later that year he took over the SUDETENLAND, a part of Czechoslovakia. A year later, on September 1, 1939, Hitler invaded Poland. The USSR also attacked Poland and then moved on to the Baltic Peninsula and Finland. Britain and France finally saw Hitler as a threat and declared war two days later.

Germany had taken over Denmark and Norway by 1940. The Germans easily invaded Luxembourg, Belgium, and the Netherlands. They fought in North Africa and Italy. Even France was overtaken, and Paris was captured by the Nazis.

But a harsh Russian winter changed everything. Ignoring the nonaggression treaty they'd created with the Soviets, the Germans entered Russian territory in 1941, only to be

defeated by near-freezing temperatures during the Russian winter two years later. In the first major defeat for Germany, 91,000 German troops surrendered at the BATTLE OF STALINGRAD (1942–1943).

The BATTLE of BRITAIN

In the summer of 1940, Hitler began his air attack on England. During the BATTLE OF BRITAIN, the *LUFTWAFFE* (Germany's air force) heavily bombed London and other parts of England. England, and BRITISH PRIME MINISTER WINSTON CHURCHILL, refused to surrender. The ROYAL AIR FORCE (RAF) attacked the *Luftwaffe* until the Germans retreated.

MEANS "AIR WEAPON"

A lot of children were evacuated from London during the bombings. This event even appears in the Chronicles of Narnia books: The main characters are sent away to live in the English countryside.

Hitler's bombing of England left many thinking that all of Europe would fall to Germany. However, Winston Churchill wouldn't give up until he stopped Hitler. Surprisingly, Hitler made the same mistake that Napoleon did. He invaded the Soviet Union only to have his troops freeze.

The HOLOCAUST

Meanwhile, the policies of Nazi Germany led to the systematic killing of six million Jews and about five million Roma, female and male homosexuals, people with disabilities, political opponents, and anyone else who opposed the Nazis, in what is known as the HOLOCAUST. Jews and others were rounded up in every region Hitler conquered and thrown into concentration camps. There were six death camps in Poland; the largest was AUSCHWITZ. Some of those sent to Auschwitz went to labor camps, where they were worked or starved to death; others were used as subjects of ghastly medical experiments. The rest were killed immediately in the GAS CHAMBERS. People who tried to hide Jews or help them escape to safe countries were also put to death if they were caught.

PEARL HARBOR

Following successful invasions in mainland Asia, Japan decided to add island territory, including the Philippines, which were protected by the U.S. After Japan attacked Indochina, the U.S. stopped selling supplies to Japan and froze any Japanese money that was in U.S. banks. On DECEMBER 7, 1941—the day that President Roosevelt famously called "A DATE WHICH WILL LIVE IN INFAMY"— Japan launched a surprise attack on the naval base at

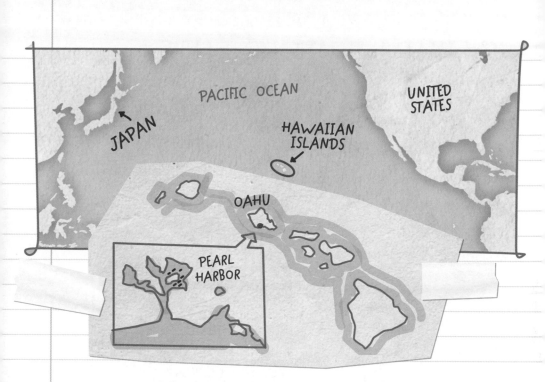

PEARL HARBOR, Hawaii. After such an attack on American soil, U.S. isolationism was done for. The next day, FDR asked Congress to declare war on Japan. Three days after that, on DECEMBER 11, 1941, Germany and Italy declared war on the U.S. and Congress reciprocated. The U.S. had entered World War II.

> The Germans had broken the Allies' code and knew their battle plans. But the U.S. had Navajo men who used their language to fool the Germans and turned the tide of the war.

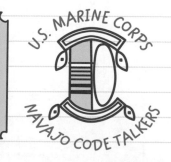

The WAR in EUROPE ENDS

On June 6, 1944, known as D-DAY, Allied warships landed in Normandy, France, in the largest **AMPHIBIOUS** landing in history. The Germans, who expected the Allies to land elsewhere, were slow to react, and D-Day marked the start of an offensive movement by the Allies to defeat the Axis powers of Italy, Germany, and Japan.

LIKE A FROG!

AMPHIBIOUS
belonging to both water and land

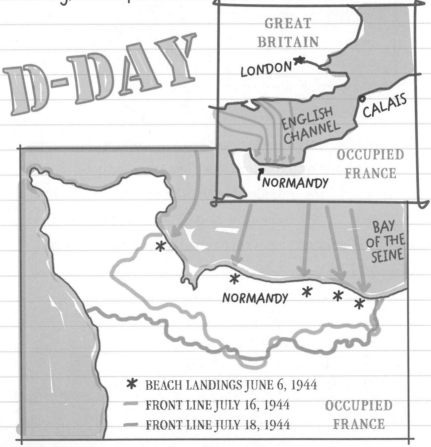

D-DAY

GREAT BRITAIN

LONDON

ENGLISH CHANNEL

CALAIS

OCCUPIED FRANCE

NORMANDY

BAY OF THE SEINE

NORMANDY

* BEACH LANDINGS JUNE 6, 1944
— FRONT LINE JULY 16, 1944
— FRONT LINE JULY 18, 1944

OCCUPIED FRANCE

France and other countries captured by the Germans were soon free, and in December 1944, the Allies defeated the Germans in the BATTLE OF THE BULGE in Belgium.

- ● FRONT LINE DECEMBER 16, 1944
- ● FRONT LINE DECEMBER 25, 1944

BELGIUM

THE BULGE →

GERMANY

FRANCE

LUXEMBOURG

THE BATTLE OF THE BULGE

is called that because of the bubble shape the Allied line formed when the Germans pushed them back in one spot. This battle is also called the Ardennes Offensive.

The Allies continued into northern Germany to join forces with the Soviets. The Soviets had advanced steadily by 1943, reoccupying Ukraine and continuing into Poland, Hungary, Romania, and Bulgaria. In January 1945, the Soviets reached Berlin.

Hiding in a bunker under the city of Berlin, Hitler wrote a final political testament, still trying to blame the Jews for World Wars I and II. On April 30, a few days after Italian resistance fighters killed Mussolini, Hitler committed suicide. On May 7, the Germans surrendered, and on May 8, 1945, known as **V-E DAY**, the Allies declared victory. The war was over in Europe, but the U.S. was still fighting Japan.

VICTORY IN EUROPE

YALTA and POTSDAM

When it was clear that the Allies would win, the

CHURCHILL   FDR   STALIN

Allied leaders met to discuss ways to prevent another world war. In February 1945, the BIG THREE—Churchill, FDR, and Stalin—had met at the YALTA CONFERENCE and decided they needed a better peacekeeping group than the League of Nations to prevent war. In July, U.S. PRESIDENT HARRY S. TRUMAN (who had been vice president, but became president when FDR died in April) met with Churchill, Clement Attlee (also from Britain), and Stalin at the POTSDAM CONFERENCE.

GERMANY
DIVIDED

○ AMERICAN CONTROL
○ BRITISH CONTROL
● FRENCH CONTROL
● SOVIET CONTROL

Berlin ★

They decided to divide Germany into four zones. The city of
Berlin would also be divided in four. The U.S., the UK, France,
and the Soviet Union would each control one zone.

The DROPPING
of the ATOMIC BOMB

On August 6, 1945, the Americans dropped an ATOMIC bomb
on Japan on the orders of President Truman. The bomb's
power came from a chain reaction of nuclear fission and
immediately destroyed the city of HIROSHIMA.

When Japan refused to surrender, the U.S. dropped a
second bomb on August 9, 1945, this time on NAGASAKI.
Tens of thousands of ordinary Japanese citizens died in the

439

explosions, and thousands more died later from exposure to horrible amounts of radiation. On August 14, 1945, **V-J DAY**, the Japanese Emperor, HIROHITO, signed a peace agreement accepting unconditional surrender. World War II officially came to an end.

VICTORY OVER
JAPAN DAY

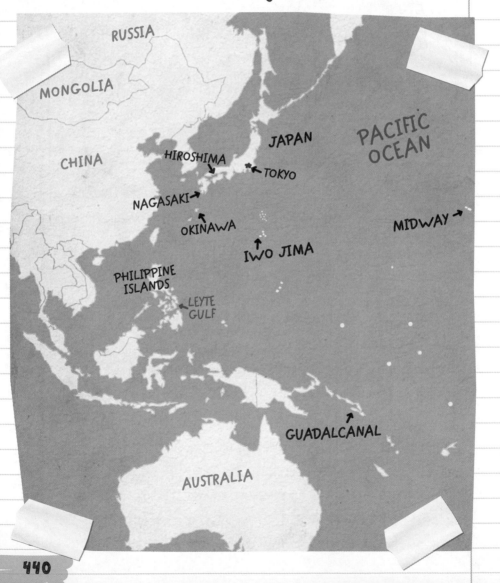

The NUREMBERG TRIALS

In November 1945, in Nuremberg, Germany, the NUREMBERG TRIALS began, trying Nazis for CRIMES AGAINST HUMANITY. In the first round of trials, twenty-two Nazis were found guilty and ten were executed. Over a hundred more were found guilty. A similar TRIBUNAL (the INTERNATIONAL MILITARY TRIBUNAL FOR THE FAR EAST)

> **TRIBUNAL**
> a court

was held in Tokyo, where Hideki Tōjō and six other Japanese leaders were convicted and executed.

COUNTING the AFTERMATH

At least forty million civilians are thought to have died during this time (some estimates are three times higher), plus at least seventeen million combatants estimated to have died in battle (again, new research puts this number much higher), making it the deadliest military conflict in history. And nuclear weapons brought in a new era of threats and warfare.

WORLD

January 30, 1933:
Germany's president Paul von Hindenburg declares Hitler chancellor and signs the Enabling Act. The Nazis begin setting up concentration camps.

1935:
The Nuremburg Laws are enacted.

May 12, 1938:
Hitler declares unification of Germany and Austria. Germany takes over Sudetenland.

March 1933:
The Nazis open Dachau, the first concentration camp.

1936:
Hitler and Mussolini form the Rome-Berlin Axis.

September 1, 1939:
Germany invades Poland, which causes Britain and France to declare war.

WAR II

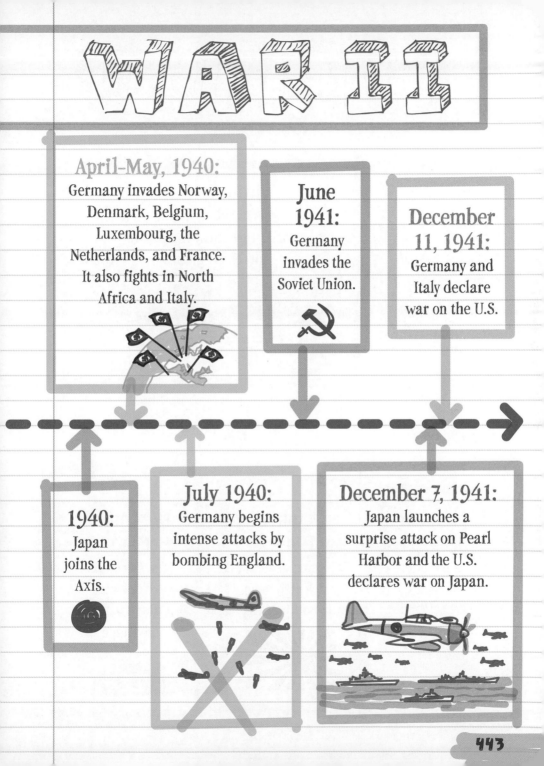

April–May, 1940: Germany invades Norway, Denmark, Belgium, Luxembourg, the Netherlands, and France. It also fights in North Africa and Italy.

June 1941: Germany invades the Soviet Union.

December 11, 1941: Germany and Italy declare war on the U.S.

1940: Japan joins the Axis.

July 1940: Germany begins intense attacks by bombing England.

December 7, 1941: Japan launches a surprise attack on Pearl Harbor and the U.S. declares war on Japan.

443

WORLD

February 1943:
After a two-year invasion of the USSR, German troops surrender at the Battle of Stalingrad.

June 1944:
Allied troops invade German-occupied France on D-Day, throwing the German forces off guard.

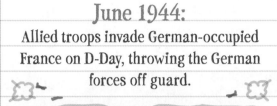

September 1943:
Italy surrenders to the Allies.

October 1944:
The Japanese navy is defeated near the Philippines.

December 1944:
The Germans are defeated in the Battle of the Bulge.

WAR II

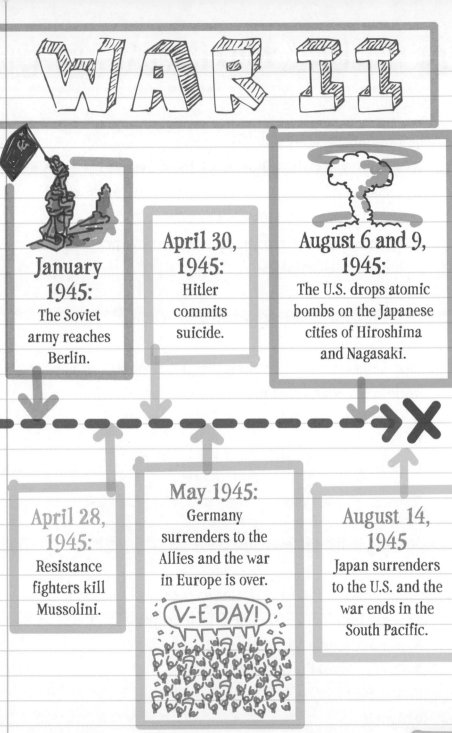

January 1945: The Soviet army reaches Berlin.

April 30, 1945: Hitler commits suicide.

August 6 and 9, 1945: The U.S. drops atomic bombs on the Japanese cities of Hiroshima and Nagasaki.

April 28, 1945: Resistance fighters kill Mussolini.

May 1945: Germany surrenders to the Allies and the war in Europe is over.

V-E DAY!

August 14, 1945 Japan surrenders to the U.S. and the war ends in the South Pacific.

CHECK YOUR KNOWLEDGE

1. The Nuremberg laws of 1935:
    A. effectively stripped Jews of their German citizenship
    B. required all Jews to be sent to concentration camps
    C. joined Hitler and Mussolini in political power
    D. gave Hitler free rein to ignore both the president and the Reichstag

2. List the groups sent to concentration camps.

3. Great Britain's initial policy toward Germany's actions in invading the Rhineland is known as:
    A. trench warfare
    B. appeasement
    C. neutrality
    D. allied reasoning

4. Reichstag is the German word for _____.

5. Britain and France first declared war on Germany following Hitler's invasion of which country in 1939?
    A. the Sudetenland
    B. Czechoslovakia
    C. Poland
    D. Austria

6. Germany's first major defeat came because of:
   A. a fierce Russian winter
   B. fierce Russian warriors
   C. the destruction of a crucial land bridge
   D. lack of food

7. When was the Battle of the Bulge, and which side was victorious?

8. Which U.S. president authorized the dropping of atomic bombs over Hiroshima and Nagasaki?

9. What were the Nuremberg Trials?

ANSWERS

CHECK YOUR ANSWERS

1. A. effectively stripped Jews of their German citizenship

2. The Nazis sent Jews, communists (and other political opponents), homosexuals, Roma, and a variety of ethnic groups that Nazis considered inferior (including Poles, Ukranians, Slavs, and Serbs), and people with mental and physical disabilities to concentration camps.

3. B. appeasement

4. Parliament

5. C. Poland

6. A. a fierce Russian winter

7. The Battle of the Bulge was in 1944, and the Allies defeated the Germans.

8. President Harry S. Truman authorized dropping the atomic bombs over Hiroshima and Nagasaki.

9. The Nuremberg Trials were tribunals meant to hold Nazis responsible for crimes against humanity. Over a hundred Nazis were found guilty during these trials.

Unit 9

Post-World War II: The World from 1945 to Today

After World War II, the world faced a period of recovery and rebuilding. Alliances from the war didn't entirely fade, and a new "war" began. This "Cold War" divided the world again and changed the path of economic and political recovery across the globe.

BRRR!

Chapter 40

CHANGES IN EUROPE AND THE MIDDLE EAST AFTER WORLD WAR II

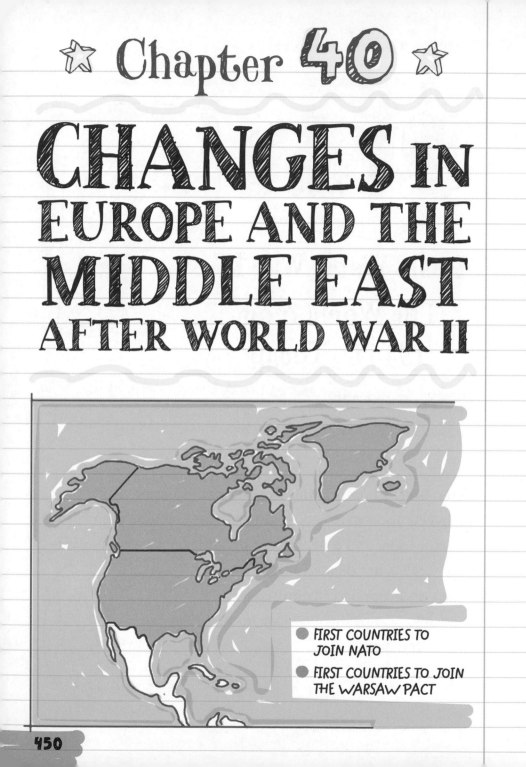

- FIRST COUNTRIES TO JOIN NATO
- FIRST COUNTRIES TO JOIN THE WARSAW PACT

Some rivalries didn't end with the war. Some became even more serious. The differences between the U.S. (the capitalist West) and the Soviet Union (the communist East) were hard to ignore.

POST-WORLD WAR II ALLIANCES

After World War II, alliances formed, with the U.S. and the Soviet Union acting as captain of each team. The U.S.'s side—Belgium, Luxembourg, France, the Netherlands, Great Britain, Italy, Denmark, Norway, Portugal, Iceland, Canada, and the U.S.—formed a pact in 1949 called the NORTH ATLANTIC TREATY ORGANIZATION (NATO). The rival team formed the WARSAW PACT with much of Eastern Europe in 1955.

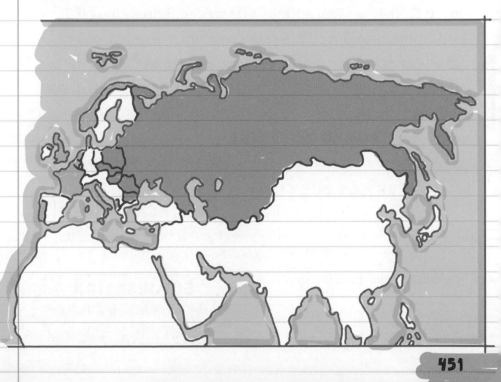

These pacts were military alliances that countries joined for security. Sort of a "you scratch my back, I'll scratch your back." (Only, scratching with diplomacy and/or guns and bombs.)

STOPPING the SPREAD of COMMUNISM

The U.S. and Great Britain thought newly liberated nations in Eastern Europe should form their own governments. The Soviets feared that these new nations would be anti-Soviet—especially Greece, which was in the middle of a civil war. Great Britain provided financial support to Greek anticommunist forces until it ran out of money. U.S. president Harry S. Truman feared that Britain's withdrawal would lead to the creation of a Greek communist country, so he asked Congress for aid for Greece as well as Turkey in 1947. It was a lot of cash to spend on another country, but President Truman made a strong case for it in what is now called the **TRUMAN DOCTRINE**.

The **TRUMAN DOCTRINE** said that the U.S. should always support free people resisting **SUBJUGATION** by armed minorities or outside pressure. The U.S. would also provide aid to countries threatened by communism.

SUBJUGATION
the act of bringing under complete control

That same year, U.S. SECRETARY OF STATE GENERAL GEORGE MARSHALL came up with the MARSHALL PLAN. Marshall believed communism took hold in countries with economic problems, so he wanted to give impoverished countries money in the hope that communism would fail. The Marshall Plan provided $13 billion to rebuild Europe after the war.

The EEC FORMS

The Soviet Union and its European **SATELLITE** states (the states dependent on the Soviet Union) refused to accept any funds from the Marshall Plan. In 1949, they created the Council for Mutual Economic Assistance (COMECON) to provide financial aid, but they didn't quite have enough cash to make it work.

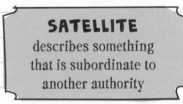

SATELLITE
describes something that is subordinate to another authority

In Western Europe, an economic plan called the EUROPEAN ECONOMIC COMMUNITY (EEC) was formed in 1957. Also known as the COMMON MARKET (and later called simply the European Community, or EC), the EEC consisted of France,

THE EC LATER GAVE RISE TO THE EUROPEAN UNION (EU), AND IT WAS DISSOLVED INTO THE EU IN 2009.

West Germany (Germany was divided after World War II), Belgium, the Netherlands, Luxembourg, and Italy. The EEC encouraged economic cooperation among member nations. Britain, Denmark, and Ireland joined the EEC in the 1970s, and Greece, Spain, and Portugal joined in the 1980s.

ORIGINAL MEMBERS OF THE EEC

NETHERLANDS

BELGIUM

LUX.

WEST GERMANY

FRANCE

ITALY

The UNITED NATIONS

The League of Nations was ineffective, but it laid the groundwork for the UNITED NATIONS, or UN, which was officially formed in October 1945 to work for peace and human dignity. The original UN charter was signed by 50 countries, and today nearly 200 countries are members.

The CREATION of ISRAEL

After the Holocaust, many Jews sought a homeland to call their own. In 1947, the UN recommended the partition of British-controlled Palestine to form a Jewish state. In 1948, by UN **MANDATE**, the state of ISRAEL was officially formed.

> **MANDATE**
> an authoritative command

The region that was formerly called Palestine (or Judaea) had a mainly Muslim Arab population that was not happy with a new Jewish state taking control.

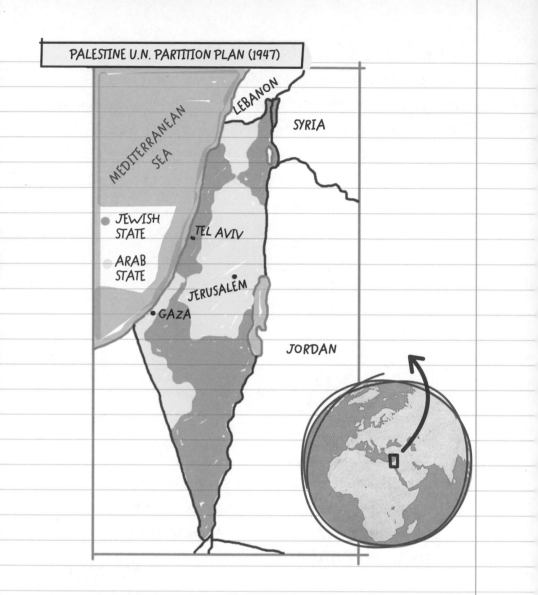

PALESTINE U.N. PARTITION PLAN (1947)

MEDITERRANEAN SEA

LEBANON

SYRIA

● JEWISH STATE

○ ARAB STATE

• TEL AVIV

• JERUSALEM

• GAZA

JORDAN

Neighboring Arab countries attacked the newly formed
Israel in 1948, but Israel fought back hard. Thousands of
Palestinian Arabs fled the area and sought refuge in the
West Bank and the Gaza Strip, two Arab-controlled lands.

Arab forces attacked again in 1967, and this time Israel gained control of the West Bank, the Gaza Strip, and parts of Syria and Egypt.

The conflict between Palestine and Israel continues to this day, despite the efforts of many great thinkers. Peace and resolution have yet to come.

CHECK YOUR KNOWLEDGE

1. _____ is a military alliance that formed between the Soviet Union and much of Eastern Europe in 1955.
   A. the Truman Pact
   B. NATO
   C. NAFTA
   D. the Warsaw Pact

2. What is the full name of the Western military pact, and what is the abbreviation?

3. Which of the following contributed aid toward rebuilding Greece and Turkey in 1947?
   A. the Truman Doctrine
   B. the Marshall Plan
   C. the European Economic Community
   D. the Warsaw Pact

4. List the countries that were involved in the Common Market.

5. Explain the significance of this economic plan.

6. What is the principal reason why the state of Israel was formed?

7. How did Arab countries respond to the creation of Israel?

ANSWERS → 459

CHECK YOUR ANSWERS

1. D. the Warsaw Pact
2. The Western military pact is called the North Atlantic Treaty Organization (NATO).
3. A. the Truman Doctrine
4. The Common Market countries included France, West Germany, Belgium, the Netherlands, Luxembourg, Italy, Britain, Denmark, Ireland, Greece, Spain, and Portugal.
5. The Common Market encouraged economic cooperation among the nations that were members and was later called the European Community, or EC. It also gave rise to the European Union.
6. After the devastation of the Holocaust and World War II, the state of Israel was formed so that Jews could have an official homeland of their own.
7. Israel was created in a region that had a mainly Muslim Arab population. The surrounding Arab countries were unhappy that a new Jewish state was taking control, so they attacked Israel in 1948 and again in 1967.

☆ Chapter 41 ☆

THE COLD WAR

The "Cold War" wasn't fought on a battlefield. It was a war of ideologies between Western democracies and Eastern communist countries over the question of communism. The "warring" countries had very different ideas about politics and economics—on one side were communists and the other side were capitalists. Communist countries in Eastern Europe were isolated from the West behind what Winston Churchill called an IRON CURTAIN in 1946.

Berlin

UK

USSR

France

U.S.

BERLIN

Fr

USSR

UK

U.S.

The DIVISION of GERMANY

After World War II, the Allied Powers divided Germany
into four zones, each occupied by one of the major powers
(Great Britain, France, the U.S., and the Soviet Union).
Great Britain, France, and the U.S. wanted to unify their
Western sections into a West German state, but the
Soviets disagreed. In June 1948, the Soviets set up the
BERLIN BLOCKADE, preventing trucks, trains, and barges
(and therefore food and supplies) from getting into the three
Western zones of Berlin. The Western
allies used the BERLIN AIRLIFT to deliver
supplies to West Berlin by plane. Ten
months later, the Soviets finally ended
their blockade.

BLOCKADE
the blocking of
something (can also
be used as a verb)

In 1949, the Allies formally created West Germany, or the FEDERAL REPUBLIC OF GERMANY. Less than a month later, the Soviets set up an East German state called the GERMAN DEMOCRATIC REPUBLIC. The capital, Berlin, was divided into East Berlin (under Soviet rule) and West Berlin (with a democratic government). Berlin became a major Cold War source of conflict. East Berlin was much poorer than West Berlin, and many East Berliners escaped and took refuge in West Berlin. To stop this, in 1961 Soviet premier (leader) NIKITA KHRUSHCHEV built a wall dividing the city. The BERLIN WALL came to symbolize the division and disagreement between communist and democratic superpowers.

In October 1989, mass demonstrations forced the communist government to open its border. On November 9, 1989, the Berlin Wall was torn down, signaling the end of Soviet-style communism. Germany's unification took place a year later.

Beijing •

CHINA

COMMUNISM in CHINA

In China, communism thrived. In 1945, there had been two Chinese governments: the nationalists in southern China and the communists in northern China. Civil war between the two sides ended in victory for communist rule under MAO ZEDONG.

MAO ZEDONG

The People's Republic of China was formed in 1949, and Mao Zedong became its first chairman.

In 1958, Chairman Mao began a new program called the GREAT LEAP FORWARD, which combined small farms into vast **COMMUNES** with more than 30,000 people living and working together. Mao promised more equal rice distribution. Communes fostered communal child care, so women could work the fields alongside their husbands. Chairman Mao hoped life in the communes would allow China to have a classless

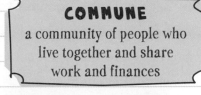

> **COMMUNE**
> a community of people who live together and share work and finances

society, but the Great Leap Forward was a great big failure and caused one of the world's worst famines. By 1960, the government abandoned the program.

In the late 1970s, Communist Party of China leader DENG XIAOPING tried to move China toward a market economy (under the communist political system) in a set of reforms called the FOUR MODERNIZATIONS. The Four Modernizations in agriculture, industry, national defense, and science and technology were intended to make China a major economic power. China's economy improved in the 1980s, when the country finally opened its doors to outside investment from countries like the U.S. When people went abroad and learned more about the West, some began to criticize the Communist Party and call for democracy, and were often put in prison as punishment for speaking up.

465

In May 1989, student protestors demanded an end to corruption. They wanted the Communist Party leaders to resign. In June, the protestors set up in TIANANMEN SQUARE in Beijing. Deng Xiaoping sent tanks and troops; between 500 and 2,000 people were killed. Even though China experienced political conflict, the country has developed into one of the strongest economies in the world in the last several decades.

KOREA and VIETNAM

In Korea and Vietnam, there were divisions between communist and noncommunist governments that worsened into military confrontations.

Before World War II, Korea had been a Japanese colony. The U.S. proposed dividing Japanese-occupied Korea near the 38th PARALLEL. The Soviets helped communists take power in NORTH KOREA, and the U.S. supported the democratic government in SOUTH KOREA. In June 1950, North Korean communist forces attacked South Korea. The United Nations put together a team of soldiers led by U.S. GENERAL DOUGLAS MACARTHUR (who had helped take Japan in World War II and had overseen its occupation) to help South Korea. When MacArthur tried to push the invaders out of South Korea, China sent troops to help their allies in North Korea. Eventually the two sides agreed to disagree—they signed an armistice in July 1953 agreeing to stop fighting and keep the country divided.

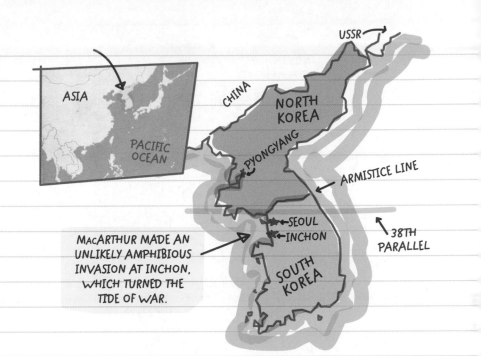

ASIA

PACIFIC OCEAN

USSR

CHINA

NORTH KOREA

PYONGYANG

ARMISTICE LINE

SEOUL
INCHON

38TH PARALLEL

SOUTH KOREA

MacARTHUR MADE AN UNLIKELY AMPHIBIOUS INVASION AT INCHON, WHICH TURNED THE TIDE OF WAR.

France had once colonized Vietnam as part of INDOCHINA (present-day Cambodia, Laos, and Vietnam). French involvement in Indochina continued after World War II until 1954, when a Vietnamese independence movement led by HO CHI MINH defeated the French at the BATTLE OF DIEN BIEN PHU. Like Korea, Vietnam was divided into a communist north and a noncommunist south. In South Vietnam, communist rebels called the VIET CONG tried to unite the entire country under communist rule. Once more the U.S. got involved, sending economic aid as well as military troops. The U.S. was afraid of seeing a DOMINO EFFECT: It believed that if the communists won South Vietnam, other Asian countries would also fall (like dominoes) to communism.

The Vietnam War lasted for years, killing thousands of Americans and Vietnamese. The U.S. launched an aggressive bombing campaign against North Vietnam called OPERATION ROLLING THUNDER, plus chemical warfare in which it sprayed the herbicide AGENT ORANGE to destroy Vietnamese jungles (to clear terrain for soldiers) and crops. In spite of all its military power, superior equipment, and large numbers of troops, the U.S. failed to defeat the North Vietnamese. Ho Chi Minh and the North Vietnamese waged guerrilla warfare; they would attack before running or hiding in the jungle; and they built underground tunnels.

Antiwar movements in the U.S. protested and called for an end to the war, especially after Americans troops killed Vietnamese civilians in the MY LAI MASSACRE of 1968 and entered another country, Cambodia, in 1970 to back up air strikes. In 1973, the U.S. withdrew its troops from South Vietnam. Fighting continued between the north and the south until communist forces captured the capital of South Vietnam, Saigon, and renamed it HO CHI MINH CITY. In 1976, they united Vietnam under communist rule.

The ARMS RACE and the CUBAN MISSILE CRISIS

Throughout this time, the U.S. and the Soviet Union built up their armies and weapons just in case they had to go to war against each other. This buildup was known as the ARMS RACE. No battles were fought between the two countries during the Cold War, but the arms race led to advancements in airplanes, jets, tanks, and other weapons systems. NUCLEAR WEAPONS became increasingly dangerous as each side tried to outdo the other with deadlier and deadlier bombs, until each nation had more than enough bombs to destroy each other several times over.

In Cuba, communist leader Fidel Castro led a revolution of workers and peasants against the right-wing dictatorship of FULGENCIO BATISTA. Castro wanted to provide education, health care, and national land rights to the

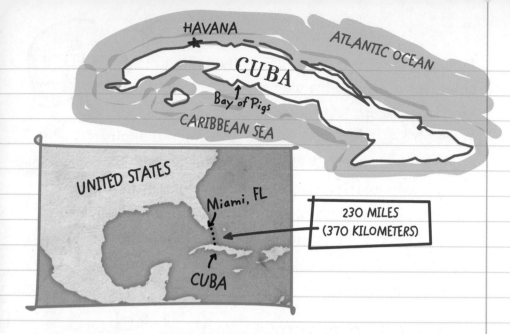

lower classes that Batista neglected in Cuba. Many of the sugar plantations were owned by foreigners. The U.S. didn't like having communism so close to home, so in April 1961 PRESIDENT JOHN F. KENNEDY (also known as JFK) supported an invasion of Cuba by exiled Cuban fighters to overthrow Castro. The BAY OF PIGS invasion was a failure and ended in the surrender of the exiled fighters. Castro remained in power, enforcing communist rule in the country, and he turned to the Soviets for support.

A year after the Bay of Pigs invasion, the U.S. discovered Soviet missiles in Cuba, which could have ended up in a nuclear weapons conflict. Luckily, the Soviets agreed to withdraw their missiles after the U.S. blockaded their fleet in the CUBAN MISSILE CRISIS of October 1962. Still, the fear of nuclear weapons being used was suddenly very realistic.

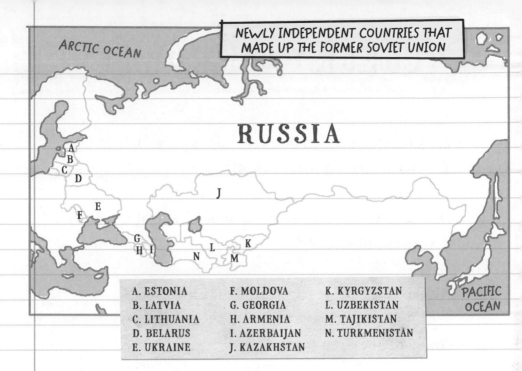

RUSSIA

ARCTIC OCEAN

PACIFIC OCEAN

A. ESTONIA
B. LATVIA
C. LITHUANIA
D. BELARUS
E. UKRAINE

F. MOLDOVA
G. GEORGIA
H. ARMENIA
I. AZERBAIJAN
J. KAZAKHSTAN

K. KYRGYZSTAN
L. UZBEKISTAN
M. TAJIKISTAN
N. TURKMENISTAN

The COLD WAR ENDS

The Cold War ended in the early 1990s thanks in part to reforms introduced by MIKHAIL GORBACHEV, who became the leader of the Communist Party of the Soviet Union in 1985. Gorbachev called for a radical restructuring of the Soviet economic and political system called PERESTROIKA. He also supported GLASNOST, a policy of perestroika that encouraged Soviet citizens to speak openly about the Soviet Union's strengths and weaknesses...which led to Soviet Republics demanding independence and the defeat of the Communist Party. In 1987, the Soviets and Americans agreed to eliminate intermediate-range nuclear weapons. The Soviet Union dissolved in 1991. The arms race between the USSR and the U.S., and the Cold War, were over at last.

CHECK YOUR KNOWLEDGE

1. Germany was divided into four zones after World War II. Who controlled these zones?

2. What was the Cold War really about? Was it a war in the traditional sense?

3. What was the arms race? Who was involved?

4. What was the Iron Curtain?

5. The Berlin Wall was built by _____ _____ in 1961 to divide the city.

6. ___ _____ was responsible for China's failed Great Leap Forward.

7. What is the significance of Tiananmen Square?
   A. It was the site of a major protest against Communist Party corruption.
   B. It marked the end of Deng Xiaoping's Four Modernizations.
   C. It was the site of a major protest against democracy.
   D. It marked the beginning of the Vietnam War.

8. Discuss why the U.S. became involved in the conflicts between North Korea and South Korea and between North Vietnam and South Vietnam.

9. Which of the following was a result of the Bay of Pigs invasion of 1961?
   A. The Viet Cong gained a major advantage over American troops.
   B. General Douglas MacArthur advanced into South Korea.
   C. Fidel Castro was removed from power.
   D. The exiled fighters surrendered to communist forces.

10. When did the Soviet Union dissolve?

ANSWERS 473

CHECK YOUR ANSWERS

1. The four zones were controlled by Great Britain, France, the U.S., and the USSR.
2. The Cold War was a war of ideologies between Western democracies and Eastern communist countries over communism versus capitalism. It wasn't a war in the traditional sense because it wasn't primarily fought on battlefields.
3. The arms race was a period when the U.S. and the Soviet Union built up their armies and weapons just in case a war was declared.
4. The Iron Curtain was a term coined by Winston Churchill to describe how communist countries in Eastern Europe were isolated from the West.
5. Nikita Khrushchev
6. Mao Zedong (Chairman Mao)
7. A. It was the site of a major protest against Communist Party corruption.
8. The U.S. became involved in both conflicts because it was afraid that if the communists took over noncommunist countries, other Asian countries might also become communist.
9. D. The exiled fighters surrendered to communist forces.
10. The Soviet Union dissolved in 1991.

★ Chapter 42 ★

NATIONALIST and INDEPENDENCE MOVEMENTS AFTER WORLD WAR II

Many countries achieved their independence after World War II.

NATIONALISM in INDIA

In India, a young Hindu named MOHANDAS GANDHI began a movement of nonviolent resistance and **CIVIL DISOBEDIENCE** to improve the lives of India's poor and gain freedom from British rule. He led the SALT MARCH with thousands of followers in 1930 to protest the British monopoly and taxes on an essential need, salt. Gandhi's followers called him Mahatma, meaning "great soul." He didn't believe in fighting and war; his peaceful ways eventually led to Indian independence from the British in August 1947. India was partitioned into two countries, one Hindu (India) and one Muslim (Pakistan). As with colonial Africa, this partition divided families and left some Hindus in Pakistan and Muslims in India.

CIVIL DISOBEDIENCE
the act of actively refusing to follow laws, usually in the form of nonviolent protest

Gandhi's peaceful protests, marches, hunger strikes, and sit-ins influenced and inspired later activists, like **MARTIN LUTHER KING JR.**, in the U.S.

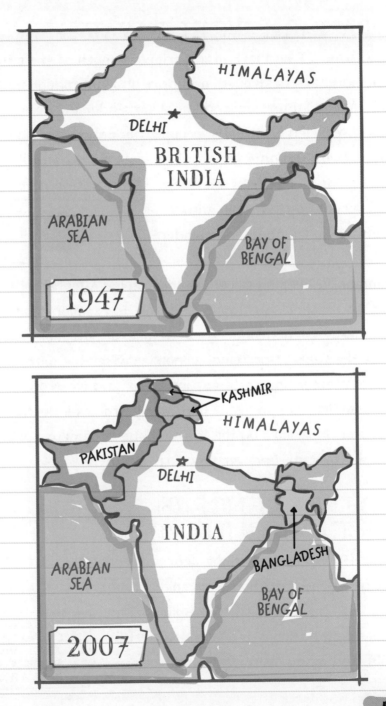

JAPAN after WORLD WAR II

World War II had left Japan crippled; much of the city of Tokyo had been destroyed, and agricultural production was down. After Japan's unconditional surrender in August 1945, Allied forces, led by the U.S., occupied Japan to distribute food, prevent Japan from developing its military, and also to make Japan more like the West. In the spring of 1952, Allied occupation officially ended. Japan was once again independent.

Beginning in 1949, by selectively borrowing Western ideas and technology, Japan was able to recover, rebuild, and emerge even stronger than before. Japan soon had one of the fastest-growing economies after the war. Its manufacturing, trade, car industry, and electronics development were so great that its electronics industry surpassed America's by the 1970s. Tokyo became a populous, vibrant, exciting—and very modern—city.

INDEPENDENCE for AFRICAN COUNTRIES

On the African continent, the years after World War II were a time of liberation from colonial rule. LIBYA became the first newly independent nation after World War II in 1951, and many countries would follow.

49 MORE COUNTRIES! INCLUDING GHANA, KENYA, AND ZIMBABWE, TO NAME A FEW.

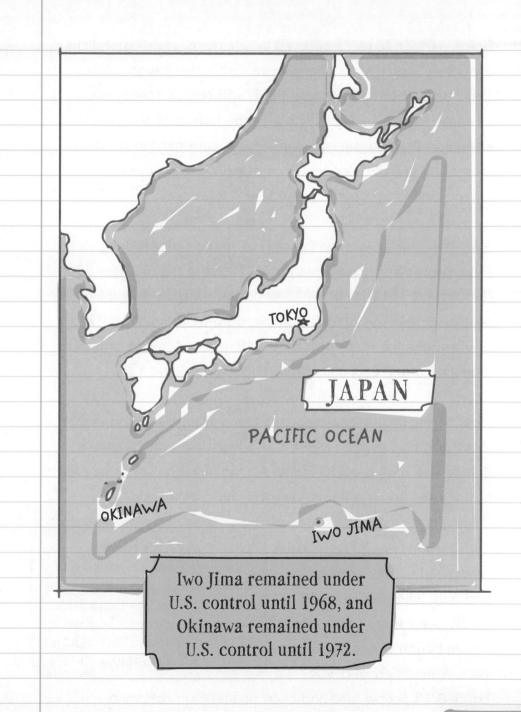

TOKYO

JAPAN

PACIFIC OCEAN

OKINAWA

IWO JIMA

Iwo Jima remained under
U.S. control until 1968, and
Okinawa remained under
U.S. control until 1972.

Some African leaders believed in Western-style capitalism, others in Soviet-style communism. Still others wanted an "African" socialism based on the traditions of community, in which wealth would be put into the hands of the people. European imperialism had divided the continent in random ways and created borders that often caused big problems when nations became independent.

PAN-AFRICANISM is the concept of uniting all Africans regardless of national boundaries. It led to the creation of the ORGANIZATION OF AFRICAN UNITY (OAU) in 1963, which supported African groups fighting against colonialism. The OAU became the AFRICAN UNION (AU) in 2002, which promotes democracy and economic growth in Africa.

Most of the new African leaders came from the urban middle class and had studied in the West; they believed Western democracy was a useful model for governing. But some new nations fell under military dictatorships, or worse.

In South Africa, **APARTHEID** separated whites and blacks, and only whites (a minority of the population) could vote. Blacks began to protest these laws in the 1950s and '60s.

> **APARTHEID**
> a system of racial segregation in which South Africans were assigned to one of four groups (black, white, mixed race, or Asian); the majority (blacks) had fewer rights than the minority (whites).

In 1960, 69 people who had been peacefully protesting

MEDITERRANEAN SEA

ATLANTIC OCEAN

INDIAN OCEAN

AFRICA

Madagascar

Johannesburg
Sharpeville

1. Tunisia
2. Morocco
3. Algeria
4. Libya
5. Egypt
6. Mauritania
7. Western Sahara
8. Senegal
9. Gambia
10. Guinea-Bissau
11. Sierra Leone
12. Guinea
13. Mali
14. Liberia
15. Ivory Coast
16. Ghana
17. Burkina Faso
18. Togo
19. Benin
20. Nigeria
21. Cameroon
22. Equatorial Guinea
23. Gabon
24. Republic of the Congo
25. Dem. Republic of the Congo
26. Angola
27. Niger
28. Chad
29. Sudan
30. South Sudan
31. Ethiopia
32. Central African Republic
33. Eritrea
34. Djibouti
35. Somalia
36. Uganda
37. Kenya
38. Rwanda
39. Burundi
40. Tanzania
41. Malawi
42. Zambia
43. Zimbabwe
44. Botswana
45. Namibia
46. South Africa
47. Swaziland
48. Lesotho
49. Mozambique
50. São Tomé and Príncipe

were killed by police in the SHARPEVILLE MASSACRE. Evidence shows that most of them had been shot in the back, meaning that they weren't approaching the police or acting aggressively. Then the government arrested NELSON MANDELA, the leader of the AFRICAN NATIONAL CONGRESS (ANC), in 1962. He was sentenced to life in prison in 1963. Mandela was kept in high-security prisons before finally being released in 1990. THAT'S 27 YEARS LATER!

In 1994, when the government agreed to hold democratic elections for the first time ever, Nelson Mandela became the first president of South Africa to be elected by the majority of all the people, black and white. Mandela's presidency and the work of human rights activist ARCHBISHOP DESMOND TUTU finally helped end apartheid.

"IT ALWAYS SEEMS IMPOSSIBLE UNTIL IT'S DONE."
—NELSON MANDELA

CHECK YOUR KNOWLEDGE

1. What movement did Mohandas Gandhi begin?

2. In what year did India finally gain independence?
   A. 1945
   B. 1947
   C. 1949
   D. 1952

3. Following India's independence from Great Britain, two countries were formed. Name them and the religions they follow.

4. Libya became an independent African nation in:
   A. 1945
   B. 1947
   C. 1951
   D. 1959

5. What is Pan-Africanism?

6. What was apartheid?

7. True or false: Archbishop Desmond Tutu was held in a high-security prison for nearly 27 years.

8. The first president of South Africa elected by a majority of all the people (regardless of race) was _____ _____.

ANSWERS   483

CHECK YOUR ANSWERS

1. Mohandas Gandhi began a movement of nonviolent resistance and civil disobedience in India.

2. B. 1947

3. After independence from Great Britain, India was partitioned into two countries: India (Hindu) and Pakistan (Muslim).

4. C. 1951

5. Pan-Africanism is the concept of uniting all black Africans regardless of national boundaries.

6. Apartheid was the policy in South Africa of segregating whites and blacks, and allowing only the small white minority to vote.

7. False. Nelson Mandela was the national leader held in high-security prisons for nearly 27 years.

8. Nelson Mandela

☆ Chapter 43 ☆

MODERN GLOBAL TRANSFORMATIONS

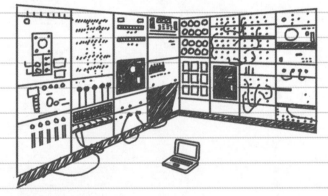

TECHNOLOGY

The first modern computers weighed around thirty tons! They were huge, and only a few places had them. But in the 1940s, these computers changed the way businesses were run; they took only seconds to do what might have taken days to do by hand. Countries around the world had to adapt to new technology to stay up to speed in the global economy.

Even in the average home, computers became incredibly important. Regular people started getting online in the 1980s, and home computers became more popular with the INTERNET REVOLUTION in the 1990s. It changed the way people communicated now that they could communicate with anyone, anywhere, at any time, in seconds.

BEFORE:

letters

shouting!

landline phones ~HELLO?

faxes

AFTER:

texting

CAPS LOCK!

DIDN'T YOU SEE MY TEXT?!?

email

Inbox

social media

Me

Another important invention of the twentieth century was TELEVISION, which became popular in the U.S. after World War II. Networks began broadcasting nightly news segments, and the television quickly replaced the radio as a major news source. The Internet is now a major news source, including sites run by television networks.

The U.S. and USSR were also locked in a SPACE RACE, starting when the Soviet Union launched the first artificial satellite, SPUTNIK, in 1957. The next year, the U.S. launched a satellite and founded the NATIONAL AERONAUTICS AND SPACE ADMINISTRATION (NASA). The Space Race led to a focus on math and science in American schools. In April 1961, YURI GAGARIN of the USSR became the first person to orbit the earth. The U.S.'s NEIL ARMSTRONG and EDWIN "BUZZ" ALDRIN were the first people to walk on the moon, on July 20, 1969, during the Apollo project.

Since then, humans have sent machines into space to explore Mars and other planets. Robots have traveled to the sun, to comets, to asteroids, and past the edge of the solar system.

MARS ROVER

The ENVIRONMENT

Humans made a lot of technological advances in the twentieth century, but they also made some pretty big mistakes. Cities grew too fast and too big. Factories and a desire for expensive products like cars and phones led us to neglect something very important: Mother Nature. We've overused land and soil, leading to **DESERTIFICATION**. We've cleared forests (DEFORESTATION) to build houses and factories. Our factories have poured harmful chemicals into our air, creating smoggy skylines, **ACID RAIN**, and CLIMATE CHANGE.

DESERTIFICATION

the depletion of plants and topsoil in semi-arid lands, causing them to become deserts; often a by-product of population growth

ACID RAIN

precipitation (such as rain or snow) with high levels of acid-forming chemicals released in the air by factories and motor vehicles

Deforestation has hit tropical RAIN FORESTS, where 50 percent of the world's species of plants and animals live. Rain forests are sometimes called the "lungs" of the planet—they're crucial to our survival because they remove carbon dioxide from the air and provide us with oxygen to breathe.

The GREENHOUSE EFFECT is the warming of the earth due to carbon dioxide buildup in the atmosphere. The greenhouse effect contributes to **GLOBAL WARMING**—which doesn't mean that everywhere is hotter all at the same time.

GLOBAL WARMING

an increase in the overall temperature of the earth's atmosphere due to the greenhouse effect

489

It's a part of overall climate change and can contribute to rising sea levels, the melting of polar ice caps, and severe droughts and storms. Climate change can cause famines when crops can't grow and, in turn, make regions of the planet unlivable, and it can even completely flood inhabited islands.

Some people consider climate change to be the most important issue currently facing humans—even bigger than the wars and political disagreements of history—because it affects the future livability of the entire planet.

SUSTAINABLE DEVELOPMENT
is development that meets our needs while also allowing us to conserve natural resources through recycling, water conservation, and other programs to reduce waste and the dumping of toxic materials.

In 2010, nearly two hundred nations made a promise to reduce carbon emissions when they signed an international agreement called the KYOTO PROTOCOL. The U.S. (which produces a lot of carbon emissions) didn't ratify this important treaty.

However, in 2015, the UNITED NATIONS CONFERENCE ON CLIMATE CHANGE (also known as the COP21 or the CMP11) was held in Paris, France. The 195 participating countries (including the U.S.) agreed to reduce greenhouse gases. The goal is to keep global warming this century to less than 2 degrees Celsius.

TODAY'S GLOBAL INTERDEPENDENCE

With today's technological advances in communication, nations and communities are more closely connected than ever before. This has led to people and nations becoming more interdependent (relying on each other). In a global economy, multinational corporations do business throughout the world. GLOBALIZATION is the process of making something worldwide, or global. There are advantages to being so connected: Organizations from different countries can work together to solve major issues like poverty, climate change, terrorism, and nuclear **PROLIFERATION**.

> A chain of restaurants that is in the U.S. and Australia and Russia and everywhere else is a sign of globalization.

> **PROLIFERATION**
> rapid spread or growth

Aside from the UN, other organizations have developed in this era of global interdependence, such as the WORLD TRADE ORGANIZATION (WTO). The WTO was formed in 1995 to increase trade by setting rules for international trade and to address other issues affecting the global economy.

The creation of the EUROPEAN UNION (EU) in 1993 established a common currency, the EURO, across European member nations. Stemming from the European Community (EC), this economic union was created to strengthen the economies of member nations and encourage trade and travel. Travel between member nations doesn't require a passport, and a person from Spain who wants to move to France can work or study there without a visa.

CHECK YOUR KNOWLEDGE

1. What were the first modern computers like?

2. How has the Internet revolutionized the modern world?

3. Name some of the downsides of all our rapid improvements in technology.

4. What is the greenhouse effect?

5. What are the consequences of climate change?

6. What document was signed in 2010 by nearly two hundred nations as a promise to reduce carbon emissions?

7. What is globalization?

8. The European Union stems from:
   A. the EC
   B. the WTO
   C. NAFTA
   D. the UN

ANSWERS 493

CHECK YOUR ANSWERS

1. The first modern computers were huge and weighed around thirty tons.

2. The Internet has revolutionized the way people communicate. There's instant communication and access to news around the world. (The Internet has ushered in online shopping, education, crime, gaming, and more!)

3. Some of the downsides of rapidly improving technology are that cities have grown too fast and products were being created without understanding their effects on the planet. Now there is desertification and deforestation, as well as smog, acid rain, and climate change.

4. The greenhouse effect is the warming of the earth due to carbon dioxide buildup in the atmosphere. The greenhouse effect contributes to global warming and climate change.

5. Climate change has many consequences: rising sea levels, melting polar ice caps, severe droughts and storms, famines, floods, and much more.

6. The Kyoto Protocol was signed in 2010 by nearly two hundred nations (but not the U.S.) as a promise to reduce carbon emissions.

7. Globalization is the process of making something worldwide, or global.

8. A. the EC

Chapter 44 ☆

GLOBAL SECURITY and MAJOR WORLD EVENTS of TODAY

In the early 2000s, the threat of **TERRORISM** moved high on the list of global concerns. New Yorkers, and all Americans,

> **TERRORISM**
> the deliberate use of violence to spread fear and achieve one's political or other goals

felt the effects of terrorism on SEPTEMBER 11, 2001 (9/11), when two hijacked planes were flown into the World Trade Center, killing thousands and creating a major worldwide scare. A third hijacked plane crashed into the Pentagon, and a fourth crashed in Pennsylvania when passengers brought it down to stop the terrorists' plans.

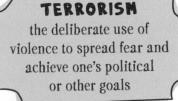

Similarly violent attacks have occurred in Britain, Spain, Egypt, Indonesia, and elsewhere. These attacks were carried out by AL-QAEDA, a radical Islamist terrorist group. Al-Qaeda are **EXTREMISTS**. Most Muslims **CONDEMN** these attacks.

> **EXTREMIST**
> a person who has extreme religious or political viewpoints, especially someone who argues for illegal, violent, or extreme action

> **CONDEMN**
> to express disapproval

WAR on TERROR

Al-Qaeda and its leader, OSAMA BIN LADEN, were being protected by the TALIBAN, the **FUNDAMENTALIST** party in power in Afghanistan. On October 7, 2001, the U.S. and its allies attacked, beginning the WAR IN AFGHANISTAN. The Taliban was thrown from power.

> **FUNDAMENTALIST**
> a person or movement that believes in strictly and literally following a set of rules or principles

> U.S. forces killed Osama bin Laden on May 2, 2011, in Pakistan.

Other threats to global security came under attack during this time—including aggressive military dictators and the spread of nuclear weapons. After 9/11, PRESIDENT GEORGE W. BUSH of the U.S. claimed that Iraqi president SADDAM HUSSEIN had WEAPONS OF MASS DESTRUCTION (WMDs) in Iraq. He also thought Iraq was linked to Al-Qaeda, but many believed he was wrong. Although many allies asked the U.S.

to allow UN weapons inspectors more time to look for WMDs, the U.S. (with the help of Britain) began the WAR IN IRAQ in March 2003. Baghdad was occupied and Saddam was ousted. The war in Iraq officially continued for more than seven years, but American troops remained in this unstable region longer.

HE WAS LATER TRIED AND EXECUTED.

In 2008, when BARACK OBAMA was elected the forty-fourth president of the U.S. (and the first African American president), he promised to bring troops home.

In 2010, President Obama also agreed with Russia to reduce the number of long-range nuclear weapons in U.S. and Russian arsenals. Fear of nuclear weapons remains. North Korea, for instance, announced in 2005 that it had nuclear weapons and periodically holds tests of them. In 2015, China, France, Russia, the UK, and the U.S. struck a historic deal with Iran to cap (limit) its nuclear program in exchange for eased **SANCTIONS**. There continue to be worries about nuclear proliferation in India, Pakistan, the Middle East, and elsewhere.

WHAT ELSE?

As the world moves further into the twenty-first century, it will face issues that divide,

> **SANCTIONS**
> measures (typically restrictions on trade) taken by nations to force another nation to follow international rules or norms

enrich, and redefine it. While many nations and international groups have made big strides in recent history, like sequencing the human genome, many challenges are still to come. These are some of the more recent major world events that continue to shape history:

On April 20, 2010, a British Petroleum oil rig exploded in the Gulf of Mexico and created the worst oil spill in U.S. history. Clean-up efforts continue to this day.

Starting with protests in Tunisia that began on December 18, 2010, the Arab world has gone through a series of major upheavals and revolutions called the **ARAB SPRING**. Antigovernment protests, uprisings, and rebellions spread across the Middle East to Egypt, Yemen, Syria, and Libya.

TURKEY

MOROCCO   TUNISIA   Palestinian Territories   Lebanon   SYRIA   IRAN

ALGERIA   LIBYA   ISRAEL   JORDAN   IRAQ   Bahrain   Qatar

Western Sahara (disputed)   EGYPT   KUWAIT   U.A.E.

MAURITANIA   MALI   SAUDI ARABIA   OMAN

SUDAN   YEMEN

SOUTH SUDAN   ETHIOPIA   SOMALIA

HOT SPOTS OF THE ARAB SPRING

CIVIL WAR	DEMOCRACY
FAILING STATE	SEMI-DEMOCRACY
DEMOCRATIC FAÇADE	ABSOLUTE MONARCHY

The most powerful earthquake ever recorded hit Japan on March 11, 2011, followed by a massive tsunami that damaged the Fukushima nuclear power plant and endangered many lives.

SENDAI

TOKYO

JAPAN

The deadliest outbreak of Ebola virus began in 2014 in West Africa and spread rapidly, creating a global epidemic.

AFRICA

After more than 50 years of no diplomatic relations, the U.S. and Cuba began restoring diplomatic relations in 2015.

CHECK YOUR KNOWLEDGE

1. What major threat did global policy leaders have to deal with in the early 2000s?

2. What happened on September 11, 2001?

3. What group was responsible for events that occurred on September 11, 2001?

4. Define an extremist. Give an example of an extremist group.

5. What sort of weapons did President Bush claim Saddam Hussein had hidden away in Iraq?

6. What did North Korea claim it had in its country in 2005?

7. What marked the start of the Arab Spring?

ANSWERS

CHECK YOUR ANSWERS

1. Terrorism was the major issue that global policy leaders dealt with in the early 2000s.

2. On September 11, 2001, a terrorist attack on the U.S. occurred: Two planes were flown intentionally into New York's World Trade Center and a third plane was flown into the Pentagon. The terrorists on a fourth plane failed when passengers crashed the plane in a field in Pennsylvania.

3. These attacks were carried out by Al-Qaeda, a radical Islamist terrorist group.

4. An extremist is a person who has extreme religious or political viewpoints and will argue for illegal, violent, or extreme actions. Al-Qaeda is an extremist group.

5. President Bush claimed Saddam Hussein had hidden weapons of mass destruction (WMDs) in Iraq.

6. North Korea announced it had nuclear weapons in 2005.

7. Protests in Tunisia that began on December 18, 2010, marked the start of the Arab Spring.

INDEX